COUNTRY-TOWN NEXUS

COUNTRY-TOWN NEXUS

Studies in Social Transformation in Contemporary India

Edited by

K.L. SHARMA
DIPANKAR GUPTA

RAWAT PUBLICATIONS
Jaipur • New Delhi • Bangalore • Guwahati • Kolkata

ISBN 978-81-7033-099-8

Reprinted, 2020

Published by
Prem Rawat for **Rawat Publications**
Satyam Apts., Sector 3, Jawahar Nagar, Jaipur - 302 004 (India)
Phone: 0141 265 1748 / 265 7006
E-mail : info@rawatbooks.com • Website: www.rawatbooks.com

New Delhi Office
4858/24, Ansari Road, Daryaganj, New Delhi 110 002
Phone: 011-23263290

Also at *Bangalore, Guwahati* and *Kolkata*

Typeset by ABC Enterprises, Delhi
Printed and bound in India

Contents

Preface

In keeping with the growing sociological awareness of the mutual interaction between country and town it was felt that an attempt should now be made to consolidate our understanding on this subject. As the scholarly contributions on this subject are quite diverse, the act of consolidation demands a controlled and disciplined handling of the material. This, in turn, would also suggest to us fresh grounds for purposive research. In the context of the sociology and anthropology of rural-urban interaction, this process of consolidation should perhaps make us more self-aware of the *country and town nexus* as a sociological category. We believe that an appreciation of this *nexus* is of crucial significance for any understanding of social transformation in contemporary India. It is not as if the country is primarily a recipient of forces emanating from the town, or vice-versa; but that there exists a nexus within which rural-urban interaction takes place. A realization of this phenomenon takes us away from isolated studies of change and forces us to take the larger context into account even when undertaking micro case studies of rural or urban transformation.

It is with the above perspective in mind that we held a national seminar on *Country and Town Nexus: Studies in Social Transformation in Contemporary India* from August 17 to 19, 1988 at the Centre for the Study of Social Systems, School of Social Sciences, Jawaharlal Nehru University, New Delhi. As the theme forces us to think both structurally and historically, it is imperative that this thinking be reflected in the selected papers presented in this volume.

We believe that the knowledge and expertise reflected in the papers will significantly contribute to our understanding of the country and town nexus in the context of social transformation in India. Our contributors in this volume have dealt mainly with rural and urban change, peasants and workers, education, migration, and mobility.

Some of the papers contribute to a theoretical (and conceptual) refinement of the term *country and town nexus*. These papers enhance our understanding on issues such as (i) the historical development of the contemporary rural-urban nexus; (ii) the specificity of the Indian variant; and (iii) the effect that the nexus has on stratification, family structure, markets, social mobility etc. The papers on peasant and working class movements also sharpen our sensitivity to the country and town nexus. Our contributors have examined the effects the nexus has had on contemporary peasant movements, on urban union collective action, as also on the development of political ideologies which hope to attract broader cross-sections of the population.

Both migration and mobility have existed down the ages. Papers on this theme lay emphasis on the *nexus* and on the extent to which this nexus influences migration and mobility. This is, of course, regardless of whether or not there is any conscious awareness of the nexus. In this context we hope that the specific characteristics of contemporary trends in migration will become salient. Social mobility too—upwards, downwards and horizontal—requires just such an examination. It is not viable to visualise social mobility today in any other fashion. The pervasiveness of the nexus is supralocal in scope though its effects may be highly localised and specific.

We also have contributions related to a domain where conscious agency and deliberate activism play an important role in the constitution of the nexus. Papers on this theme enhance our understanding of how sensitive the educationists and educational material are to the dynamics of the nexus. This provide us with a fresh opportunity to examine the kinds of social images that the educational system forwards.

As will be readily apparent, there are many themes that can be legitimately included in a volume on *country and town nexus*. We have taken just a few and hopefully done some justice to them through this volume. In fact, we longed to incorporate many more papers on these and some other related themes, but due to paucity of funds our ambition had to remain unfulfilled. We hope to carry on the exercise in the future to do fuller justice to the subject and bring together more studies on social transformation in contemporary India.

The national seminar on the country-town nexus was possible mainly because of the provision for holding seminars under the Department of Special Assistance of the Centre for the Study of Social Systems. We are grateful to Professor Yogendra Singh, Coordinator of the DSA, for giving us a free hand in using the grant of Rs. 30,000 for this purpose. The Indian Council of Social Science Research also provided us a grant of Rs. 10,000 and we sincerely thank the ICSSR. Professor M.S. Agwani, Vice-Chancellor, Jawaharlal Nehru University, encouraged us in myraid ways for organising the seminar. We are grateful to Professor Agwani for his many acts of generosity and scholarly advice. We are grateful to Professor Iqbal Narain, formerly Member-Secretary, ICSSR, for conducting the inaugral session. Professor Yogendra Singh delivered the keynote address, and we are once again grateful to him.

Our sincere thanks are due to all the participants and particularly to the contributors of papers. In particular we wish to thank our senior colleagues: Professors, A.R. Desai, Y.B. Damle, A.M. Shah, B.R. Chauhan, Indra Deva, C.P. Bhambhri, S.N. Jha, Krishna Bhardwaj, S. Bhattacharya and several others who made the discussions and deliberations of the seminar intellectually stimulating and absorbing. We also wish to thank our colleagues and students in the Centre without whose cooperation it would not have been possible for us to organise the seminar. Dr. H.N. Singh was the backbone of entire organisational set up, and we express our sincerest thanks to him for his keen interest in the seminar. Lastly, we thank Rawat Publications for showing interest in the publication of this volume right from the inception of the seminar.

K.L. Sharma
Dipankar Gupta
Jawaharlal Nehru University
New Delhi

1st May, 1991

Contributors

A.M. SHAH, Department of Sociology, Delhi School of Economics, University of Delhi.

ANJAN GHOSH, Centre for Social Sciences, Calcutta.

ATIYA HABEEB KIDWAI, Centre for the Study of Regional Development, Jawaharlal Nehru University, New Delhi.

DIPANKAR GUPTA, Centre for the Study of Social Systems, Jawaharlal Nehru University, New Delhi.

D.N. DHANAGARE, Department of Sociology, University of Poona, Pune.

ILA SHAH, Tata Institute of Social Sciences, Bombay.

INDRA DEVA, Department of Sociology, Ravi Shankar University, Raipur.

K.L. SHARMA, Centre for the Study of Social Systems, Jawaharlal Nehru University, New Delhi.

MANORAMA SAVUR, Department of Sociology, Bombay University, Bombay.

M.K. PREMI, Centre for the Study of Regional Development, Jawaharlal Nehru University, New Delhi.

PRADIP KUMAR BOSE, Centre for Social Sciences, Calcutta.

SHARIT BHOWMIK, Department of Sociology, Delhi School of Economics, University of Delhi, Delhi.

SHEOBAHAL SINGH, Department of Sociolgy, Gorakhpur University, Gorakhpur.

YOGENDRA SINGH, Centre for the Study of Social Systems, Jawaharlal Nehru University, New Delhi.

Introduction

Relations between village and town have always attracted the attention of social scientists, political workers, activists and policy-makers. In most such cases it is generally assumed that the town/city exercises a near hegemonic control over the destiny of village life. The two, i.e. town and country, are depicted as polar opposites, or unmatching contrasts, in terms of population composition, density of population, professions, civic amenities, occupations, life styles, etc.

However, in our opinion village and town are obverse sides of a structural process that implicates both and has a telling impact on the broader civilization, culture and history of a society. Thus, country and town are necessarily interacting units, and the pattern of interaction is such that neither the country nor the town is privileged as the epicentre of social transformation. Both country and town mutually influence each other, but not on the basis of an *ad hoc* format, but rather on account of supra local forces of transition. These supra-local forces need to be conceptually understood and appreciated so that a more refined approach towards the *country—town nexus* may emerge which will have greater empirical validity for our times.

In all there are fourteen papers in the volume. The first four by Yogendra Singh, A.M. Shah, K.L. Sharma and Indra Deva deal with general and conceptual issues relating to the country-town nexus keeping in view the nature of social transformation in contemporary India. Dipankar Gupta and D.N. Dhanagare discuss in detail the emergence of 'peasant power', in particular the Bhartiya Kisan Union (BKU) and its leader, Mahendra Singh Tikait. The analysis of agrarian classes in the context of their linkages with outside financial agencies and other non-rural institutions and organisations finds detailed expression in the papers by Pradip Bose, Manorama Savur, Anjan Ghosh, Sheobahal Singh and Ila Shah. It is particularly illustrative to read these pieces for they enlarge our understanding of the nature of industrialization in rural and semi-urban settings which in turn highlights the significance of the country-town nexus. M.K. Premi and

Atiya Habeeb Kidwai provide lucid accounts of the multiple patterns of social mobility and migration in a diachronic framework in order to demonstrate the extent of the effect of the country-town nexus on the patterns of migration today.

In the opening paper of this volume Yogendra Singh examines country-town interrelationships within the framework of broader theoretical and methodological developments in sociology and social anthropology. The development of sociological sensitivity in India is related to these broader developments and further the studies of country-town nexus are seen as a part of this development of sociology in India. In earlier studies village autonomy was erroneously emphasised without recognising its civilizational base. In the 1950's, however, studies of both village and town were guided by the theoretical presuppositions of functional-structural sociology: but these were also devoid of macro-sociological orientations. In the 1960's neither the functional-structural orientation, nor the autonomy of village/town remained central concerns in sociological studies. Studies focussing upon conflict and contradictions with social interaction as the major concern were highly appreciated. To go beyond the village and/ or to go beyond the town for a fuller comprehension of social reality became a focal theme in both rural and urban studies. Yogendra Singh hence emphasises in this fashion the relevance of the country-town nexus as a sociological category.

The thrust of Singh's keynote address is to understand the country-town nexus within the framework of macro-social transformation in India. Keeping in view the colonial legacy he refers to the policy of industrialisation as a critical factor which has contributed to the peculiar form of urbanisation in India. A new middle class has emerged signifying a new form of socio-economic inequality. Also a self-conscious new middle class has emerged in the countryside posing a threat at times to the privileges enjoyed by its counterpart in towns and cities. Both are products of the same forces and processes of macro social transformation. The hiatus between these two and other segments of population is due to the unequal and lop-sided development of villages and towns. Singh concludes by saying that today the country-town nexus in India tends to intensify the alternative rather than integrative forces in our polity, economy, culture and social system. Segmental identities based on social and cultural cleavages have increased their hold on the institutional appratuses of society. The emerging new middle classes have provided the momentum to this situation in our society.

A.M. Shah in his paper— "The Rural–Urban Networks in India" explodes several age-old motions regarding exclusivity of village and town, caste and class, joint and nuclear family, corporateness and individualism Shah's study of rural-urban networks is based on his analysis of society and culture in Gujarat. However, its relevance for studying the same elsewhere in India is undeniably immense. The links between villages and towns are not confined to caste, kinship and marriage alone, there are links also in regard to religion, culture, trade and commerce.

Shah highlights commonality and difference regarding the structure and functioning of the basic institutions such as caste, family, kinship, religion, trade and commerce. The main thrust of Shah's paper is that despite the commonality of these institutions in the two settings, there are crucial differences in their functioning which in turn implicate differential patterns of change. This commonality is brought about by the linkages between the village and town. The linkages are generally bilateral and reciprocal, and they are never completely hegemonic in nature as it is believed by some scholars.

How were a large number of caste groups in the town inter-related? What was the nature of interaction among the people of different castes? From where did village people acquire tools and raw materials, sacred books and account books? Shah has dealt with these and several other questions in depth. His analysis of migration, particularly inter-urban migration, urbanisation, sectarianism and individualism and of the process of interlinkages between village and town has successfully established links between sociology and history.

K.L. Sharma refers to country-town nexus both as a historical and contextual reality concerning relations between village and town. The nexus is defined by Sharma as a set of ties (in terms of connections) between village and town which explains both the structural and cultural changes in the two settings. Macro-structural changes, social stratification and specific conditions of given villages and towns determine largely the country-town nexus and the consequent structural and cultural changes in the two. Sharma makes an attempt to spell out the country-town nexus as a viable conceptual tool for analysing social transformation in contemporary India. In this context Sharma brings out the limitations of the existing frameworks, dichotomies and continua for analysing the country-town nexus.

Moneylenders, artisans, shop-keepers, salaried workers, non-agricultural wage earners, priests, white-collar workers constitute an important element in the country-town nexus. Migration, mobility and change in both the settings could be actualised by these sections of society. Today a large number of new social categories such as school teachers, revenue officials, village-level workers, peons, bank officials, etc., have emerged ushering in a new era in the pattern of country-town nexus. However, there is an uneven impact of policy measures, planning and infrastructural inputs upon the people living both in villages and towns. A hierarchy of country-town nexus thus becomes an unavoidable feature of our society because of the variatons in structural changes, social stratification, and local conditions.

Indra Deva examines the role of country-town nexus in the context of social change in rural India. He finds the existing conceptual and methodological tools inadequate for analysing the changing character of peasant society and culture. There have been traditionally established bonds between villages and towns as integral parts of the wider Indian society. Deva underlines the economic-technic, the Politico-Legal and the cultural-ideological forces as the main spheres of life in which the nexus between villages and towns has witnessed change in modern India. Deva's analysis of the changing character of the country-town nexus requires special mention as it is based on his understanding of folk-culture and oral tradition. Further, he observes that folk forms have the capability of finding new avenues of survival and growth in the wake of modern technological, political and cultural forces.

Dipankar Gupta's paper entitled "The Country-Town Nexus: Situating the Bharatiya Kisan Union...", endeavours to understand the farmers' movement in west U.P. in the context of the "country-town nexus". He begins by arguing that it is important to analytically overcome the "rural-urban interaction" framework for it does not quite appreciate the two-way dynamism between town and country. This two-way dynamism is such that the town implicitly assumes the country, and vice-versa, but not always in a harmonic fashion. Indeed, the "country-town nexus", more often than not, generates conflict and tension which are multi-dimensional in their effects. In addition Gupta also. In addition Gupta also underlines the importance of conceptualising the "country-town nexus" as a structural and supralocal category not limited by reasons of contiguity. In other words, it is not as if the analysis is confined to an examintion of the effects that a town has on the contiguous countryside, but to be able to see town and country as structural impulses that mutually impinge and influence each other. By drawing on the literature on peasant movements and on rural-urban interaction Gupta attempts to demonstrate that the stylized notion of "Bharat vs. India" does not really operate on the ground. The two, i.e., country and town, or, Bharat and India, are not mutually exclusive options but are bilaterally implicated. The country remains strong in the Bharatiya Kisan Union (BKU) led farmers' movement in west U.P., but not without active inputs from the town. This is true inspite of the overtly rural and *jat* character of its membership.

The next paper by D.N. Dhanagare is also on the Bharatiya Kisan Union (BKU), but it has a somewhat different concern. According to Dhanagare the BKU's political options are severely limited by its insistence on staying away from politics. He contrasts the BKU's leader Mahender Singh Tikait to Maharashtra's Shetkari Sangathan leader Sharad Joshi to make the point that while the former is apolitically fritterring away the chances of forging an all India peasant combine, the latter is sensitive to the needs of just such an all India body. In pursuance of this objective Joshi also advocates the cause of the rural poor. In the background Dhanagare figures in the effects of the green revolution on the countryside and the demands that the farmers, particularly the richer ones, are making on the Indian state. Dhanagare's evaluation of the potentialities and constraints of Tikait's apopulist populism gains salience and richness because of this larger canvass.

In keeping with the broad understanding of the "country-town nexus" as a supralocal category with significant conflict potential, Pradip Bose presents an analytical essay to demonstrate how different classes in rural India are responding to this nexus. Rural industrialisation is not simply mimicking urban industrialisation but finds its dynamic instead in the recent modernization of agriculture. Nevertheless, Bose argues, the rural rich are linking up with external financial agencies through the medium of the market. The middle peasants, however, do not present a clear picture as many of them (but not all) have ended up rather worse off than before. The peasants seem to have borne the brunt of agrarian modernization and have become particularly vulnerable to the rural rich. In contrast to mainstream modernization theses Bose relates the conflicts and contradictions that the contemporary rural-urban interaction has wrought on the countryside. Bose, thus deliberately, dismisses the received bland format which only assimilates variations in the `positive' impact of modernization while ignoring its "negative", non-consenusal, and disharmonic dimensions.

Towns and cities at the intermediate level not only attract migrants from villages and other urban areas, they also represent a synthesis of tradition and modernity In his paper on education, migration and social change M.K. Premi notes that the rural links of migrants to intermediate towns are quite strong. These linkages vary with the destinations of migration and with the places of birth of the migrants. These in turn depend upon the socio-economic status of the migrants and the size of the city. The nexus is thus never expressed in a monolithic fashion: it is highly differentiated and rooted in the social background of the people and the nature and size of the towns.

From peasants we now move on to the working class. Sharit Bhowmik's essay is based on his field work among the workers in Bokaro Steel Plant. We get an extremely interesting picutre of the rural-urban nexus for Bhowmik richly illustrates how urban employment has an effect on the working class, who are often of rural origin. Though the village is still there in the industrial worker, he has nevertheless moved quite decisively towards the town in terms of his future and projected image of himself. By carefully sifting through the results of his detailed survey Bhowmik provides us with a rounded picture of the pressures on, and the characteristics of, different kinds of workers. Though the workers generally come from peasant backgrounds, their orientation today towards the village is very calculated, and not primordial or sentimental, as is popularly believed. We thus get a detailed understanding of the contradictory influences of the "country-town nexus" and the differential impact it has on a working class which in turn is fairly well differentiated internally in terms of background, education, and skills.

Manorama Savur examines the "country-town nexus" from the perspective of the food processing industry. Here, too, though the cases under study are particular food processing units, she is forced to connect them to the wider national and global economy. Only then, she argues, is it possible to comprehensively understand the ramifications of the nexus. Food processing industries, whether dealing with apple, cocoa, milk, fish or mango, have selectively benefitted the more privileged classes. The poorer sections of the rural popualtion have generally been victims of this nexus for they have not only lost significant chunks of their autonomy but also those natural resources over which they had relatively greater access. Savur's essay relates the stages by which international food processing moguls gradually penetrate the countryside and irreversibly alter the social lives of many.

A study of labour mobilization in the Raniganj-Jharia coalfields by Anjan Ghosh highlights the emergence of the country-town nexus. The study covers the coalfields located in Burdwan and Dhanbad districts of Bengal and Bihar, respectively. Detailed caste and tribe-wise information is provided by Ghosh in his paper on the people employed in non-agricultural occupations in the two districts in relation to the total employment in the respective states. Ghosh concludes that the mining settlements are of a quasi-urban nature. The articulation of interests in the coalfields is comparable with what one finds between villages and towns. The rural links of the industrial work-force prove to be a source of strength for the workers in the articulation of their interests against the employers in the coalfields.

Sheobahal Singh's paper is another illustration of the role of small-scale industrialisation, entrepreneurship and urbanisation in fostering the country-town nexus. Singh's study of the carpet industry in Bhadohi town of eastern Uttar Pradesh reveals the complex and multidimensional character of the country-town nexus. Even though carpet manufacturing is a cottage industry, it has a world market and is based on the capitalist system of production. The nature of production is such that it inevitably brings together people from villages and towns under the same roof. Singh has dealt with this aspect of his study at length. The workers engaged in carpet manufacturing can retain their links with their rural households and agriculture. A hierarchical involvement of the people from among different castes and communities as observed by Singh reveals the coexistence between country and town and the absence of polarity between tradition and modernity. The findings of this study stimulates Singh to suggest that a systematic policy of industrial growth that ensures the interdependence between villages and towns could perhaps provide solution to India's gigantic problems of unemployment, over-crowding of towns and cities and the exodus from villages.

The differentiated rural market has been much discussed both by economists and sociologists. Ila Shah's paper adds to this valuable corpus of literature by empirically linking different classes of cotton growers to the variety of merchants who trade in this commodity. The market is not only differentiated at the rural end but it has corresponding hiatuses at the urban end as well. By highlighting the role of credit manipulation Shah is able to bring out the unequal exchange between town and country, and more interestingly, finds the causes of rural backwardness related to the control that the more prosperous town-based merchants and entrepreneurs exercise over the credit market.

Based on a case study of a Muslim family tree in Uttar Pradesh Atiya Habeeb Kidwai suggests a research design for the study of the country-town nexus. Kidwai considers the nexus as a multifaceted phenomenon and a conceptual tool for sociological inequiry. Her study has been designed as a longitudinal micro study of actors, who are in this case, members of a family genealogy. An attempt is made here to relate macro-processes with the micro-situation.

Kidwai highlights four factors which she considers important in the life of her actors i.e. members of the Kidwai family. They are: (i) birth in terms of time and generation, (ii) education in terms of the place and the level, (iii) marriage fields, and (iv) livelihood positions. Being a geographer Kidwai has enriched her paper with maps and charts to show the country-town linkages of five generations of Kidwais spreading over a period of about 140 years. She traces the changing bonds of the rural gentry with supra-local spaces. She finds that the links with the country begining to weaken in the fourth generation, and it exists only in a symbolic form in the current generation. Lastly, Kidwai raises questions about the suitably of the concept of the nexus for studying social transformation both historically and contextually.

The essays in this volume, whether conceptual or empirical, or a blend of both, all reinforce the claim that the term "country-town nexus" makes as a sociological category. In conclusion it is worthwhile to reiterate what we see as the advantages of employing the category "country-town nexus" as opposed to "modernization" or "rural-urban interaction". Firstly, the "country-town nexus" forces one to visualise the town and country as mutually implicated. Secondly, the "nexus" also sensitises the scholar to the fact that the interaction between town and country is fraught with contradictions and that is why it influences different social classes differently. Thus there is a very self-conscious move away from the "modernization" scheme which is partial to the so-called benevolent effects of modernization and tends to ignore the elements of tension and social conflict that come with it. Finally, "the country-town nexus" goes beyong micro exchanges to the macro level where contiguity does not limit the universe of rural-urban interaction. It is for these reasons that the term "country-town nexus" aspires to supercede the perspectives hitherto provided by the conventional frameworks of "modernization" and of "rural-urban interaction".

CHAPTER 1

Country-Town Nexus: Social Transformation in Contemporary Indian Society

—*Yogendra Singh*

The process of social transformation today generates many serious contradictions. The emerging pattern of country-town relationship constitutes one such aspect. It is, therefore, timely that a Seminar is devoted to analysing this problem from perspectives that are both theoretical and substantive. One is particularly impressed by theoretical sensitivity in Indian sociology to recognise the relevance of this problem for understanding the processes of social change. There have existed two kinds of theoretical and methodological impulses in Indian sociology and social anthropology: first, indigenous and second western-inspired. The theoretical and methodological advances that Indian sociologists and social anthropologists have made so far, have been a result of interaction between these two historical conditions. Broadly, one could hypothesise that centrality of focus on macro-sociology, or on studying linkages among structures and institutions that constitute the reality of Indian society, its culture and civilization as a wholistic entity has fluctuated depending upon either of the two frames of reference in theory and methodology. The focus upon nexus or on binding relationship between country-town, or other levels of inter-relationships were wanting in the works of British administrators-cum-sociologists or social anthropologists. We find that during early 1920's "many British and European writings on Indian society and culture used conceptual categories which were Eurocentric in cognitive and value terms; some of these also tended to distort history and imputed meanings to Indian reality in the abstract...Concepts such as 'caste' 'tribe', 'village', 'community', 'family and kinship' were defined as segmentary entities, often analogous to their socio-historical equivalents in European society. The emphasis was on showing how each of these social entities affirmed the principles of segmentation or autonomy rather than being parts of an organic whole. The elements of discreteness was over emphasised and the linkages, both social and cultural, which bound these entities into an organic system of social structure and civilization were neglected." In contradistinction to this, we witness a macro-sociological perspective in the study of Indian social structure and cuture in the writings of G.S. Ghurye, Radhakamal Mukherjee, D.P. Mukherji, N.K. Bose and other founders of sociology. The basic categories of sociology that we find in the analytical scheme of their writings are those of region, civilization, cultural area and rural-urban interactions. Individual forms of social structure are no doubt the focus of observation but from the perspective of social and cultural linkages.

This theoretical and methodological tradition of indigenous sociology was weakened during the decade of the 1950's, when the era of single village studies began in India largely under the inspiration of Americal social anthropology. The village studies generated useful data on the functioning of individual social institutions; they even focused upon the inter-institutional relationships or linkages but within the boundary of the village as an autonomous system. Erroneously, the autonomy of tribal or rural settlements found in other societies was taken for granted in such studies to be also applicable to the Indian society, without recognising its civilizational base and institutional linkages developed over several millenia. This period also saw the growth of urban studies based largely on the methodology of social surveys. These generated some useful empirical statistical data but without much sensitivity in respect of organic linkages among social systems within the city or between country-city inter-relationships. The studies both of the village and towns during the decade of the 1950's shared a feature in common: both of them were grounded in the theoretical presuppositions of functional-structural sociology and both such studies were devoid of macro-sociological orientation.

By the middle of 1960's new developments in the global shape of sociology and social anthropology took place which contributed to disenchantment both from functional-structural theory and the tendency to treat micro-structures such as village, town, tribe, caste, class etc. as autonomous entities. Several historical factors were responsible for this development in sociology. First, the tensions of social and cultural alienation that swept most countries of Europe and north-America during the mid 1960's culminating in a series of strifes of youth, students and working classes rendered the basic postulates of functionalism, such as consensus, integration voluntarism and autonomy of structures or cultural systems obsolescent. Not consensus but conflict or contradictions both at the levels of social interaction and ideology seemed to govern the processes of society. Hence, Marxism and conflict theory in different modes of their manifestation began to emerge as dominant theoretical traditions in sociology and social sciences. This tendency also coincided with new traditions of researches in history, political science, economics and social psychology where analysis of social institutions and structures were conducted in wholistic and comparative historical settings. The contributions of Indian historians, economists and political scientists during this period offered sociologists rich material for their more meaningful treatment of social institutions and their linkages from a macro-sociological point of view.

Sociological and social anthropological researches from the middle of 1960's onwards increasingly demonstrated the concern for explorations of nexuses among institutions and sub-systems of society. Even the writings of European and American sociologists on India can be observed to have shown this orientation. Louis Dumont, Milton Singer, Bernard Cohn among many others recognised the need for a historical, comparative and systemic approach for understanding of specific institutions such as caste and kinship, town and country and economy and culture in India. These studies, reinforced the work of Indian sociologists and social anthropologists who had already been using macro-sociological and comparative theoretical perspective in their studies. In most of these studies, not only the assumption of autonomy of the village or city as a social unit was challenged but doubts were also expressed on the validity of these as sociological categories. A momentum was thus created for adopting macro-sociological and comparative historical perspective in the studies of social structures and cultural elements of the Indian social system. In early 1970's, the Indian Institute for Advanced Studies, Simla organised a national seminar of sociologists, and social anthropologists, with the theme "The 'Macrosociology of India" and its proceedings were appropriately titled "Beyond the Village: Sociological Explorations." This seminar made concrete methodological contributions as each member participants had to report from an empirical study of his own. It did not directly deal, however, with country-town nexus, but made contributions to some aspects of methodology and theory of macro-sociology. Later, more systematic studies followed using the conceptual frameworks of macro-sociology. These demonstrated the linkages between micro and macro-structures and little and great traditions of the Indian society. Similarly, many studies on folk-urban cultural continuum were conducted from a cross-regional and comparative theoretical point of view. These clearly demonstrated the deeper cultural interdependence and linkages between country and town and between one linguistic region and another. Moreover, the folk culture perspective on the study of Indian society also enriched the theoretical and methodological dimensions of Indian sociology.

The direction of these theoretical and methodological developments in macro-sociology of India constitute one area of relevance for the study of country-town nexus. Another important dimension of this relationship belongs to the emerging processes of social transformation that Indian society is going through today. The concrete direction of this change gives urgency to undertaking a thorough and systematic analysis of this problem. Historically, country-town relationship had a pattern of interdependency in India that was governed by tradition and economy. The traditional Indian cities throughout history had a near symbiotic relationship with countryside. Their economic relationship was complimentary, the occupational specialisations and division of labour offered opportunities for continuities as well as change and mobility. Folk-elite cultural tradition and its role structures established meaningful nexuses between country, town and capital cities. Commerce, political administration, ritual and religious practices and art and aesthetics constituted nodal principles around which this country-town relationship was maintained. Commensurate with the level of technology and modes of production and distribution a near equilibrium between country-town relationships had traditionally evolved.

Colonialism disrupted this pattern of interdependent relationship. The fiscal, industrial and political policies persued by the British regime in India contributed to the decline of both country and town through increasing deindustrialization. The large scale pauperization of artisans, and peasantry took place as a result of massive disruption of traditional Indian economy and its social base. The pattern of country-town relationship that emerged during the colonial and post-colonial periods of Indian history, despite release of new forces of modernization could not restore the balance between the country-town relationship. The preeminent place that village oriented ideology was accorded in Gandhiji's social and economic agenda for reconstruction of Indian society was probably in recognition of this historical distortion between country-town relationship. Ironically, the process of modernisation in India took a highly segmentary form as a result of colonial distortion. The pace of modernization grew mainly from urban metropolitan centres, and had a narrow base in class and caste structure in specific areas of economy. It was only after Independence that attempt was made to broad base the process of development. Successive plans endeavoured to implement a development policy which aimed at a balanced growth of social strata but its ideological framework made it difficult to achieve quick results.

The policy of industrialization encouraged a form of urbanisation which only contributed to enlargement of social contradictions. It led to massive migration of rural poor to cities without their integration in the urban-industrial economy. The result is growth of slums and street corner population in cities which is rapidly outnumbering the rest of the urban population. Industrialisation has not been without its successes, but its social consequence remain uneven and its social base remains narrow, groved in a class character which increases the hiatus between country and town and rich and poor sections of society. The un-intended consequence of urbanization and industrialization have led to social alienation and encourage exploitation. No doubt, the rapid pace of industrialization has given strength to Indian economy. The technological and economic growth has set in new forces of social stratification and social mobility. A substantial urban middle class has emerged in cities; new entrepreneurial and professional groups have rapidly enlarged their numbers, but the social character of these classes does not promote a balanced relationship between country and town. The ideological orientation of these middle classes alienates them from establishing fruitful linkages with the countryside. Rather, the institutional set up in the rise of these classes is such that promotes and strengthens the dependency of village upon the city. We witness the paradox of industrial and professional growth without social justice.

Industrialization, technological advancement and processes of reform in the rural agrarian structures have contributed to development in agriculture in various parts of the country, popularly known as 'green revolution.' The leaders of green revolution in most cases come from the traditional peasant castes, the former tenants of village landlords or feudal nobility. The emergence of this group in villages has had a dual consequence for country-town relationships. On the one hand, the dependence of modern agriculture on urban industrial inputs, banks, market and pricing mechanisms etc. has enlarged the nexus between city - and country, but on the other, this relationship itself has precipitated a crisis in country-town relationship in general. The spurt in political, cultural and physical levels of communication and contact between the two social entities has intensified self-consciousness and identity of the new rural middle classes. Their relative economic strength has given them access to some opportunities in education, political power and political participation. It has strengthened their voice in the developmental processes of the rural society. This awareness is often compounded by the solidary character of these middle classes in villages on caste and kinship lines. Most of them come from similar caste background and enjoy numerical advantages in rural population. They dominate over village panchayats and its block and district level representations. They constitute powerful political resource on which the professional politicians must depend for electoral successes in state legislatures, and often in parliamentary elections. In some states, such as Maharashtra, Gujarat, Punjab, and Andhra Pradesh etc. where such agricultural development is linked also with production of cash crops, their political and economic clout has been further enlarged.

There are many levels of relationship that these rural middle classes tend to establish within and outside the village scene. Within the village their relationship with weaker sections and landless labourers ranges from outright indifference to pugnacity. This increasingly alienates the working classes who undertake urbanward migration, not in all cases due to attraction for the city life, but in order to escape from rural exploitation. These rural middle classes have ideological affinity at one level with the urban middle classes as both these groups share conservative and narrow utilitarian ethos. But peasant middle classes, anchorage in this ideology also generates at another level a feeling of intense conflict with the urban middle classes, entrepreneurs and professional groups. There is historical basis for this contradiction. The process of development in agriculture has after a period of time slowed down due to structural and technological stagnation. Even the so called rich peasants have over the past few years confronted the prospect of downward mobility in terms of social and economic status due to unfavourable price policy, stagnation in productivity of agriculture, fragmentation of landholding due to population pressure in the family and non-availability of other avenues of employment for their youth. This post green revolution underdevelopment in agriculture further reinforces the alienation of middle class peasantry from the urban and industrial middle classes as it constitutes a set back to their level of aspiration, having already reached a high peak during the early periods of green revolution. The existing policies of communication and media exposure further aggravates their sense of relative deprivation. This has resulted in a series of farmers' protest movements in most parts of our country, which views country-town nexus from a highly negative ideological perspective. This perspective is based on facts about highly uneven levels of rural-urban development and inequitous availability of resources, fiscal and market opportunities.

The ideological stance of the middle class peasant movements is to draw support from starkness of the unequal development between country and town in India. Indeed,it is held that cities and industries have grown in India at the cost of villages and agriculture. This is supported from developmental statistics as well. Of the total energy generated in the country the share of villages is only slightly above 9 percent where more than 70 percent population resides. It is said, "that most villagers being illiterate are voiceless. Taking advantage of these circumstances, the new (urban-based) rulers of India have succeeded in imposing a system, in which the rural masses have been reduced to the status of "captive-producers and captive consumers." They are left with no choice but to sell their produce at the cheapest, and buy their requirements at the highest prices. Besides exploitation through price twists, the rural masses have also been denied their due share in plan expenditure, supplies of power and credit, and facilities for proper education and medicare. Agriculture has been contributing from one half to one third to the national income, yet combined allocation for all the rural programmes from III to VI plan has never exceeded 23% of the total public sector plan expenditure. Allocation for education was brought down from 7.7% of the total to 2.7%, and for medical services from 2.6% to 1.8% during the same period. And these reductions have been made at the cost of the rural population, because no one can see any reduction of these facilities in cities." If one were to draw a statistical profile of the country-town differentials in levels and quality of development and allocation of developmental resources, the unequal pattern in favour of cities and discriminatory to villages can be clearly outlined. These indicators of unequal development are today increasingly being converted into an ideology of rural-urban opposition which despite being relevant is being made use of from a class point of view. This results in farmers movements and protests, which some times takes violent forms. It gets entwined with political processes and party ideologies as we witness today.

Where does this leave us in terms of the country-town nexus? Obviously, there is need for a systemic perspective which could diagnose the nature of these problems more objectively and introduce corrections in ideological uses of indicators of development and underdevelopment. A simple correction that could be introduced in this analysis is of replacing the categories rural and urban by sociological categories of rich and poor, privileged and under-privileged or propertied and propertyless groups or classes. One could not deny that the model of economic and social development that the country has adopted during the past decades has contributed to an elitist pattern of development, encouraged consumerism in a small section of about 10 percent, mostly urban population. It did not create effective institutions for equitable distribution of resources to different sectors and sections of society. From another point of view, however, one could not be oblivious of the fact that massive investments made in infrastructures, e.g. power, irrigation, fertilizers, transport and capital goods industries has contributed to the growth in agriculture and these benefits were made available to rich farmers more than smaller ones or the landless workers. The policy of industrial development could not, therefore, be considered discriminatory in terms of country-town divide. It could however, be treated as discriminatory from the normative perspective if we introduce the categories of rich and poor in India. It cannot be denied that development model within the framework of a mixed economy contained built-in contradictions, but most of these contradictions were envisaged as resolvable by suitable orchestration of policies.

These policies have not worked as effectively as it was anticipated. Development activities in villages reinforced the strength of the better-to-do classes, activated caste and kinship solidarities along new lines of cultural and political alignments. It affected the legitimacy both of the democratic institutions and principles of social justice in society. The skewed pattern of economic development both in villages and cities led to distortion of the political and cultural ideologies. Uneven development of groups and classes both in cities and villages has hindered the effective role that democratic institutions could play in socially purposeful implementation of social and economic reform policies. It has contributed to strengthening of a political culture in the country which is increasingly losing its ability to be responsive to genuine needs of the people. Instead, it relies increasingly on politicial manipulation of sectional interests, generally through the dominant classes both in cities and villages, the political nexus between country and town clearly articulates this hegemonistic relationship.

The country-town nexus as it has emerged in the process of social transformation in India during the past four decades tends to intensify the alienative rather than integrative forces in our polity, economy, culture and social system. Segmentary identities based on social and cultural cleavages have increased their hold on the institutional apparatuses of society. Communalism, regionalism and casteism, the forces that pose maximum challenge to our national ideology can be seen establishing new alliances across country and town. The momentum for it is being provided by the emerging new middle classes in our society. No doubt, these classes have demonstrated their entrepreneurial and economic dynamism by selective adoption of utilitarian rationality. But it is devoid of a social ethic, commensurate with national ideology, the ethic of democracy, socialism and secularism. The country-town category as a sociological phenomenon suffers from this uneven and negatively ideological process of development. The problem is deeply structural and ideological.

This seminar is meeting at a crucial stage of our development. It should offer us an occasion to examine the roots of our structural and cultural contradictions, distortions and errors in our development policies, or strategies. From this possibly we might gain insights about how to mend our approach and move towards a balanced form of social and economic development in our society. Firstly, we might examine the approach to development itself, more particularly the nature of linkages between decision making and implementation of policies. These linkages have their weaker points in our social setting, administration and political initiatives at the grass-root levels of society. Secondly, we might also analyse how decentralization in decision making, specially through local elected bodies both in cities and villages could be strengthened in order to effectively implement policies of development and to suggest corrections to these policies wherever necessary. It may be well to undertake intensive study of the ideology of the emerging new middle classes to diagnose the cultural crisis that we encounter through the rise of communalism, casteism, genderism and superstition. I believe that we are passing through a phase of development where we encounter major ideological challenges. The impact of our cosmopolitan nationalist ideology has weakened over the past few decades due to ascendancy of a narrow utilitarian culture, in politics, profession, business, administration and agriculture. The new middle classes are products of this culture and serve as its carriers. They do demonstrate entrepreneurial ability and skill in manipulative operations but there is a certain short sightedness to their cultural ethos. It tends to be non-empathic and non-cosmopolitan in nature.

Such ideology can prove dangerous in a country where large majority of people are poor, without shelter or availability of basic necessities of life. We need to combat this ideology through suitable responses from our education, communication and media policies. We might like to examine the contribution that education and media are making to give a proper direction and balance to the country-town relationships in our society. A closer examination of this might bring to light many anomalies. Finally, we may also examine the ecological, demograhic and physical side of the problems of country-town nexus in society. At present we prepare master plans for cities, without taking into consideration planned development of villages. We might consider how far an integrated physical, ecological and institutional planning process could be evolved which is anchored in the perspective of a country-town nexus, their mutual binding relationships, and not in opposition.

CHAPTER 2

The Rural-Urban Networks in India

—*A.M. Shah*

I

With the urban population in India constituting 23.7 per cent of the total population in 1981 and with the projected growth rising to 27.5 per cent in 1991 (Registrar General of India 1986) India can no longer be described as a land of villages.[1] (Not that there was much justification for such description in the past, but I shall say more about that later). The urban centres are playing an increasingly important role in Indian society as a whole, including rural society. The importance of understanding rural-urban relations, therefore, can hardly be overemphasised. This paper is a modest attempt to contribute to an understanding of these relations.

[This paper was first published in *South Asia,* Vol. XI, No. 2, 1988, pp. 1-27. The editors are grateful to Professor A.M. Shah, the author, and to Professor H.V. Brasted, Editor of *South Asia* for permission to reprint the paper in this volume. The paper is being reprinted in its original form except the changes in the manner of providing notes and references to harmonise with the other papers in this volume eds.]

[1]This paper was incubating for a long time. It was written during my Visiting Fellowship at the Institute of Development Studies, Sussex, and presented at seminars at the School of African and Asian Studies, University of Sussex, and the London School of Economics in 1976-77. Later its revised versions were presented at Gujarat Vidyapeeth, Ahmedabad, at the seminar on 'Nehru and the Village' organised by the Nehru Memorial Fund at Madras, at the University of Pennsylvania, Philadelphia, and at the seminar on 'Gujarat Society' at the Centre for Social Studies, Surat. Its present version was delivered as a 'guest lecture' of the South Asian Studies Association of Australia and New Zealand at the Seventh National Conference of the Asian Studies Association of Australia held at Canberra in February 1988. I am thankful to the participants in all these gatherings and to Professor M.N. Srinivas for comments.

My competence to talk about urban society in India is limited. I have not carried out any empirical investigation in urban centres. I have done fieldwork mainly in villages. However, as the villages in which I worked had several towns in their vicinity since at least the eighteenth century, I could not help observing relations between villages and towns, and this led me to read and think about these relations. My recent work on castes as horizontal units also involved study of castes in the urban context.[2] All this work does not amount to much, but I hope this little intrusion into the urban field will be tolerated by those who have really specialised in it.

Anyone who surveys the literature on urban India will be struck by the fact that it is dominated by demographers, geographers and town planners.[3] Also, it is well known that the sociology and social anthropology of urban India is not as developed as that of rural India. First of all, the volume of empirical research done on the former is much less than that on the latter. Secondly, the approaches to the study of urban society and its relations with rural society, and the consequent views of structure and change in Indian society as a whole, leave much to be desired. That a general theoretical understanding of a social structure or institution improves with the growth of volume of good research on it is well known, but frequently a lack of proper approach also leads to a lack of proper direction in research. One of the aims of this paper is to plead for a reorientation of approach to the study of urban society and its relations with rural society in India.

In many sociological and social anthropological writings on urbanisation, industrialisation, modernisation, development, and change in India - all involving notions of past and present - certain processes are assumed to be new although they may really be continuations of old and established processes. Until recently many writings on Indian society assumed that urbanisation in India was itself a new process. According to them, India was a land of villages, which came under the impact of urbanisation only since British rule. Some have stated that Indian cities and towns - particularly small towns - are extensions of villages, or that they are overgrown villages. Terms such as 'rural town', 'rururban', 'rural urbanite' and 'urban ruralite' have been used to describe people and society in small towns. Many have stated that although people live in towns their social structure and institutions are rural in character. Many have considered such basic institutions as caste and joint family as essentially rural in character, or as having their origin in rural society and therefore rural even if they recur in cities. For example, Beteille writes in one essay, 'Caste merely represents a systematisation and elaboration of ideas and values which are present as important ingredients in most agrarian societies'.[4] In another essay he writes, 'One cannot help being struck by the remarkable association between caste or caste-like organisations and the agrarian way of life'.[5] He then quotes with approval Michael Young's statement, 'The soil grows castes, the machine makes classes'.[6] Apart from such statements involving the view that the Indian village consists of only agricultural castes, they assume that castes are rural in origin and therefore rural wherever they occur.

Fortunately there is now an increasing realisation among sociologists of the fact that India has had urban centres since the time of the Indus Valley Civilisation several centuries before Christ, and that towns and cities - small and large - existed in all parts of India throughout its recorded history. But welcome as such awareness is, it has not changed the formulations of the nature of social structure and change in India. Frequently the importance of urban centres is either minimised or altogether ignored on account of the small proportion of population living in them. Frequently the formulations of the nature of social change posit change from the rural past to the urban present, ignoring the urban past.

In recent years, however, there has been a tendency to promote urban studies. This is indeed welcome, but it has led mainly to a juxtaposition of rural and urban studies. Just as village studies have tended to deal with intra-village structures and institutions, urban studies have tended to deal with intra-town structures and institutions. It is necessary to go beyond such juxtaposition, and to study structures and institutions which link the two - which are supra-village and supra-town, or which are networks linking villages and towns.

Let us take an example. That members of a caste live in many villages and towns, forming what Srinivas has called a horizontal unit, is well known.[7] Certain important questions arise from this fact. What was the nature of the network formed by a large number of such horizontal units linking a large number of villages and towns in a region? What changes have taken place in the local and the regional structures, and what is their significance for understanding social change in general? It is not sufficient to say that the village has castes and the town has castes. What is necessary is to understand the total matrix of castes as horizontal units cutting across villages and towns.

Pocock has rightly pointed out that 'city and village are elements of the same civilisation'[8] and that the same institutions - caste, kinship, religion, and so on - exist in both villages and towns.[9] He argues, on this basis, not only against the idea of rural-urban dichotomy and the division of the sociology of India into rural and urban sociologies, but also against the idea of rural-urban continuum since it assumes rural-urban dichotomy. If his emphasis on the sameness of institutions in villages and towns means that there cannot be any institution whatsoever distinctive of towns, then the words village and town cannot be used as social categories. He, however, seems to recognise some difference between village and town when he states: 'the city stood for the most complete and abiding expression of the essential social values. At the ideal level, the city was the centre of caste ... the place where castes both in number and in hierarchical order most nearly corresponded to a Brahman's ideal'.[10] This formulation shows that Pocock subsumes the entire urban society under caste. Not many would agree prima facie with this formulation, even if they disregard the assumption of the equation of urban society with Hindu society throughout history. It may be considered at best a hypothesis, in view of meagre research on urban society.

Rao tried to meet the inadequacy of Pocock's formulation by trying to posit that although there were certain structural continuities between village and town in traditional India, there were significant organisational differences.[11] This amounts to hardly any disagreement with Pocock, because organisational differences can always exist within structural similarities. Nevertheless, Rao made a good case for studying traditional urbanism.

Lynch tends to confirm Pocock's hypothesis that it is false to presuppose a dichotomy of rural and urban sociologies, but adds the qualifications that 'this seems true of some castes, in some cities, and at certain historical periods.[12]

One of the aims of this paper is to show that an understanding of the rural-urban networks in the past is essential for an understanding of the rural-urban networks, urbanisation, and social change in recent time. I must add here, however, that I am not a professional historian but I have been working on some historical records about villages in Gujarat in which I have done fieldwork, and this work has led me to the study of some records about towns in the area. I am using this limited experience to say something in general about Gujarat and, by extension about India. This exercise has involved considerable historica speculation, but I believe that sometimes speculation is essential for academic advancement. I shall deal mainly with the question: what was the nature of urban society in the past and what was its relation with rural society? I shall refer mainly to the situation obtaining at the beginning of the nineteenth century when the British began to rule over India and initiate a number of changes.[13]

Demographers and geographers have done a considerable amount of work on urban centres in India, and sociologists should of course use this work, but they should also keep in mind the special meaning demographers and geographers, and many others following them, attach to the concepts of 'urban growth' and 'urbanisation'. For a dismissal of these concepts see *Ashish Bose*, 'Six Decades of Urbanisation in India, 1901–1961', *Indian Economic and Social History Review*, III (1965) 23–41. The former indicates absolute increase in urban population and the latter increase in the proportion of urban to total population in a given country or a part of it. Theoretically, there can be urban growth without urbanisation. If both the rural and the urban populations grow at the same rate - for example, there is no rural-urban migration at all and the natural increase in population is the same both in the rural and the urban areas - there is growth of urban population but not of urbanisation, in as much as the proportion of urban to total population remains constant in spite of growth in urban population. This distinction between 'urban growth' and 'urbanisation' is useful. But it takes care of only aggregates for a whole country or a region in it and ignores increase or decrease in population of individual towns and cities. We shall come back to this issue later.

Sociologists and social anthropologists use the concept of urbanisation in a more general sense. It would of course include the growth of urban population both absolutely and relatively to rural population, but it would also include, as Srinivas has done, the diffusion of urban institutions and ways of life in rural areas, resulting in some cases in transformation of villages into towns[14] or as Redfield and Singer[15] have done, the role of cities in the formation, maintenance, spread, decline, and transformation of civilisation.[16]

II

The degree and character of urban growth varied from one part of India to another. The coastal areas - from Karachi to Kanyakumari and from there to Chittagong - were dotted about with a number of trading towns, and here also some areas such as Gujarat, Konkan, Malabar and Coromandel, had many more towns than did the other areas. Within the inland areas too, the plains areas with developed agriculture and arts and crafts - which meant numerous Hindu castes with specialised occupations - had many more urban centres than did the hilly and jungle tracts inhabited by the primitive tribes. Similarly, desert areas provided a poor base for urban growth.

The distribution of urban population in an area is an important factor in the pattern of rural-urban relations. This population could be concentrated in one large city and only a small proportion of the urban population could be found in smaller towns, so that there would be a lot of distance between village and town, as well as a lot of contrast. On the other hand, the urban population could be dispersed over a large number of medium and small size towns, so that every village would have several towns in its vicinity in different directions, and there would be an absence of sharp contrast between village and town. Gujarat has been largely an area of the latter kind.

It is well known that three basic factors played varying roles in the making of an urban centre in pre-industrial India: economic (trade, commerce and manufacture), political (court and administration), and religious (pilgrimage)[17]. The economic factor was, however, much more important than the other two in the case of Gujarat. Gujarat has a long coast line, which had as many as 27 ports for big ships and 45 for small boats during the 16th-18th centuries.[18] Secondly, ports of Gujarat served a vast hinterland in central and north India. Thirdly, the coast line has in its immediate vicinity a rich plainland. Due to all these favourable factors Gujarat was involved in various kinds of trade: international trade with other parts of the world; coastal trade with other parts of Indian coast; trade among towns on Gujarat coast itself; trade with inland towns in other regions of India; trade between one inland town and another within Gujarat; trade between town and village; and trade between villages.

Economic historians have given much attention to the study of Gujarat's international and inter-regional trade,[19] but hardly any to that of its intra-regional trade. This is partly due to the paucity of historical sources, but partly also due to the unstated assumption of intra-regional uniformity. As a matter of fact, there was a great deal of geographical diversity within Gujarat, not only between the plains and the highlands but also within each of them. The plainland was divided traditionally into a number of tracts, such as Bhal, Charotar, Chorasi, Chumval,

Daskosi, Kanam, Mal and Vakal, to name only a few.[20] There was considerable specialisation of agricultural production between these tracts: they produced not only different commercial crops such as indigo, cotton, tobacco, sugarcane, spices, and oil seeds, but also food crops such as rice and wheat, and dairy products such as ghee. Such specialisation in agricultural production encouraged trade between one agricultural tract and another. Frequently the villagers of one tract themselves carried their produce on head, on pack animals or in carts to sell directly to villagers in another, usually an adjoining tract. However, they also sold a great deal of their produce to traders in a nearby town, in a weekly market, or in a fair, who in turn marketed it to other towns and villages. This point needs to be emphasised because although the old theory of the self-sufficiency of each individual Indian village has virtually died, it has been substituted by the theory that the rural sector as a whole was self-sufficient.[21] We shall return to this point in another context later.

A noteworthy feature of urbanisation in Gujarat was the development of a considerable number of villages into towns since the beginning of the Commerical Revolution in the 16th century. Certain villages became rich due to the cultivation of commercial crops such as indigo, cotton, tobacco, sugarcane, spices and oil seeds. The increasing wealth and power of the principal peasant caste, namely, Patidar, in these villages attracted a large number of traders, artisans, craftsmen and servants, thus adding an urban component to these villages and converting them into towns. In Central Gujarat, Nadiad was perhaps the first such town to develop, and quite a number of others such as Sojitra, Mahudha, Savli and Vaso followed later.[22]

The political history of Gujarat from the 16th to the 18th century was marked by gradual increase in the number of small Rajput as well as Muslim princedoms, each with a small capital town. This was a feature particularly of Saurashtra, Kachchh and the highlands.[23] It was one more factor behind the existence of a large number of small towns in Gujarat during this period.

Although higher or 'great traditional' religion characterised every town and city, it was a primary characteristic of a few small towns: Dwarka and Somnath in Saurashtra, Siddhpur in north Gujarat, and Dakor in central Gujarat.

Gujarat was divided into two major geographical and socio-cultural regions: one, the fertile plain adjoining the coast line, inhabited by many Hindu castes, and people of other religions, i.e., Jains, Muslims,

Parsis, Jews and Christians; and two, the bordering hilly and jungle tracts, inhabited mainly by tribal groups such as Bhil, Naikda, Chodhra, Dubla, Dhodia, Gamit and others. There were very few urban centres in the hilly tracts, and as we shall see, the rural-urban relations here were also of a different kind.[24] In the plains, on the other hand, there were a large number of urban centres and they were evenly distributed so that a village would have several towns in its vicinity. For example, at the beginning of the nineteenth century, the village which was the subject of my study in central Gujarat, had two towns within a radius of five miles and two more within a radius of ten miles, and so on. This situation was not at all atypical of plains Gujarat.

While agricultural, pastoral and such other pursuits were the basis of the village economy, non-agricultural pursuits were the basis of the urban economy. Village society had a great deal of division of labour: besides the agricultural castes there were the priestly Brahmans and a number of artisan and servant castes. Although every tract used to have one caste considered as the peasant caste par excellence, agriculture was an open occupation, so that several castes could have agriculture as their main occupation.

There was a great diversity of occupations in urban centres. The population of the town included, first of all, the families of the king, chief or governor, and of his nobles, courtiers, officials, clerks, retainers, soldiers and policemen. The second major category of urban population was comprised of cultural specialists, such as priests, scholars, musicians, dancers, artists, genealogists and so on. There were not only ordinary priests for ordinary people but also learned priests for the elite. The third major category of ubran population was comprised of shopkeepers, traders, money-lenders and bankers. The fourth category was composed of a variety of specialised artisans and craftsmen. A large quantity of textiles was produced in towns. Cotton textiles involved cotton-cleaners, carders, spinners, weavers, dyers, printers and others. Silk textiles involved even more specialised artisans. Moreover, there were goldsmiths, cutlers, brick-makers, masons, lime-workers, tailors, bangle-makers, cobblers, saddlers, potters, oil-pressers, and so on and so forth. The fifth important category of urban population was composed of specialised servants, such as barbers, washermen, drummers, grain parchers, rice pounders, florists, vegetable sellers, betal-leaf sellers, leather-workers, scavengers, and so on. The special life-style of the urban rich required special types of servants and workers.

Every town had, besides the preponderant Hindu population, at least some population of other religious groups. Although there were Muslim peasants in villages, most of the Muslim population used to live in towns, practising a variety of occupations. There were Muslims belonging to almost all the major occupational categories mentioned above. The Jains, mainly traders, generally lived in urban centres. Moreover, there were Parsis, Christians and Jews, though the latter two were represented in very small numbers. Each of these religious groups, except the Parsis, was further divided into sects and castes. A high degree of religious, ethnic and caste heterogeneity was one of the basic characteristics of the social structure of the town. Such marginal groups as Hijadas (eunuchs), Khavas (progeny of Rajput kings and their concubines) and prostitutes added to the heterogeneity of the town.[25]

III

As I have explained elsewhere at some length,[26] an understanding of relation between villages and towns, and inter alia of the social structure of both, requires us to distinguish three categories of Hindu castes: (i) castes found almost entirely in towns, (ii) castes found almost entirely in villages, and (iii) castes found both in towns and villages.

Some castes were to be found only in towns: (a) Several castes engaged in occupations requiring high literacy, if not learning, lived only in towns. Kayasthas and Brahmakshatriyas, two such castes, were employed mainly in the bureaucracy at different levels. Barots (bards, genealogists and mythographers) were another such caste. (b) Vanias (traders) were primarily an urban caste, and so also were the smaller trading castes of Bhatia, Lohana and Bhansali. Although a small proportion of Vanias kept shops in villages, they rarely struck social roots there - unless there were prospects of a village developing into a town, as mentioned earlier. In the case of many of these village shopkeepers the man would stay in the village but keep his wife and children in the town where his caste fellows lived in large number. Vanias began to strike roots in villages in a big way in the early 19th century when the British began to enforce their law that when a landowner who had mortgaged his land to a moneylender did not repay the loan, the title of ownership of land should be transferred to the moneylender. While the Vania acquired land, frequently through British law courts, he rarely cultivated it himself. The modern land reform legislation against absentee and non-cultivating landowners has uprooted many Vanias from villages and they are again back to the town where they originally belonged. Many Vanias also worked as bureaucrats at various levels, from the king's minister downward to petty clerk, and a few in commercial firms (*pedhis*) and in Jain and Vaishnavite sectarian organisations. (c) A number of specialised artisan and craftsmen castes lived almost entirely in towns, as for example, Soni (goldsmith), Kansara (brazier), Chudgar (bangle-maker, ivory-worker), Chhipa (dyer, printer), Bhavsar (weaver, dyer, printer), Khatri (cotton weaver), Salvi (silk weaver), Kadiya (brick-layer), Salat (mason), Chunara (clay-maker, brick-layer), Kandoi or Sukhadia (sweets maker), Kharadi (skilled carpenter and wood-carver), Dabgar (maker of drums, saddles and such other goods of leather), Ghanchi (oil presser), and Darji (tailor). (d) The towns had their distinctive specialised servant castes, as for example, Gola (rice pounder, domestic servant), Kachhia (vegetable seller), Tamboli (betel leaf and areca nut seller), Mali (florist), Dhobi (washerman), and Mochi (cobbler).[27]

In some cases, as far as the major caste division was concerned, the caste population would be divided between towns and villages, but at the level of the caste subdivision - the most effective unit for endogamy - some caste subdivisions could be entirely urban in character. We shall return to this issue later.

The castes whose population was divided between towns and villages were highly differentiated internally. Brahmans were found in both towns and villages. The urban Brahmans were involved in occupations requiring a high degree of literacy, and many of them learned Sanskrit. They were domestic and temple priests, teachers, astrologers, practitioners of Ayurvedic medicine, and bureaucrats at various levels. A considerable number of Brahmans had also taken to banking, money lending, and trading. The village Brahmans, on the other hand, practised priesthood with very little knowledge of Sanskrit, and many of them were involved in agriculture, frequently as owner-cultivators.

The caste of Rajputs included at one end the royal and chiefly families and the families of their nobles, courtiers and soldiers, all of whom lived in towns, and it had at the other end cultivators (even tenants and labourers) living in villages. The caste practised hypergamy, i.e., girls were married upward from the lower to the higher status families. The royal, chiefly and noblemen's families living in towns were of course the highest.

Another caste of the same kind was Kanbi (now called Patidar), traditionally the caste of cultivators. Their richest and most powerful landlord families lived in towns and the rest of the population in villages. This caste was also hypergamous, with the rich urban families enjoying the highest status. Their so called 'Six Villages' enjoying the highest status were really towns.

The population of certain lower castes, such as Chamar (leather worker), Bhangi (scavenger), and other untouchable castes, was also divided between towns and villages, and they too practised hypergamy. When an artisan caste, like that of carpenters or of blacksmiths, was divided between rural and urban sections, the two sections usually did different kinds of work though in the same broad field.

There were a few but populous castes almost all of whose population was found in villages. The most important of these was Koli, the largest single caste in Gujarat, constituting about 25 per cent of the total population. They were mainly small landholders, tenants and labourers, and occupied a rather low position in the ritual hierarchy of castes.

The large tribal population living in the highland areas was even more predominantly rural than were the Kolis; they were rarely, if ever, found in towns. In terms of ethnic composition, therefore, there was a clear contrast in rural-urban relations between the plains and the highlands. In the former there were caste links between the town and the village. In the latter the urban population (which was mainly caste population) had hardly any 'ethnic' links with the tribal population. The caste population in towns in both the areas was of course inter-linked.

Viewing the totality of the caste pattern, there was a proportionately greater population of higher and more Sanskritised castes in towns than in villages. The town was the locus of higher forms of Hindu religion and culture - a centre of 'great tradition', to use Redfield and Singer's term. This was reflected in the life style, including many customs and institutions, practised by the urban population.

We have so far considered large caste divisions, what I have elsewhere called 'caste divisions of the first order'.[28] I have discussed there at some length the complexity of the internal organisation of these divisions. Briefly, on the one hand there were some divisions with a great deal of internal hierarchy and a strong emphasis on hypergamy. They had either weak internal subdivisions (called *ekda*, *gol*, or *dharo*) each claiming to be endogamous but never really achieving the ideal of endogamy, or they had no such subdivisions at all. On the other hand, there were caste divisions of the first order each of which was divided into divisions of the second order, and each of the latter could be further divided into divisions of the third order, and so on. The divisions of the smaller order were the most effective endogamous units. For example, the Vanias, a first-order division, were divided into 30 to 40 second-order divisions, such as Khadayata, Lad, Modh, Nagar, Nima, Porwad, Shrimali, Vayada, and Zarola. Each of these was further divided into third-order divisions called *ekadas* or *gols*, some of which were each divided into *tads* (lit., splits). The *ekdas* and *tads*, the most effective endogamous units, were usually small in size, some as small as composed of about 200 households.

Let us now return to the distinction between the primarily rural, the primarily urban, and the rural-cum-urban castes. As far as the first-order divisions were concerned, the population of a division could be distributed between towns and villages, but some of its second-order divisions could be almost entirely urban. For example, while Brahmans were a rural-cum-urban first-order division, the Bhargav and Khadayata Brahmans were entirely urban second-order divisions. Similarly, some of the third-order divisions of a second-order division could be entirely urban (as for example, Nadiad-Petlad *ekda* among Modh Vanias in Central Gujarat), and so also some of the fourth-order divisions of a third-order division (as for example, Motu *tad* within Nadiad *ekda* within Khadayata Vania division). Usually the population of each of such small urban divisions was found distributed in a few nearby towns. But in the case of a large town such as Ahmedabad, Baroda or Surat, the entire population of a small division could be confined to just one town.

Such a division was a highly integrated unit, because almost all the kinship and affinal relationship were confined within the town, and most of the members practised more or less the same occupation, resided on a single street (sometimes a fortified one), possessed corporate property, regulated the corporate affairs through a panchayat, and worshipped a tutelary deity. There was considerable elaboration in urban centres of what is called the community aspect of caste.

All the urban castes and most of the rural-cum-urban castes permitted intra-town (also, of course, intra-caste) marriage. Marriages even between households living on the same street were not uncommon. This was in sharp contrast to the rule of village exogamy which prevailed in Gujarat as in the rest of north India. We need not discuss here the issue as to whether this was really a rule or only a pseudo-rule, a shorthand statement of some more basic facts of kinship in villages in north India. Nor need we discuss the complications of the rule for the rural-cum-urban castes. But certainly it did not make sense in the urban context. Intra-town marriages contributed a great deal to the cohesiveness of each such urban caste division.

A large town could have living in it two or more of the fourth-order divisions of a single third-order division, and similarly two or more of the third-order divisions of a single second-order division, and two or more of the second-order divisions of a single first-order division. For example, in a medium size town such as Nadiad in central Gujarat in the nineteenth century the Vanias were divided into at least three second-order divisions, Khadayata, Modh and Porwad; the Khadayatas of this town formed a third-order division (*ekda*) as opposed to other Khadayata *ekdas* in other towns; and this *ekda* was further divided into two fourth-order divisions (*tads*).

The Hindu population of any large town was thus divided into a large number of small endogamous units. James Campbell, who compiled the Bombay Gazetteers in the latter half of the 19th century, states about Gujarat: 'In no part of India are the subdivisions so minute, one of them the Rayakval Vania, numbering only 47 persons in 1891. When Mr. H. Borradaile in A.D. 1827 collected information regarding the customs of the Hindus, no less than 207 castes which did not intermarry were found in the city of Surat alone'.[29] This was at a time when Surat's population was declining. The number of castes was probably higher during the earlier period.

There was a clear contrast between the pattern of caste groups in the village and in the town. Usually the village had a small population, divided into a small number of first-order divisions. The population of each such division was also small, some divisions having just one or two household each. Even the largest divisions could not be as large as to constitute separate endogamous units. Usually the population of a caste was homogeneous, belonging to only one of the various second-order divisions. In other words, the population of two or more subdivisions of a caste was rarely found living together in a single village, while such coexistence was a common feature of the town. Social interaction between persons belonging to two or more lower-order divisions in a higher-order one commonly found in the town was rarely found in the village. The former makes the whole notion of inter-caste relations more complex.

A great deal has been written about the principle of hierarchy governing the relation between castes. Some scholars hold the view that this is an all-encompassing principle, governing not only inter-caste but also intra-caste relations. I have, however, shown elsewhere at some length how this view has limited applicability.[30] While there were certainly a number of castes, i.e., first-order horizontal units, with strong intra-caste hierarchy, there were also a number of others within which the relations between subdivisions were marked more by juxtaposition than by hierarchy and a sense of being different and separate rather than being higher and lower. This was particularly true in urban centres since co-residence of lower-order divisions within a higher-order one was a prominent feature of the urban community. As regards inter-caste hierarchy in the village, there is by now a lengthy bibliography of works, indicating a great deal of sophistication achieved in observation and analysis of this hierarchy. As regards inter-caste hierarchy in the town, however, there is not even an exploratory work available. Nevertheless, a few broad observations may be made here about differences between the two.

Inter-caste relations in the village operated in a small face-to-face community and overlapped with relations of a number of different kinds; in brief, they were multiplex. A town, on the other hand, was large enough an entity to make impossible to work out a rank order of all the castes in the town - even of the first-order divisions, let alone the smaller-order ones - the kind of which is worked out by sociologists and anthropologists for village communities. This does not mean that the principle of hierarchy did not operate among castes in the town, but only that the operation of the principle there needs to be studied systematically. The members of one caste would interact there with members of only some of the other castes and that too with different degrees of intensity. There were many different spheres of interaction, with partial or minimal overlap between them.

IV

The above discussion of caste in rural and urban areas indicates that Indian society always included a section of population which was hereditarily urban - groups which lived from generation to generation in urban centres. These groups were the carriers of an urban culture, with a distinctive style of life, customs, institutions, and possibly also modes of thought and perceptions. Urban society included many people who were born and brought up in urban centres, spent all their life there, and were involved in such occupations that they had hardly anything to do with rural people - who were, one might even say, alienated from the rural people. The modern alienation of a large section of the urban population from the rural masses has deep roots in the past. Moreover, the traditional urban population covered a wide economic spectrum: the rich, the poor, the not so rich, and the not so poor. To think, as is frequently done, that the urban poor of today are entirely a creation of modern industrialisation and urbanisation would be incorrect.

The hereditarily urban population used to migrate from one town to another whenever necessary. In this context, it would be worth knowing if during pre-industrial times there was urbanisation in the demographers' sense of the term, i.e., whether there were periods of rural-to-urban migration. We know for certain that individual towns and cities grew and declined, some even completely disintegrated (like Vijayanagara in Karnataka and Champaner in Gujarat), but I wonder if historians can tell whether there was net addition to urban population in the country as a whole at different periods of time by migration from rural areas. Ashish Bose shows, on the basis of a detailed study of census data from 1881 onwards, how the rate of urbanisation was more or less constant up until 1911.[31] This suggests that individual towns and cities grew and declined mainly due to inter-urban rather than rural-urban migration up until 1911. Frequently population from foreign lands came to settle in urban centres in India, as when Muslim traders from West Asia and then European traders settled in towns all along the West coast, including Gujarat. Similarly, urban population from one region of India migrated to another region of India. For example, Gujarati traders, artisans and craftsmen migrated to towns in other parts of India. Many Gujarati silk-weavers migrated to towns in Tamilnadu, most probably via Maharashtra and Karnataka.[32]

The Kayasthas of north India went to several parts of India, including Hyderabad.[33] There was also a great deal of inter-urban migration within Gujarat. The ancient port of Broach declined and Cambay grew, then Cambay declined and Surat grew, then Surat declined and Bombay grew. Similarly in the inland area, the capital city of Patan declined and Ahmedabad grew, and when Champaner disintegrated its population migrated to several nearby towns such as Baroda and Godhra.

The point is that inter-urban migration meant migration of the hereditarily urban population. Their migration remained the pronounced feature of urban centres not only throughout the nineteenth century but also during the first few decades of the twentieth century. Thus, the growth of Gujarati population in the neighbouring metropolis of Bombay during this period was mainly due to migration of traditionally urban population from a number of towns in Gujarat.

Historians frequently refer to hordes of peasants flocking to cities during periods of rural distress such as famines. But this can hardly be considered as genuine urbanisation. The same peasants would return to their villages as soon as the period of distress was over. Whenever genuine urbanisation took place, i.e., rural people migrated for long term settlement in urban centres, it must have been a slow process. Since most occupations were hereditary - even menial occupations were hereditary - it was not easy for most villagers to change over to urban occupations. Migration was easiest in the case of castes whose population was distributed in both rural and urban areas. For example, if there was a greater demand for barbers, carpenters, blacksmiths, scavengers or such other artisans and servants in a town, the rural members of their respective caste could move easily to the town. Also, if there was greater demand for more skilled artisans or craftsmen of a certain category, it was easier for the less skilled village artisans or craftsmen of the same caste to take advantage of the opportunity.

V

How were the large number of caste groups in the town interrelated? What was the nature of interaction among the people of different castes? It is impossible to answer these questions in the present state of research on the subject. We can only think of some parameters of discussion.

The nature of relations among the Hindu castes cannot be understood fully without taking into account the non-Hindu groups in the town. There was hardly any town in Gujarat without Jains and Muslims; many towns in south Gujarat included Parsis; a few large towns included Jews; and every town began to have Christians particularly after the establishment of British rule in the early 19th century. A large number of occupations in the town were not only caste-free but also religion-free. Although the hereditary element in occupational specialisation was important, there were very few economic activities which could be considered as the exclusive preserve of a particular caste. Apart from the fact that more than one Hindu caste would be involved in a single economic activity, non-Hindu groups would also be involved in it. Trade and commerce were open to a wide variety of religious and caste groups. The increasing opportunities for trade and commerce had brought members of a number of traditionally non-trading castes such as Brahmans, Kanbis and Khatris into this field.[34] It was quite common for some members of an artisan or craftsman caste, such as Goldsmith, Brazier, Blacksmith or Weaver to develop into traders in goods and services connected with their traditional art or craft, and might even become moneylenders and financiers. A number of arts and crafts were practised by Hindu as well as non-Hindu groups. For example, there were both Hindu and Muslim weavers, oil-pressers, tailors, musicians, washermen, barbers, and so on. There was even a caste of Jain weavers: the general impression that Jains in Gujarat were only Vanias is not correct.

The jajmani type of relationships between members of different castes found typically in the village - about which anthropologists have written so much - were also found in the town but only between a small number of castes in certain narrowly defined fields. It was observed most commonly in the field of ritual services performed by the Brahman priest and the Barber and to some extent in the supply of goods and services by the Potter, the Washerman, the Florist and the Scavenger. There were also patron-client ties between members of different castes and religious groups. Otherwise the economic relations in the town were far more contractual, commercial and monetised, than those in the village.

Every small town had a market place (bazaar) and every large town, such as Ahmedabad or Surat, a number of general as well as specialised market places. Not only that, there also existed markets as impersonal institutions permitting competition.

The number of castes was much larger in a town than in a village. They did not interact with one another in the same intensive way as in a village. In the case of some castes, the contact between their members and those of other castes was casual or confined to a simple economic transaction. Often, the castes concerned lived in streets far removed from each other, so that they could not have intensive interaction.

We have little information on production relations in the urban centres. Most of the arts and crafts were of course practised in the family. However, there were the so called *karkhanas* (workshops), about whose internal organisation we have little information. Moreover, we do not know how the various specialised workers in the field of cotton and other textiles coordinated their activities before the product reached the consumer.

It is well known that *mahajans* (guilds) prevailed in all towns, but there is hardly any research done on them. By and large scholars have dismissed them as nothing but castes in another form. However, the situation was more complex and closer examination is necessary. First of all, we should distinguish between guilds in small towns and in large cities. While each small town had one multi-occupational guild, a large city like Ahmedabad or Surat had a number of guilds for different occupations as well as a general one for the city as a whole. We have to examine these guilds in the context of certain general features of urban society mentioned earlier: (1) participation of members of several different religions and castes in a single occupation, (2) occupational diversification within a caste, and (3) existence of subdivisions within a caste division of the first order. For example, the guild in one small town in Central Gujarat I know, included all trading castes - Vania as well as Lohana, Hindu as well as Jain, and all the subdivisions within them. In addition, it included several skilled craftsmen castes such as Soni (goldsmith), Kansara (brazier), one subdivision of Suthar (carpenter), and Bhavsar (weaver and dyer). The guild performed important functions and owned corporate property, and was presided over by the Nagar-Sheth who was a Jain Vania. Significantly, in the 1940s it admitted one member from the Kachhia (vegetable seller) caste because he had established himself as a leading trader in a variety of goods. He was the only one from his caste to achieve this position. The guild thus was not just another form of caste.

VI

Every caste was a multi-faceted group, binding its members by various kinds of links. In the case of primarily urban castes, it linked members living in different towns, and in the case of rural-cum-urban castes it linked members living in both villages and towns. The most important intra-caste link was that of kinship and marriage. In almost every rural-cum-urban caste there used to be hypergamy between the urban and the rural section, the rural section trying to get daughters married into towns and the urban section rarely reciprocating. Such hypergamy meant various relationships flowing from marriage between rural and urban people: mother's brother and sister's son/daughter; father's sister and her brother's son/daughter; cross-cousins; son-in-law and parents-in-law; wife-givers and wife-takers; and so on. The network of relationships would became wider and stronger if a number of village girls related with one another were married in several different towns. That there was, in addition, hierarchy between small towns and large cities may also be mentioned.

Although dispersal of male members of the family (i.e., father and son, and brothers) between village and town was not common in the past as it is today, it was not altogether absent. For example, a rich landlord living in a town might own a lot of land in a number of neighbouring villages - this, called absentee landlordism today, was in fact quite common in the past - and consequent upon partition of his estate one of his sons might settle down in the village in which he inherited land, with a view to cultivate that land himself or to get it cultivated under his direct supervision. I found a number of such cases in the late eighteenth and early nineteenth century in central Gujarat.[35] On the other hand, a village priest's, artisan's, craftsman's or servant's son might venture to go to a town to pursue his occupation there. Anyway, genealogical records show many cases in which the members of a single partrilineage were dispersed in towns and villages. This in turn meant that the members of a lineage would maintain social relations with one another at least for a few generations after dispersal.

The rural-urban kinship and affinal relationships meant coming and going of relatives between village and town; exchange of money, of other forms of wealth, and of goods and services between relatives by way of, for example, inheritance of property, giving of dowry and bride price and gifts; and most important, exchange of information and ideas. In addition to such individual relationships among members of a rural-cum-urban caste, there were also meetings of the members of the caste as a collectivity and of its panchayat and such other representative bodies. Frequently, such meetings were held in 'neutral' places like pilgrim centres. All in all, the rural-cum-urban castes provided an important strand, a live wire, so to say, in the network of rural-urban relations.

VII

The links between villages and towns were not confined to caste, kinship and marriage only. There were other links as well.

Towns were centres of great traditions of Hindu religion and culture. A number of religious and cultural specialists lived there and provided their specialised services to villages. This is the burden of the many writings of Robert Redfield, Milton Singer, M.N. Srinivas, McKim

Marriott, and others on Great and Little Traditions, Universalisation and Parochialisation, Sanskritisation, and so on. While most village Brahmans performed all 'ordinary' rituals, learned Brahmans had to be called from the town to perform any special ritual in a 'truly' scriptural manner in the village. For example, a rich peasant might like to raise his status by getting the wedding rituals performed by a learned Brahman from the town. Performance of a grand sacrifice (*mahayagya*) in propitiation of Visnu, Siva or Devi, or installation of a deity's image in a new temple would require a team of learned urban Brahmans. The village Brahmans had to send their sons to learn not only Sanskrit but even the local language in *pathsalas* or with individual *gurus* in towns. Frequently, a trip to a pilgrim centre meant a trip to a town, since many pilgrim centres were also towns. Many urban temples had lands donated to them in villages, management of which entailed regular village-town contacts. Narrators of tales from sacred literature (*kirtankar*, *kathakar*, *purani*), bards (Bhats and Charans), genealogists and mythographers (Vahivanchas), eunuchs (Hijadas), drama troupes, and a number of other religious and cultural specialists living in towns visited villages from time to time.[36] Some of them had hereditary or some other form of long term relationship with villagers.

As regards rural-urban economic relations, historians have written extensively about the extraction of agricultural surplus from villagers by way of taxation by the ruling elite living in urban centres. Moreover, the urban population had to subsist on food grains supplied by the rural population, and the urban artisans and craftsmen had to use raw materials supplied by the rural population. These are incontrovertable facts, but they have generated a view that there was one-way traffic of goods and services from the rural to the urban communities. The villages, as it were, did not receive anything in return. This view fits well into the theory of self-sufficiency of the Indian village community propounded by such influential figures as Thomas Munro, Charles Metcalfe, Henry Maine, Karl Marx, and their many modern followers, including Mahatma Gandhi, Vinoba Bhave and Jayprakash Narain. This view, however, needs to be examined carefully.[37]

Writings by historians as well as sociologists during the last thirty years or so have led to the rejection of the idea of every village being self-sufficient. However, as mentioned earlier, the theory still persists in the minds of the people that the rural sector as a whole was more or less self-sufficient. This idea needs critical examination. First of all, it assumes that the rural sector was undifferentiated. As a matter of fact, however, it was highly differentiated. Every village was divided into a number of castes. The specialised occupations of a number of castes required tools and raw materials, and we should ask: from where did they get their tools and raw materials? For example, from where did the carpenter, the blacksmith, the oil presser, the musician, and the barber get his tools? From where did the village priest get the various sacred books required in performing his function? From where did the village Vania get his account books? Anyone with an eye for detail who has observed village artisans, craftsmen and servants performing their functions would know that they got many of their tools and raw materials from the town. It is remarkable how social scientists and historians have neglected the study of non-agricultural groups in village society in India, and how the whole of it is branded simplistically as agricultural, agrarian, or peasant. 'Agrarian social structure' and 'peasant society' are much abused though fashionable terms in the study of village society today.

That there was inequality of property and income in agricultural groups is well known, but its full implications need to be worked out. The richer agricultural families must have exhibited their wealth in diet, clothing, housing, pots and pans, vehicles, gold and silver jewellery, and so on, and all of these must have involved goods purchased in the town. Besides the differentiation of caste and class, there was a differentiation of yet another kind. Whether rich or poor, every villager's life was marked by rites of passage and other special occasions, such as birth, initiation, wedding, death, festival, religious ceremony, and so on. Such special occasions required special foodstuffs, special clothings, and many other special things. Many of these things had to be purchased in the town.

Finally, there were the needs of the village community, caste group, and lineage group as collectivities: village, caste and lineage temples, the festivals of village gods and goddesses, the village council house, and the charitable institutions of the village. All of these involved purchase of goods and services available in the town.

The economic implications of various social institutions in the village should thus be kept in view while considering economic relations between village and town. In the case of food, for example, while most of the daily items were available in the village, the villagers had to depend on the town for special food stuffs (for example, spices and dry fruits) required on special occasions. While the poor villagers might make do with whatever was available in the village, the richer villagers would obtain special food stuffs from the town. And so also would the village, caste or lineage as a collectivity.

The demand and supply of textiles should be looked into carefully. Cotton was cultivated only in a few tracts where suitable soil was available. Even in a tract growing cotton, every village did not grow it. This led to considerable intra-regional specialisation of cotton textile manufacturing. There was also considerable specialisation in the various processes of textile manufacture. Weavers were not found in many villages. They were concentrated in towns and large villages. We have very little knowledge about the organisation of the processes preliminary to weaving, i.e., cotton cleaning, carding, spinning, etc. Did every household cultivate cotton for its needs? How far is it true to say that every household produced its own cotton cloth? Did every household clean and card cotton and then spin as much yarn as it needed for its normal requirement of cloth? If not, who were professional cleaners, carders and spinners? What was the relation between the spinner and the weaver? Even if it is assumed that the normal requirement of ordinary cloth was met in the villge itself, there was always some import of even ordinary cloth from the town. And special cloth for special occasions (such as a good *sari* or *dhoti* for bride and groom, and for a god or goddess in temples, respectively) had to be obtained from the town. The richer villagers obtained cloth even for their daily requirement from the town. All superior varieties of cotton textiles and all silk textiles were made by urban craftsmen.

The villagers had to obtain certain specialised services from the town. For example, if a villager wanted to construct a *pukka* house or well with brick, mortar, etc., he had to bring bricklayers, masons, mortar-makers, and other specialised workers from the town. Construction of such collective buildings as temples, *dharmasalas*, and council houses also required these specialised workers. Pots and pans made of metal, jewellery made of gold, silver and ivory, even simple bangles made of wood and laquer, saddlery, cuttlery, musical instruments, gods' images, and a myriad of other things were made by urban artisans and craftsmen. Everyone of them had something to offer to the villager for his use. The villagers either went to a town, a weekly market or a fair to purchase these things, or the peripatetic trader from the town went to villages to sell them at the villager's door step. Rural society in general was certainly not as self-sufficient as it is assumed to be by many scholars.

It was stated earlier that the town was the centre of the higher level of Hindu religion and culture - of Sanskritic Hinduism, of the great tradition of Hinduism - and this level entailed a number of religious and cultural specialists and the literati who lived in the town and operated from this base. Their role both in the town and in the countryside was important.

Sectarianism was another structural feature associated with the higher level of Hinduism in the town. In our article on 'Hinduism', Srinivas and I tried to work out, rather briefly, the relation between sectarianism and Sanskritic Hinduism[38] (see the sections on 'Sectarianism' and 'Non-Sectarian Hinduism'), and I repeat it even more briefly here. The vast majority of Hindus were non-sectarian, both in villages and in towns. The sectarian Hindus, belonging exclusively to one sect (*sampradaya*, *marga*, *panth*) or other, had a relatively small number and were concentrated in towns. The Vaishnavites belonging to Vallabhacharya's Pushtimarga, for example, lived almost exclusively in towns in Gujarat. The Jains were also predominantly urban. Not only that, on account of the necessity of every sect to elaborate its exclusiveness with reference to the sacred texts of Hinduism, the sectarian Hindus were also usually highly Sanskritic. Pushtimarga Vaishnavism drew its followers only from the upper Sanskritised castes. The small number of Pushtimarga Patidars also belonged to the highly Sanskritised urban section of the caste. The non-sectarian Hindus were found in both villages and towns, but those in towns tended to be more Sanskritic than those in villages. Thus both the sectarian and the non-sectarian population in towns were highly Sanskritic, making the town the centre of Sanskritic Hinduism. The rural population was predominantly both non-sectarian and less Sanskritic.

Normally, membership in a sect, unlike that in a caste, was not hereditary but came through initiation. Even though frequently - though, certainly not always - children remained members of the same sect as their parents', they had to be formally initiated into it, unlike their acquiring membership of their caste by birth. And every sect was composed of members drawn from more than one caste. Sectarianism which was prominent in towns, therefore, provided strong social links cutting across castes in towns. Similarly, wherever sectarianism had penetrated villages, like the Swaminarayan sect, it provided links between the members of the sect living in villages and in towns.

The sociology and anthropology of India have for long beeen dominated by the view that caste, village, and joint family were the fundamental structures of traditional Indian society. Since the joint family operated within caste and village, and since the village was dominated by caste, caste is considered to be the all-encompassing fundamental structure. In other words, there is presumed to be a totalitarian regime of caste. When we consider the urban situation we realise serious limitations of this view.

Frequently it is said that Hindu society did not provide scope for individualism. A close study of the urban situation - the special characteristics of caste in towns and the several structures cutting across caste - would, I believe, show that Hindu Society provided sufficient scope for exercise of individual initiative and freedom.

VIII

We have so far dealt with rural-urban relations in the taditional or pre-modern set-up. So many changes have taken place in this set-up during the modern times that we cannot deal with them here. I shall only try to illustrate how some of the ideas developed above could be used to analyse these changes.

Important changes have taken place in the demography of rural and urban areas since 1911: the ratio of urban to total population has increased; rural-urban migration has increased; the existing urban centres have grown in size; a small number of new planned cities, like Gandhinagar in Gujarat and Chandigarh in Punjab, have come up; and a large number of large villages have become small towns. The earlier rural-urban network has played an important role in these changes.

No understanding of changes in the present condition of urban life in India is possible without studying social life in the old sector of the present urban settlements. While people have moved in and out of this sector in every town, there is still a large population which was born and brought up in it, retaining a great deal of the older life style. It would be a mistake to consider this population and its social organisation and culture as rural.

When a new planned town comes up or a large village becomes a small town, it involves migration of the population of existing urban centres to these towns. When an existing urban centre grows in size, it involves, besides natural increase in population, migration of population from other urban centres. A large part of inter-urban migration is 'step migration' of people from a small town to a large town, and finally, from the latter to a metropolis. There is always some distress migration of rural population to cities (due to, for example, drought in villages) and also some adventurous migration, but usually such migration results in what is called floating population (people living on pavements and in slums and in uni-member households). Normally very few rural people migrate straightaway to large cities, and if they do they follow the existing rural-urban links.

As Asish Bose see Ashish Bose, op. cit., 1965, has shown, the rate of urbanisation, which implies the rate of rural-urban migration, was practically nil up until 1911, and then it was slow till 1951. These figures, however, disguise the fact of inter-urban migration which was going on throughout the period of British rule. This migration was a continuation of the propensity of the traditional urban groups to migrate wherever opportunities took them. These groups took advantage of the opportunities created by British rule in the fields of industry, trade, administration, professions and education. The traditional network of caste, kinship and marriage played an importnt role in this process. The urban and the rural-cum-urban castes were the first to take advantage of the new opportunities. From the rural areas, the rural component of the rural-cum-urban castes was able to take advantage on account of its links with the urban component. The rural castes with the least urban component were the least and the last in taking advantage. They therefore continue to have the least urban component today. The tribal folk have even less of such component.

D'Souza reports: 'The information about the over-representation of the higher castes and the under-representation of the lower castes, especially the scheduled castes, in the urban areas has been well documented by the National Sample Survey's 14th round of inquiry and several urban studies which have looked into this problem.[39] This is indeed a continuation of the old established pattern, mentioned earlier, wherein the higher castes formed a larger proportion of the population in urban than in rural areas.

Along with this continuity, however, there is an important change. Even though the lower castes are under-represented in the urban areas, the little representation they have now is definitely higher than what it was in the past. Almost entirely rural lower castes like the Koli and the tribal groups like the Bhil in Gujarat have now recognisable representation in towns, and this has far reaching consequences for the future trends of change in these castes and tribes and in the villages in which they live.

On the other hand, my impression is that the representation of higher castes such as Brahmans and Vanias in villages has declined, making them even more alienated than they were from rural society and culture.

Since the old established links between towns and villages played an important role in the process of migration from villages to towns, the migrant villager was not a total stranger to the town. He came through the pre-existing links and got absorbed into the world of caste and kinship in the town. A Gujarati migrating to even a large city like Bombay took no time in getting absorbed in the world of his caste and kinship in the city.[40]

While rural-urban migration is important, urbanisation should not be looked upon, as noted earlier, as a process only of migration of people from rural to urban areas. Its another dimension is the diffusion of customs, institutions, ideas, etc. from urban to rural areas by various means of communication, including social links such as those of caste and kinship. Since urban areas had already had their own traditional modes of thought and action - not to be equated with the Western modes of thought and action - a great deal of taditional modes of thought and action would diffuse to the villages. It is also important to realise that the Western and modern modes of thought and action got transformed, modified and refracted through the traditional urban society before they reached the villages.

The thinking on the effects of urbanisation on the Hindu family has been affected by false assumptions about the nature of the Hindu family in villages as well as in towns in the past. It has been assumed for long that urbanisation leads to disintegration of the joint family. [This assumption is based on another assumption, that there is a stronger emphasis on the joint family in villages than in towns and that the joint family did not at all exist in towns because towns as such did not exist or because the joint family was a product of agrarian society.] The gradually increasing evidence shows that the towns rather than villages were the stronghold of the joint family system.[41] This is related to the fact that the higher and more sanskritised castes formed a greater proportion of the population in towns than in villages. Therefore, when the villagers migrated from village to town, they were not going into an environment hostile to the joint family. When they settled down in the town, they continued with the same norm of joint living, possibly with greater vigour. Secondly, the process of urban migration was itself helped by the joint family system. The male villager usually went alone to the town and left his wife and children back in the village home, to the care of the members of the joint family. Even when the wife and children joined him, they left considerable household and landed property behind to be looked after by members of the joint family in their absence, and they could return to the village home from time to time.[42]

The use of pre-existing links in the process of migration re-affirmed, if not strengthened, caste groups in towns. It is no wonder towns are strongholds of caste in modern India. It is here that caste links are reinforced by the formation of caste associations with their manifold activities. The caste associations provide a new kind of leadership to the caste, not only to its population living in the town but also to that living in villages. They are endowed with huge funds and use them to provide various services to the members of the caste in both towns and villages.

Since the late 1950s there has been considerable debate on the view that caste is changing from whole to parts, from system to elements, from structure to substance, from cooperation to competition. A fundamental problem with this view is that it is based on a partial conception of the whole - partial because it does not take into account caste in urban centres in the past. Even those who take account of it tend to presume that its nature was the same as in villages.[43] A comprehensive understanding of changes in caste is possible only by comparison of caste in past and present in both rural and urban areas (including rural-urban linkages).

As I have argued above and elsewhere[44] the principle of division (or separation, difference, repulsion) competed with the principle of hierarchy in caste in urban areas in Gujarat in the past. There are many indications of the growing significance of the principle of division and of gradual decline in the strength of the principle of hierarchy in the modern times. This change is becoming increasingly significant in the society as a whole in view of the growth of urban population in absolute numbers and in relation to the total population.

I would suggest that the emphasis on the principle of division in urban caste, the existence of many cross-cutting social groups in urban centres, and the well-known general tendency of urban culture to encourage innovation, provided the ground - however diffuse that ground might be - for a favourable response to the anti-hierarchical and individualistic ideas coming from the West. Significantly, a large number of social thinkers and workers who propagated against the hierarchical features of caste and in favour of individual freedom came from urban centres.[45]

NOTES AND REFERENCES

1. Registrar General of India, *Report of the Expert Committee on Population Projections,* New Delhi, Publications Division, 1986.
2. A.M. Shah, 'Division and Hierarchy : An Overview of Caste in Gujarat', *Contributions to Indian Sociology* (N.S.), 16 (1982), 1-33; Shah, A.M. and Desai, I.P., Division and Hierarchy : An Overview of Caste in Gujarat, Delhi, Hindustan, 1988.
3. Victor S., D'Souza, *'Urban Studies : A Trend Report', in Indian Council of Social Science Research, A Survey of Research in Sociology and Social Anthropology,* I, Bombay, Popular Prakashan, 1974; V.S. D'Souza, 'Urban Studies', in Indian Council of Social Science Research, A Survey of Research in Sociology and Social Anthropology, I, New Delhi, Mayur, 1987.
4. Andre, Beteille, Studies in Agrarian Social Structure, Delhi, Oxford University Press, 1974, p. 39.
5. Ibid, p. 60.
6. Ibid, p. 64.
7. M.N. Srinivas, Religion and Society among the Coorgs of South India, Oxford, Clarendon Press, 1952, p. 31; M.N. Srinivas, Social Change in Modern India, Bombay, Allied, 1966, pp. 9, 44, 92, 98-100, 114-117.
8. D.F. Pocock, 'Sociologies - Urban and Rural', Contributions to Indian Sociology, IV (1960), p. 81.
9. Ibid, p. 65.
10. Ibid, pp. 66-69.
11. M.S.A. Rao, 'Traditional Urbanism and Urbanisation' in M.S.A. Rao (ed.), Urban Sociology in India, Delhi, Orient Longman, 1974, p. 16.
12. Owen M., Lynch, 'Rural Cities in India : Continuities and Discontinuities', in Philip Mason (ed.), India and Ceylon : Unity and Diversity, London, Oxford University Press, 1967, pp. 156-57.
13. The historical portion is based on a variety of sources: gazetteers of British districts and princely states, recent historical works, early nineteenth century local records for central Gujarat, family and caste histories, ethnographic data, etc. Since this paper involves mainly interpretation of well-known facts, I shall not cite sources except where required by the context.
14. M.N., Srinivas, 'The Industrialisation and Urbanisation of Rural Areas', Sociological Bulletin, 5, (1956), 2, pp. 77-78.
15. Robert Redfield, and Milton Singer, 'The Cultural Role of Cities', Economic Development and Cultural Change, 3(1954), pp. 53-73.
16. I am aware of the problem of definition of 'urban' and 'rural' involved here but have left it untouched.

17. To define the pre-modern city entirely on the basis of 'the manner in which material wealth is generated', as Ravinder Kumar has done in his essay on urban history, would be to take a narrow view of the city. As I have argued elsewhere, although there could be one dominant factor - economic, political, administrative, or religious - in the making of a town, the other factors coexisted with it in a dynamic relationship. Any attempt to define the city or to trace its origin in terms of a single factor cannot take us far, if it is not totally futile. *See* Ravinder Kumar, 'The Changing Structure of Urban Society in Colonial India', in Ravinder Kumar (ed.), Essays in the Social History of Modern India, Delhi, Oxford University Press, 1983, and A.M. Shah. and I.P. Desai, Division and Hierarchy : An Overview of Caste in Gujarat, Delhi, Hindustan, 1988, 107-109.
18. Tapan Raychaudhuri, and Habib Irfan (eds.), Cambridge Economic History of India, I, Cambridge, Cambridge University Press, 1982, p. 352.
19. There are at leat five full-length works: Balkrishna Govind Gokhale, Surat in the Seventeenth Century, London, Curzon Press, 1978; Gopal, Surendra, Commerce and Crafts in Gujarat : 16th and 17th Centuries, New Delhi, People's Publishing House, 1975; Nightingale, Pamela, Trade and Empire in Western India, 1784-1806, Cambridge, Cambridge University Press, 1970; Pearson, N. Michael Merchants and Rulers in Gujarat; the Response to the Portuguese in the 16th Century, Berkeley, University of California Press, 1979; and Ashin Dasgupta, Indian Merchants and the Decline of Surat, 1700-1750, Wiesbaden, Franz Steiner Verlag, 1979.
20. For an account of these tracts, *see* Bharat L. Bhatt, 'The Cultural Regions in India', in David Sopher (ed.), Exploration of India, Ithaca, N.Y., Cornell University Press, 1982.
21. *See* Ray Tapan Chaudhuri, and Habib Irfan , (eds.), op. cit., pp. 83, 247, 248, and 327.
22. For historical and ethnographic accounts of villages and towns in Central Gujarat, *see* C.F. Shah, and Shah P.C. (eds.), Charotar Sarvasangraha, 2 vols., Nadiad, Lokmat Prakashan, 1960 (in Gujarati).
23. *See* A.M. Shah, 'Eighteenth Century Political System in Gujarat', Enquiry (N.S.), I (1965), pp. 88-95.
24. Apart from several gazetteers and such other works for information on these tribal areas, there are two useful recent studies of towns in the adjoining tribal areas in Rajasthan and Madhya Pradesh. *See* G.S. Aurora, Tribe-Caste-Class Encounters : Some Aspects of Folk-Urban Relations in Alirajpur Tehsil, Hyderabad, Administrative Staff College of India, 1972; Brij Raj Chauhan, Towns in the Tribal Setting, Delhi, National, 1970. I also did fieldwork in the merger zone between

the plains and the highlands and made a few brief field trips to the latter in 1953.

25. For an account of the Hijadas, see A.M. Shah, 'A Note on the Hijadas of Gujarat', American Anthropologist, 63, (1961), 6, 1325-1330; on Khavas see Spodek, Howard, Urban Rural Integration in Regional Development : A Case Study of Saurashtra, India, 1800-1960, Chicago, University of Chicago, 1976, Department of Geography, Research Paper No. 171; and on a similar group in Rajasthan see B.R. Chauhan, op. cit., 1970.
26. A.M. Shah, op. cit., 1982; and A.M. Shah, and Desai, I.P. op. cit., 1988.
27. See Spodek, Howard, op. cit., for a similar classification of castes, though based mainly on their political role, in towns in Saurashtra on the eve of British rule.
28. A.M. Shah, A.M., op. cit., 1982; and A.M. Shah, and Desai, I.P. op. cit., 1988.
29. Gazetteer of the Bombay Presidency, 4.1, Gujarat Population, Hindus, Bombay, Government Central Press, 1901, p. xii.
30. A.M. Shah, op. cit., 1982; and A.M. Shah, and Desai, I.P. op. cit., 1988.
31. Bose, Asish, 'Six Decades of Ubanisation in India, 1901-1961', Indian Economic and Social History Review, II(1965), pp. 23-41.
32. *See* Ramaswamy, Vijaya, Textiles and Weavers in Medieval South India, Delhi, Oxford University Press, 1985.
33. *See* Karen I. Leonard, The Social History of an Indian Caste : The Kayasthas of Hyderabad, Berkeley, University of California Press, 1978.
34. For evidence on castes of merchants in Surat, see Lakshmi Subramanian, 'Capital and Crowd in a Declining Asian Port City: The Anglo-Bania Order and the Surat Riots of 1795', Modern Asian Studies, 19, (1985), 2, pp. 205-237, and 'Banias and the British: The Role of Indigenous Credit in the Process of Imperial Expansion in Western India in the Second Half of the Eighteenth Century', Modern Asian Studies, 21, (1987), 3, pp. 473-510; Michelguglielmo Torri, 'In the Deep Blue Sea : Surat and its Merchant Class during the Dyarchic Era (1759-1800)', Indian Economic and Social History Review, 19, (1982), 3-4, pp. 267-299, and 'Surat During the Second Half of the Eighteenth Century : What kind of Social Order? A Rejoinder to Lakshmi Subramanian', Modern Asian Studies, 21, (1987), 4, pp. 679-710. See also Dvijendra Tripathi, (ed.), Business Communities of India : A Historical Perspective, Delhi, Manohar, 1984.
35. For an account of dispersal of members of lineages and clans between towns and villages in Uttar Pradesh, see Richard G. Fox 'Rajput 'Clans' and Rururban Settlements in Northern India', in Richard G. Fox (ed.), Urban India: Society, Space and Image, Durham, Duke University, 1970

36. For an account of Vahivancha Barots, see A.M. Shah, and R.G. Shroff, 'The Vahivancha Barots of Gujarat: A Caste of Genealogists and Mythographers', Journal of American Folklore, 71(1958), pp. 246-76. Reprinted in Milton Singer (ed.), Traditional India: Structure and Change, Philadelphia, American Folklore Society, 1959, pp. 40-70.
37. There is by now extensive debate on this issue. For an earlier statement from sociologists, see M.N. Srinivas, and A.M. Shah, 'Myth of Self-sufficiency of the Indian Village', Economic Weekly, 12, (1960), 37, pp. 1375-1383. For recent statements from historians, see Eric Stokes, 'The Return of the Peasant to South Asian History', South Asia (Old Series), 6(1976), 96-111, and Ravinder Kumar, 'The Changing Structure of Urban Society in Colonial India', in Ravinder Kumar (ed.), Essays in the Social History of Modern India, Delhi, Oxford University Press, 1983.
38. M.N. Srinivas, and Shah, A.M., 'Hinduism', in L. David Sils (ed.), International Encyclopedia of the Social Sciences, New York, Macmillan and Free Press, 1967.
39. Victor S. D'Souza, 'Urban Studies', op. cit., 1987.
40. See Frank Conlon, 'Urbanism and Indian Society: The Aspect of Caste', in Allen G. Noble and Ashok K. Dutt (ed.)., Indian Urbanization and Planning: Vehicles of Modernization, Delhi, Tata McGraw-Hill, 1977. Conlon first shows how several trends in thought and research over the last more than one hundred years led to the hypothesis that 'the city would be inhospitable to the continued operation of traditional social institutions such as caste and family'. He cites evidence from several recent studies, particularly of the Nadars of Tamilnadu by Robert Hardgrave, of the Jatavs of Agra by Owen Lynch, and of the Saraswats of Konkan by Conlon himself, to show how urban India is 'at least not incongenial' to caste. While this conclusion is useful, what is more important is Conlon's rather incidental statement: 'To speak of caste associations, reform movements and/or efforts at status mobility as strictly urban phenomena is to miss the linkages which existed between cities and countryside. Caste was itself one such linkage,.

The role of caste in Bombay during the earlier phase of its growth is well documented in Christine Dobbin, Urban Leadership in Western India : Politics and Communities in Bombay City, 1840-1885, London, Oxford University Press, 1972; Jim Masselos, Towards Nationalism: Group Affiliations and the Politics of Public Associations in Nineteenth Century Western India, Bombay, Popular Prakashan, 1974; and William L. Rowe, 'Caste, Kinship and Association in Urban India', in Aidan Southall (ed.), Urban Anthropology: Cross-Cultural Studies of Urbanization, New York, Oxford University Press, 1973. Masselos mentions significantly that several Gujarati caste associations in Bombay sent delegates to the fourth session of the Indian National Congress held at Allahabad in 1888.

41. A.M. Shah, The Household Dimension of the Family in India, Berkeley, University of California Press and Delhi, Orient Longman, 1973.
42. For detailed accounts of persistence of the joint family in towns, see I.P. Desai, Some Aspects of Family in Mahuva, Bombay, Asia, 1964; Singer, Milton, 'The Indian Joint Family in Modern Industry'; in Milton Singer and Bernard S. Cohn (ed.), Structure and Change in Indian Society, New York, Wenner-Gren Foundation for Anthropological Research, 1968; and Vatuk, Sylvia, Kinship and Urbanization: White Colalr Migrants in North India, Berkeley, University of California Press.
43. See, for example, the chapter on 'Caste in the City' in Pauline Kolenda, Caste in Contemporary India: Beyond Organic Solidarity, Menlo Park, Benjamin/Cummings, 1978, and Frank Conlon, op. cit.
44. A.M. Shah, 1982, op. cit., and A.M. Shah and I.P. Desai, op. cit.
45. It is noteworthy that Romila Thapar explains the rice of heterodox sects in ancient Indian with reference to the growth of urban centres. See Romila Thapar, From Lineage to State: Social Formation in Mid-first Millenium B.C. in the Ganga Valley, Bombay, Oxford University Press, 1984, pp. 109 and 153-154.

CHAPTER 3

Country-Town Nexus in India: A Macro-View

—*K.L. Sharma*

INTRODUCTION

Country-town nexus refers to myraid historical and contextual relations between village and town. It is difficult to know with exactitude the nature of nexus between village and town at a given point of time or in a time-series mainly due to complex nature of relations between the two. Nexus is defined here as a set of ties in terms of connections which becomes the basis of structural and cultural changes in both either proportionately or otherwise. Therefore, there is no necessary symmetry of relations in regard to causation, effectiveness and repercussions of change. Interdependence and/or dependence, interlinkages, hegemony etc. regarding relations between village and town are a focal point of observation and analysis rather than an antithesis. To know the "core" and the "peripheral" aspects of the nexus, it is necessary to know how much the "core" is really "core", and the "peripheral" aspect is really "peripheral", or not so peripheral in the context of the village and town nexus.

Our emphasis in this paper is limited to the analysis of some notions which have perpetuated mainly about the structural connections between country and town. The two have never been antithetical entities. The relationship between village and town has always been dynamic, and it is influenced by the internal structure and external forces, namely, macro-structural changes, social stratification and specific conditions of given villages and towns. Macro-structural changes refer to constitutional provisions, governmental policies and actions, science and technology etc. Social stratification in terms of castes, classes and power groups acts as a mechanism to accept or reject partly or wholly the macro-structural social transformation. Size and social composition of the village and its distance from town and infrastructural facilities like road, electricity, means of transport and communication too determine specific linkages with the town (s) in the vicinity.

There is nothing like cause-effect relationship between a set of factors and a given number of effects. Dynamics of macro-structural factors, social stratification and specific conditions of given villages and towns determine the nexus at a given point of time or over a period of time. Role of factors like migration and education, infrastructural inputs such as roads, irrigation and electricity, and specific historicities and contextualities of towns and urban centres can be examined based on a holistic account of these factors.

PERSPECTIVES REGARDING THE STUDIES OF VILLAGE AND TOWN

In the studies conducted prior to Independence the Indian village was considered as a "closed" and "isolated" system. It was characterised as monolithic, atomistic and unchanging entity. Metcalfe describes village communities as "unchanged, unshaken and self-sufficient, little republics."[1] Distortions have crept into our understanding of India's villages from such a characterisation. The studies conducted in the fifties and sixties were based on the assumption that the Indian village was not "static", "isolated" and "homogeneous"; it was changing, had connections with the wider society, and had social differentiation.[2]

Village exogamy, migration, inter-village economic ties, dependence upon towns for markets, division of labour etc. link members of a village with other villages and towns. Today village people are perhaps more dependent upon towns than the villages in which they live, and similarly the townsmen depend also more today upon villages than before. However, the nature of dependence of village upon town and of the town upon village is determined by wider societal changes, and by the changes in social stratification and in the specific local conditions.

The classifications such as "folk", "peasant" and "urban",[3] and "tribal", "folk" and "elite",[4] assume that "folk","tribal", "peasant" and "urban" societies are worlds apart from each other and they can be seen as constellations on a continuum. Robert Redfield uses the term "folk society" for "primitive" and "preliterate" people. They are the people who existed before the rise of cities and have remained unaffected by the great civilization. Redfield writes:

> In the folk society the moral order is great and the technical order is small.... Neither the formal regulation of the state or Church nor the normal ordering of behaviour which occurs in the market plays an important part in these societies. It is civilization that develops them. [5]

The distinction between tribal, folk and elite cultures is also based on the idealization of social and cultural life of the people. Although the village community in India is not perceived as "little community",[6] and "yet tribal culture" is seen as a whole in terms of its small size, homogeneity, distinctiveness and all-pervasive self-sufficiency.[7] The folk—tradition bears a widespread pan-Indic character like the elite tradition, but tribal culture is a local phenomenon.[8] Rural and urban, and tribal, folk and elite are not monolithic cultures or constellations. Oommen observes that there are considerable variations within rural and urban communities, and the rural and urban elements are found in differing proportions in both.[9]

Thus, structural pattering of social relations is crucial in terms of being more urban or less urban or more rural or less rural for a proper understanding of the country-town nexus and its transformation. Even heuristically the conceptual formulations analysed above are not adequate enough. Our study of the Jharkhand region in Bihar shows that the tribes of this region have been interacting for centuries with each other despite geographical barriers and problems of means of communication. The Hindu zamindars, Bengali money-lenders and the British administration posed a threat to them through their exploitative mechanisms even to the extent of their extinction and utter dehumanization.[10]

Inter-tribal isolation and cultural exclusiveness were never so conspicuous aspects as they have been made out. Mobilization of tribals against their "exploitors" and their interaction with the state administration, town elites and with the non-tribal communities have been an unalienable part of the tribal history. The main issues of the tribals of Bihar are related to agriculture and forestry like the non-tribal people in the Jharkhand region and elsewhere.

There are two distinct points which link the tribal people with the non-tribal people in the Jharkhand region. These are: (i) the "outsiders" exploit the native people and the material resources of the region, and (ii) the ethnic differences between the tribal people and the north Biharis and migrants from Rajasthan and Panjab are distinctly recognised.[11] Between 1765 and 1857 as many as five reformative revolts took place to improve the pathetic situation in the tribal Bihar. Christian missions not only created new organizations, they also brought about normative changes in the traditional tribal socio-religious organization. Today towns like Ranchi, Chaibasa, Dhanbad, Dumka and Hazaribagh are the centres for launching tribal movements and reformative programmes.

Tribal society was tranformed by colonialism despite its uneven impact. K.S. Singh mentions new patterns of social stratification, sanskritization and role of christianity as notable features of the colonial period.[12] Exploitation and alienation from land have resulted into a shift in identity from ethnicity to class among the tribal people, and this shift itself unites different tribes as a class against their exploitors.

We had single-village studies in the 1950s, and these were followed by a shift towards multi-village comparative studies.[13] Despite shifts from synchrony to diachrony and holism to comparison, the frameworks of "little community" and "folk-urban continuum" remained central along with alternate dichotomies, trichotomies and continua.[14] Sharma observes that most of the alternative suggestions were "reactive" rather than "emanative".[15] The understanding of social reality receives a subordinate place in the scheme of these studies, and the frameworks or classifications are accorded primacy over the knowledge-view of social reality.

Questions have been raised about cognitive and ontological bases of the village studies. Several other questions and doubts are discussed in Sharma's study regarding apriorism, methods and techniques, historicity, ideology etc.[16] Questions regarding nature, areas, content and goal, channels, sources of social change in village India are not adequately answered in the studies guided by the frameworks which have originated from the experience of societies and cultures alien to Indian soil.[17]

There are some other serious limiations of the studies of the village community in India. Social stratification is erroneously equated with "caste hierarchy" or "agrarian stratification". In either case, it amounts to the exclusion of non-caste and non-agrarian relations. The role and significance of caste and agrarian relations in the village community cannot be underestimated, but at the same time village community is a larger phenomenon than caste and agrarian relations, and in fact encompasses both. The point is that "peasant studies" are not "village studies". The former fall short of the latter. Peasantry is a very crucial segment of rural society. But the peasants are not a monolithic lot as they are differentiated in terms of ownership of land, self-cultivation, hired labour and contacts with wider society and power-alliances.

Frykenberg observes that there are socially structured land control relationships with gradations between two theoretically absolute polarities.[18] He writes:

> At one extreme is the lord over land and labour, absolute in authority so long as there does not sit above him some greater lord. At the other end of the spectrum is the labourer on land, absolute in servility so long as beneath him there is no lower level of subjection. Between the two are innumerable strata of lesser lords and larger labourers.[19]

Admitting complex relationship between land control and social structure Frykenberg observes that at some points some lords may be forced to labour and some labourers may have the opportunity to "lord". Also the same person could be both landlord and tenant to another person.[20] All varieties of zamindars, jagirdars and ryots were intricately linked to definite socio-ceremonial and communal as well as economic and political roles.

W.H. Moreland's study of the agrarian system of Moslem India explains that there were landowners who enjoyed certain rights, interests and privileges and they were in fact intremediaries between the rulers and the peasantry. Besides the intermediaries and peasants, there were landless labourers, village servants and recipients of charity.[21]

In the British period we find those agrarian classes in somewhat transformed form. However, British rule in India also changed the character of the merchant, artisan and landed classes and created conditions for the emergence of "new middle classes" through its policies regarding trade and commerce, industry, education etc. New professional classes also emerged during the British period which continue even today except in terms of some change in their self and societal awareness particularly due to the national movement and achievement of Independence.[22]

DYNAMICS OF COUNTRY-TOWN NEXUS

Thus, "country" cannot be defined in opposition to "town" and vice-versa, and similarly a villager or a peasant is not opposite of a townsman. A village is not a stable and isolate entity independent of a town. Village people, though in differentiated forms, have had always connections with rulers, officials, leaders, merchants and craftsmen living in towns and cities. Due to codifications of law, recourse to courts, bureaucratization and increased governmental interference and demands, inputs of capital etc. towns have come closer to villages since the dawn of British rule. Whenever there is a departure or deviation from the established pattern of norms and social relations, a change in the country-town nexus takes place.[23] Peter Robb writes about rural transformation in the British India as follows:

> In the countryside cultivation expanded, the value of production grew, and holdings were increasingly subdivided or fragmented. Competition became more open, over land, in tenures and rents, and for labour; and there is at least the possibility that disparities in income widened. Attitudes also changed, or the expression of them did. People tried to improve status or defend religion; landlords complained of unruly tenants and tenants of rapacious landlords. People became readier to appeal to the government's 'duty' to look after rights, but also to resent its interventions.[24]

Thus, it was not a system simply based on tradition and superstition. We find a great deal of dynamics and discontinuities within the village community and between the country and town. People grew for subsistence as well as for commercial purposes. Robb's following question seems quite convincing: "How complete is the division between urban and rural when few economic or social activities are restricted to one arena or the other, and when the same trading, credit and social or religious network pervade both?"[25] But at the same time cultiviators were practically under the command of Zamindars and money-lenders. Rural people were inferior materially to townsmen. Despite such inequalities, communications and exchanges improved. There were remarkable changes in agrarian relations, production system, transport, law and socio-religious and political spheres. A new nexus between country and town emerged in the British period.

Today it is widely acknowledged that Indian society has not been as rigid and unchanging as it is generally believed to be. The question is: what was the nature of change? Was it a fundamental change? Did such a change make it possible for some people to move up and forced others to slide down? What were the factors of change in the social order? We could say that both continuity and change were there, and factors like population growth, invasions, migration, culture-contact and contradictions within the existing social order brought about social change. Inequalities, injustices, unequal access to opportunities created contradictions in Indian society. Social tensions, movements, uprisings, role-conflicts and social mobility are natural consequences of such contradictions and external influences.[26]

Indian village consists of a complex hierarchical system with individuals, families and groups superimposed upon each other. Relations between these units are found simultaneously in terms of caste gradation, money-power, landownership, intellectual calibre and political power. A complex matrix of these factors in a given situation and at a particular point of time is the basis of status–determination. Therefore, status-incongruence besides being a common feature of the village community, also explains contradictions, mobility and falsity of "reductionsim" in the understanding of India's social stratification.

Caste does not imply essentially only "tradition" and class does not refer to "modernity" alone, nor village stratification is reducible to caste hierarchy, and urban stratification to class hierarchy. Caste has inhered class, and class has inhered caste for centuries in Indian society.[27] Also today the two are found in an inseparable complex mix. Both are found active simultaneously as an effective mechanism in elections, marriages and other socio-cultural situations. Caste is not simply a ritualistic system, nor class is found as an open system. Since such a "mix" of the two is found in both rural and urban settings, the country-town nexus is found in regard to social stratification.[28]

COUNTRY-TOWN NEXUS IN POST-INDEPENDENT INDIA

Let us now look at the nature of nexus between country and town in terms of change in the village community in the post-independent India. It is evident from the following analysis that agrarian relations have been considered as the focal point of village community. Money-lenders, artisans, shop-keepers, salaried workers, non-agricultural wage-earners, priests, salaried white-collar workers outside their village constituted an important segment of rural society at the start of the post—independence era. Their linkages with various sections of pesantry certainly mattered a lot. Migration, mobility and change were actualised through these sections of rural society.

In north-western Rajasthan, Brahmins and Banias have had a tradition of migrating to Assam, Bengal and Bihar to work initially as accountants and shop-assistants in private business firms owned by the people from their own areas and generally by the members of their own caste community. These people generally did not settle down at the places of their work. They used to visit their families normally once a year, and after spending two to three months would return to the places of their work.[29]

Artisans and other illiterate people used to go to Ahmedabad, Bombay, Kanpur and other towns for employment in cotton mills. Not only people sought employment, but also saved a lot and spent their savings on buying land, marriages, construction of houses, and also invested in money-lending. New ideas and knowledge about urban styles of life filtered to their families through them, and through their families to other villagers. What particular knowledge/information was transmitted depended upon the social background of the migrants and the nature of employment and surroundings of their place of work and residence.

Not only Brahmins, Banias and artisans had linkages with towns and cities, the village feudal lords too had linkages with their superiors who had headquarters of their jagirs, thikanas and states in towns and cities. They passed on materials and messages to them and received orders from them. Almost every jagirdar had a "house" at the headquarters of his Princely State. Impact of urban life on rural people could be seen through such connections. Several other examples of rural-urban connections can be cited.

The post-independent India has witnessed significant change in the traditional pattern of country-town nexus. The character of both countryside and urban settings has undergone tremendous transformation as a result of some very basic structural innovations. These include constitutional provisions, developmental planning, green revolution, expansion of higher education, new avenues of employment and infrastructural inputs like roads, electricity, irrigation etc. A large number of village people are working in the rural areas as school teachers, clerks, patwaris, gramsevaks, compounders, peons, ayurved physicians etc. Also we find a good number of the village people working in banks, offices of state and central governments, colleges and universities.

Consequent upon such a structural change, the number of people who used to go to far off places in Assam, Bengal and Bihar has come down considerably. A large number of them from upper castes who migrate to these areas today are school and college dropouts. Those who used to go earlier for employment have established their own business, and they have even settled down at the places of their work. Another new feature is that these migrants shift their families too to these places, and hence their visits to the native places have reduced considerably. However, rural-urban connections have increased enormously within a given district/state due to the structural factors analysed earlier.

What has happend in the recent years is quite different from what existed in the past. School teachers, patwaris, gramsevaks, peons, managers of cooperative societies etc. prefer to work in their own villages. Alternatively, they prefer to work at the nearby places from where they can commute daily or visit their families at the week-end. Other people are those who prefer to work at the headquarters of tehsil/ block, district and the state depending upon their respective positions, interests and preferences. However, there are always some exceptions in regard to the preferences for work at some places outside from one's own state. Many people have permanently settled down in various small, medium and large towns in their own states, but there are others who have built houses and settled down at far off places in Assam, Bengal, Bihar, Madhya Pradesh, Uttar Pradesh, Delhi, Gujrat, Maharashtra etc. These people have not severed their connections with their kith and kin in their native villages.[30]

It is not that only the upper or lower castes have moved out of their villages. A larger number of better off members from the middle caste's peasant families have also migrated to the nearest towns and the State headquarters. A good number of them have taken up white-collar jobs at the lower and middle levels, and some have also become petty traders and shop-keepers. Such a situation has also affected power-politics in the countryside. However, we do not intend to dwell upon this point here.

One obvious conclusion is that country and town are not "independent" variables of social change. The "independent variables" are, for example, policy measures, planning and infrastructural inputs which transfom village and town, and rechannelise agents of social change such as education, economic resources, migration, employment avenues and opportunities. All these are affected unevenly for different sections of society because of the persisting unevenness among people. Equal measures cannot have even consequences on uneven social structure. Persisting social inequalities become an obstacle in social transformation.

Before we analyse trends of social change in both the settings, namely, country and town, we would like to mention that efficacy of resourcefulness is not different in these settings provided a person has also cognitive ability about its proper utilization. Country and town are two different but interlinked structural patterns of living. People with certain economic standing and cognition send their wards to towns and cities for higher education. Others try to get the sick members of their families treated at the best possible hospitals irrespective of distance from their places of residence. The poor in towns and cities might be living just close to a good college/university, but they may not be able to send their worthy wards for higher education. Similarly, a poor person may remain deprived of treatment even after knowing that he is just there at the threshold of a hospital.

Agrarian Change and the Country-Town Nexus

Mencher in her study of a village in the South Arcot district of Tamilnadu which was earlier studied by Gilbert Slater in 1916 personally and later in 1937 and 1961 by others, analyses change and continuity in living conditions, technology, landownership and the village power structure.[31] Slater found "dualism" in the village based on acute distinctions between Brahmins and Harijans. Economic inequality, social discrimination and physical segregation were vividly visible in the village. The survey conducted in 1961 shows that land ceiling legislation has resulted in the divestiture of about ten per cent of the landlord's holdings. Mencher observes as follows:

> The plutocrat's economic power has given him effective control over the village commons. He is in a position to promote or prevent anything happening in or to the village. His support has been forthcoming for primary education, health care, veterinary services, and temple renovation and maintenance in the village. But he has stood in the way of anything that would make the Harijans more self-reliant, e.g., house-sites and milch cattle; nor, has he shown interest in securing simple welfare needs for them, e.g., drinking water and street lighting. He has taken the fullest advantage of the "new technology". As a dominant employer in the labour market, he has been able to keep wages down.[32]

However, the plutocrat today faces tension and threat to his dominant position. Resentment against his tyranny is openly expressed. Higher wages are demanded. The emergence of the non-Congress government has severed his ties with state level leaders affecting adversely his political standing in the village. Introduction of a new mode of irrigation has spread the new technology of high yieldinig seeds and fertilizers. Besides helping only more affluent landholders due to cost involved, the new technology has created more employment in the village in both agricultural and non-agricultural sectors. The growth of public services has increased cosiderably. As we have pointed out earlier the benefits of these new openings and services have remained uneven and quite limited for the poor and Harijans in the village surveyed by Mencher.

There is a close interrelation between agrarian structure and rural development. Institutional factors create obstacles in the process of modernization and development as they do not allow equal distribution of the fruits of development, and perpetuate economic disparities.[33] Appu observes:

> ..."the ownership of land is still generally confined to the members of the upper and the upper middle castes, and those who belong to the bottom rungs of the caste hierarchy are, by and large, agricultural labourers."[34]

A similar observation is made by us in our study of six villages conducted in mid-sixties regardiing modernization and rural stratification.[35] Modernization depends upon two basic characteristics of society, viz., institutionalization of modern values and adaptability of the community concerned. These two attributes are closely associated with stratification and cultural legitimation. A pervasive and acute lack of means among the non-privileged to adopt and internalise the modern values is the basic difficulty in modernization in rural India. Ultimately, value-change is not found as a barrier in the process of modernization, the unequal or differential accessibility to the attributes of modernization is found as an obstacle in the emergence of egalitarian relations.[36]

Mencher's findings reported in another article corroborate our observations in the context of six villages in Rajasthan. She writes: "a social system, because of the ways in which the various strata within society relate to one another and to scarce resources, may itself impede aspects of modernization in some way."[37] Despite the perpetuating congruity between the traditionally entrenched sections of village community and the distribution of resources and benefits from schemes of rural development,it is being asked: What is being produced, by whom, and to whom the benefits are or are not flowing.[38] D.N. Dhanagare asks rightly in this context: "Has the green revolution succeeded in reducing socio-economic inequalities in rural India?"[39] Productivity and growth have increased sufficiently as a result of green revolution, but its percolation effects have not helped in reducing problems of unemployment and poverty in India. Dhanagare's emphasis is on the socialization of productive assets and more egalitarian distribution of resources and facilities through the cooperative endeavour.[40]

The infrastructural inputs in agriculture are of a recent origin and they symbolise incorporation of industrial capitalism. Role of indigeneous capital has also been found in 19th century western India.[41] The role of capital (urban) in growing of sugar is emphasised by Shahi Amin in terms of "unequal antagonisms" between peasants and capitalists because of their mutually opposed interests in the Gorakhpur region.[42] In Maharashtra and Gujarat, unlike eastern Uttar Pradesh, a "cooperative capitalism" is building up.

It has been observed that today villages depend more on cash, and rural moneylenders have acquired urban interests, hence capital from villages flows to the town. But also money flows from the town banks to the village people in the form of subsidies and loans.[43] Even small farmers are involved in the town-markets for disposal of their produces, and in return buy agricultural inputs.[44] The introduction of new technology in agriculture can be seen in terms of role of capitalism, polarisation of classes and class antagonism.[45]

Another notable trend, which we have mentioned earlier, refers to the transformation of well-off farmers and village shop-keepers into urban shop-keepers, traders, entrepreneurs and small-scale industrialists. The swelling of urban population after India's independence is mainly due to two reasons: (i) diversification of economic activities; and (ii) migration of those sections of rural society who have settled down in towns and cities. Carol Boyack Upadhyay's study of the Coastal Andhra Pradesh explains the rise of a new class of businessmen out of the class of capitalist farmers.[46] He writes:

> The emergence of this class is explained by reference to the convergence of several historical processes: the development of a productive and commercialised agrarian economy in the late nineteenth century and the emergence of a "rich peasant" class, the integration of town and countryside, an early interest in education on the part of the rural elite, the politicization of caste identity and, later, the green revolution and land reforms.[47]

Thus high production and profit in agriculture have resulted into surpluses which the rural elite by migrating to urban centres and diversifying their economic activities have invested into business, and have also transformed themselves into a class of businessmen entrepreneurs and industrialists. Several other researches also corroborate Upadhyay's findings regarding the consequences of green revolution in terms of the emergence of the capitalist farmers and their subsequent transformation into the new urban business class. While analysing peasants, migrants and paupers in South Gujarat in the late 1970s Jan Breman observes the emergence of exploitation and alienation of labour due to the accumulation of capital within and outside agriculture. The caste-class nexus plays an important role in this triangular relationship between migrants, local landless people and dominant landowners who are the principal employers.[49]

Breman observes education and migration as inseparable processes for the rural elite. Once education is accomplished, preference for urban living as a cherished value compels the educated youth to shun rural life. However, it is found that business enterprises and agriculture are pursued simultaneously by the same household. Most of the migrants owned land in their native villages, and about half of the cases owned land jointly with rural or urban-based fathers and/or brothers.[50] Thus, urban migrant businessmen retain important social and economic ties with their village–folk through frequent visits on social occasions, marriages and funerals. Undivided land also constrains the migrants to keep close connection with their kinsmen and relatives who have remained in the village.

Migration, Mobility and the Country-Town Nexus

Two most significant factors responsible for rapid urban growth in India are: (i) in-migration from villages; and (ii) expansion of urban centres by inclusion of villages and small towns located in the hinterland of big towns and cities.[51] These two factors explain better the rural-urban connections and the emergence of new structures and relations. We are not dealing here with density, spatial concentration of population and cultural aspects such as values, attitudes and behavioural aspects of urban people and their impact on the rual population. The only point which can be stressed here is that India's urbanization consists of a great deal of rural material and cultural inputs.

The towns which have witnessed maximum growth during the decade 1971 to 1981 are Banglore, Jaipur and Delhi, and the abnormal growth is through the process of migration from rural areas mainly to these capital towns. Why such an unidirectional process of change? Who are the migrants? What attractions the migrants find in towns? Biplab Dasgupta and Roy Laishley also pose two questions in this context: (i) which social, economic, and demographic factors in village life are associated with migratory movements?; and (ii) who are the migrants? Their study reveals that while the unequal distribution of resources in the village is a key factor in inducing migration, necessarily the landless or the poorest do not migrate. There is a dualistic pattern of migration, consisting of young and old, poor and rich, illiterate and highly educated, harijans and upper castes.[52]

We can work out a hierarchy of country-town nexus based on the sociometry of the migrants from villages to towns, and on the basis of transmission of the styles of life, cultural values and norms, and material activities and technological devices. In fact, migration is not simply a seasonal, cyclical, temporary or permanent phenomenon; it is representative of the social hierarchy in the village.

There is a range of the educated migrants, including the school and college drop-outs, educated with poor, moderate, good and excellent performances and technically trained persons. Caste and class background also matters in determining migration and mobility. Pre-existing connections and political patronage sometimes make migration and mobility easier. There are also push and pull factors, sometimes found singularly and sometiems combined in a given situation. Acute unemployment, poverty and pauperization are more of a push factor in Indian villages. The poor may migrate more in numbers than the rich, the illiterate may leave their native places more than the educated people, and the lower caste people may have to migrate more often than the upper castes. But it is not that the poor, illiterate and the lower caste people, because of their numerical preponderance in regard to migration to towns and cities, establish more rural-urban connections compared to the rich, the educated and the upper caste migrants

The construction workers from Rajasthan in Delhi, though substantial in number, are poor, illiterate and belong to lower castes. Their existential conditions are comparable with worst slum-dwellers in the city. They have been pushed out of their native places becaue of poverty, unemployment and indebtedness. There is hardly anything they give to the town except their labour, and they get hardly anything except the barest means for their survival. Their migration is also dependent upon the institution of zamadar (middleman).[53] No doubt the country-town nexus has this element, but there are also other elements which determine the nature of country-town nexus.[54]

Migration necessarily implies social and occupational mobility irrespective of caste, class and educational background of the migrants.

It is not that only paupers and the educated unemployed people migrate to towns and cities from villages. Some people also migrate to towns and cities for fulfilling those cherished aspirations and ambitions for which there are no ample opportunities available in their native villages. Some migrate to towns for more comforts and facilities, and they generally settle down there. Rural elite, including the political elite from among the caste Hindus, Scheduled Castes and Scheduled Tribes, have a tendency to settle down in towns and cities. We have noted earlier that the beneficiaries of green revolution shift to towns and cities for upgrading themselves as businessmen and entrepreneurs.

CONCLUSION

Country-town nexus is dependent on historical as well as contextual relations between village and town. Macro-structural factors, social stratification and specific conditions pertaining to specific villages and towns are the most important considerations in the study of country-town nexus. Country-town nexus has several layers and levels dependent upon the role of three sets of factors, namely, structural changes, social stratification and specific conditions pertaining to particular villages and towns. Keeping these factors in view we have analysed in this paper the relevance of frameworks regarding the study of village and town, the nature of country-town nexus in the British and post-independence periods, and the continuity and change in the nexus. We have also analysed, though not quite systematically, the role of education, migration and mobility mainly as offshoots of macro-structural changes in Indian society.

REFERENCES

1. See Bernard S. Cohn, "Notes on the History of the Study of Indian Society and Culture" in Milton Singer and Bernard S. Cohn (ed.), *Structure and Change in Indian Society*, Chicago: Aldine Publishing Company, 1968,pp.7-23. See also Louis Dumont, "The Village Community from Munro to Maine",*Contributions to Indian Sociology*, No. 9, 1966.
2. Surendra Sharma, *Sociology in India: A Perspective from Sociology of Knowledge*, Jaipur:Rawat Publications, 1985. See particularly Chapter 6, "Village Studies: Theoretical and Methodological Orientations", pp.115-44.

3. Robert Redfield *The Folk-Culture of Yucatan,* Chicago: The University of Chicago Press, 1941; and *Little Community and Peasant Society and Culture,* Chicago: The University of Chicago Press, 1951.
4. T.K.N. Unnithan, Indra Deva, Y. Singh (ed.),*Towards a Sociology of Culture in India,* New Delhi: Prentice-Hall of India (Pvt) Ltd., 1965.
5. Redfield , Robert , *op.cit.,* 1951.
6. See Robert Redfield, op.cit., 1951; Marriott, McKim, (ed.), *Village India,* Chicago: Chicago University Press, 1955; Chauhan, B.R., A *Rajasthan Village,* New Delhi: Associated Publishing House, 1967.
7. Robert Redfield, *op.cit.,* 1951.
8. T.K.N. Unnithan, Deva , Indra, and Singh, Yogendra, *op.cit.,* p.29.
9. T.K. Oommen, "The Rural-Urban Continuum Reexamined in the Indian Context", *Sociologia Ruralis,* Vol. vii, No.1, 1967, pp.30-48.
10. K.L. Sharma, "Folk-Culture of Jharkhand Region in Bihar",in Buddhadeb Chaudhuri (ed.), *Tribal Development in Inida, Delhi:* Inter-India Publications, 1982, pp.105-15.
11. K.L. Sharma, "Jharkhand Movement in Bihar", *Economic and Political Weekly,* vol.xi, Nos. 1-2, 1976, pp.37-43.
12. K.S. Singh, "Colonial Transformation of Tribal Society in Middle India", *Economic and Political Weekly,* vol.xiii, No. 30, 1978, pp.1221-32. See also Sengupta, Nirmal, "Class and Tribe in Jharkhand" *Economic and Political Weekly,* vol,xv, No.14, 1980, pp.664-71.
13. See, for example , S.C. Dube *Indian Village,* London: Routledge and Kegan Paul, 1955; M.N. Srinivas, (ed.), *India's Villages,* Calcutta: Government of West Bengal Publication, 1955; D.N. Majumdar, (ed.), *Rural Profiles,* Lucknow; Ethnographic and Folk-culture Society, 1955; Mckim Marriott, (ed.), *op.cit.,* 1955; B.R. Chauhan, *op.cit.,*1967. See also, Andre Beteille, *Caste, Class and Power,* Bombay: Oxford Univeristy Press, 1966; R.K. Mukherjee, *Dynamics of a Rural Society,* Berlin: Akademie-verlag, 1957; F.G. Bailey, *Caste and Economic Frontier,* Manchester: Manchester University Press, 1957; Epstein, T.S.,; *Economic Development and Social Change in South India,* Manchester: Manchester University Press, 1962; K.L. Sharma, *The Changing Rural Stratification System,* Delhi: Orient Longman, 1974. See, Sharma, Surendra, *op.cit,* 1985 for a detailed commentary on the village studies.
14. Surendra Sharma, op.cit.,1985.
15. Ibid., p.119.
16. Ibid.
17. Ibid.
18. Robert Eric Frykenberg, (ed.), *Land Control and Social Structure in Indian History,* New Delhi : Manohar Publications, 1979, p.xiv.
19. Ibid., p.xiv.
20. Ibid., p.xiv.

21. W.H. Moreland, *The Agrarian System of Moslem India,* Delhi: Oriental Reprint, 1968, p.160.
22. B.B. See, Misra, *The Indian Middle Classes,* Delhi: Oxford Univeristy Press, 1961.
23. Peter Robb, (ed.), *Rural India,* New Delhi: Segment Book Distributors, 1986.
24. Ibid., p.2.
25. Ibid., p.3.
26. See, S.C. Malik, (ed.), *Determinants of Social Status in India,* Shimla: Indian Institute of Advanced study, 1986.
27. K.L. Sharma, (ed.), *Social Stratification in India,* Delhi: Manohar Publications, 1986, p.56
28. K.L. Sharma, Caste, Class and Social Movements, Jaipur: Rawat Publications, 1986, p.18.
29. See, Thomas A. Timberg, *Marwaris: From Traders to Industrialists,* New Delhi: Vikas, 1978.
30. Recently I have conducted a study of the nexus between caste, peasantry and feudalism in the Shekhawati region of Rajasthan in which country-town nexus has been found as the major dimension of social change.
31. S. Guhan, and Joan P. Mencher, "Iruvelpattu Revisited", I and II, *Economic and Political Weekly,* vol.xviii, No. 23, and 24, 1983, pp.1013-22; and 1063-74.
32. Ibid., p.1072.
33. See, Gunnar Myrdal, *Asian Drama:* An Inquiry into the Poverty of Nations, vol.I, Penguin Books, 1968.
34. P.S. Appu, "Agrarian Structure and Rural Development", *Economic and Political Weekly,* vol.ix, No. 39,1974, pp.A-70-A-75.
35. K.L. Sharma, "Modernization and Rural Stratification", *Economic and Political Weekly,* vol.V, No.37, 1970, pp.1537-43.
36. Ibid., pp.1537-43.
37. Joan P. Mencher, "Change Agents and Villagers", *Economic and Political Weekly,* vol. v, Nos.29-31, 1970, pp.1187-97.
38. Barry H. Michie, "Variations in Economic Behaviour and the Green Revolution", *Economic and Political Weekly,* vol.viii, Nos.26, 1973, pp.A-67-A-75.
39. D.N. Dhanagare, "Green Revolution and Social Inequalities in Rural India", *Economic and Political Weekly,* vol. xxii, Nos. 19-21, 1987, pp.AN-137-AN-144.
40. Ibid., P.AN-143.
41. See, Jairus Banaji, "India and the Colonial Mode of Production: A Comment,"*Economic and Political Weekly,* vol.x, No.49,1975, pp.1887-92.
42. Shahid Amin, "Unequal Antagonists," *Economic and Political Weekly,* vol.xvi, Nos. 42-43, 1981,pp. PE-19-PE-31.

43. Karl Kautsky, cited from John Harriss (ed.), *Rural Development,* London: Hutchinson University Library, 1982.
44. John Harriss, *Capitalism and Peasant Farming,* Bombay: Oxford University Press, 1982.
45. See, Jan Breman, *Patronage and Exploitation,* New Delhi: Manohar Publications, 1974.
46. Carol Boyak Upadhyay, "The Farmer-Capitalists of Coastal Andhra Pradesh", *Economic and Political Weekly,* vol.xxiii, No. 28,1988.
47. Ibid., p.1376.
48. Gail Omvedt, "Capitalist Agriculture and Rural Classes in India", *Economic and Political Weekly,* vol,xvi, No. 52, 1981, pp.A-140-A-159.
49. Jan Breman, *Of Peasants, Migrants and Paupers,* Delhi: Oxford University Press, 1985, pp.xiv-xx.
50. Gail Omvedt, *op.cit.*, 1981.
51. V. Nath, "Urbanization in India", *Economic and Political Weekly,* vol. xxi, No. 8, 1986, pp. 339-52.
52. Biplab Dasgupta and Laishley Roy, Migration from Villages, *Economic and Political Weekly,* vol.x, No.42, 1975, pp.1652-62.
53. Maren Bellwinkel, "Rajasthani Contract Labour in Delhi: A Case Study of the Relationship between Company, Middlemen and Workers" *Sociological Bulletin,* vol,22, No.1, 1973, pp.78-97.
54. Lionel Caplan, "Class and Urban Migration in South India: Christian Elites in Madras City", *Sociological Bulletin,* vol.25, No.2, 1976, pp.207-24.

    See also, M.S.A. Rao, "Some Aspects of Sociology of Migration", *Sociological Bulletin,* vol.30, No.1, 1981, pp. 39-53.

CHAPTER 4

The Country-Town Nexus and the Study of Rural Change in India

—Indra Deva

Historicity of the Country-town Nexus

The existing conceptual and methodological tools of social science are far too inadequate for a proper understanding of rural society and culture in peasant civilizations like India. Most of the village studies are essentially based on the "little community" approach and treat peasant villages as scoio-cultural wholes notwithstanding statements to the contrary in their Prefaces. The failure to relate a peasant village to the civilization of which it is a part, precludes the study of rural dynamics in a broad historical perspective.

Apart from this, the conception of single village as a socio-cultural whole had a cramping influence on the study of rural dynamics in a more fundamental sense. By positing rural-urban (or folk-urban) polarity the emphasis centred on the differences between the village and the town. The country-town nexus was almost wholly forgotten. The fact, however, seems to be that the key to the understanding of much of the rural socio-cultural dynamics lies in a proper insight into the changing nature of this nexus.

First of all it must be clearly recognized that the existence of a relationship between peasant villages and towns is not a new phenomenon. It is not the modern means of transport and communication that have related the peasant village to town for the first time. Modern technology and other modern forces have undoubtedly brought about a basic change in the rural-urban relationship, but they have certainly not begotten this relationship. Institutional, cultural, religious, political and economic ties have existed between the peasant villages and urban cultures since the beginning of historical times. In fact cities and towns could not have come into being, or continued to exist without this relationship. The urban centres had to depend necessarily on villages for agricultural products and other rural surpluses. Even for the continuance of these primary supplies a stable pattern of rural-urban relationship was a pre-requisite. The bases of this relationship, however, were much wider. The bonds were not only economic but also political, and cultural. A majority of the town-dwellers as well as villagers of the adjoining regions shared one and the same cultural tradition. It would be utterly erroneous to think that the tradition of folk-culture was confined to villages. A large majority of the urban people as well were its active bearers. Only the male population of the upper classes in urban centres was usually the carrier of the elite tradition. Women even of the aristocratic and royal families were closer to the culture of the folk. This can be seen from the fact that in many Sanskrit dramas it is only the upper class men who speak Sanskrit. Even royal ladies, as well as the lower class male attendants, spoke Prakrit. Obviously, even in large towns the majoirity of the population shared essentially the same stream of folk- culture with rural people in the adjoining regions.

Apart from the stream of folk-culture which bound up the rural and a large section of urban population, the elite and folk traditions have themselves not remained unrelated. They were based on a fundamentally common worldview, which resulted in essentially similar manifestations in the two domains. For instance, the themes found in elite literature (e.g. the frolics of Krishna) are found also in folk-literature. The difference between the two streams of culture is chiefly that of degree of refinement, systematisation and articulation.Traditionally there has been no basic conflict between the values underlying the two traditions. It is this sharing of values which explains why the traditional elite-culture did not imperil the folk-culture even though both were interacting with each other constantly. As we shall see, the modern forces have changed the nature of this interaction, with the result that the very existence of folk-culture is threatened.

The rural and urban sectors have also been related through established pattern of institutional relationship. No caste is confined to a village. Every caste normally includes people living in towns as well as villages of the region. The higher tiers of caste panchayats exercised social control not only over villagers but also over urban people belonging to their respective castes. The kinship bonds too extended far beyond the villages, and most families living in traditional urban cultures had some relatives in the countryside too.

Thus there have been traditionally established bonds between villages and towns in all important spheres of life. It has to be clearly seen that these bonds cannot be regarded merely outside influences on the society and culture of the village. They have been integral parts of the socio-cultural system of the peasant civilization which included the rural and urban aspects as its dimensions. Traditional rural-ruban interaction has been radically different from the process of acculturation which a tribe undergoes as a result of outside influences. While the former is essential to the sustenance of rural culture, the latter is incidental and at times damaging. We have therefore to consider modern influences on rural society in terms of the basic changes that the pattern of rural -urban relationship have undergone. Mere assessment of the impact of particular traits won't do. Just as the collection of data regarding the past of a village is no substitute for a broader historical background of the civilization of which the village is an integral part, so also the study of the rural social change merely in terms of particular influecnes from outside would not be adequate.

This paper seeks to analyse briefly how the change that the rural-urban nexus has undergone in modern times may account for the pattern of change witnessed in various aspects of rural society and culture. For the sake of convenience the economic-technic, the politico-legal, and the cultural-ideological forces, which in fact are dimensions of the same process, have been taken up one by one.

The Economic-Technic Forces

For an adequate evaluation of the impact of the modern economic and technological forces on rural society and culture attention must be paid to the changes in the country-town nexus. Modern technology is exerting a profound influence on the rural way of life by effecting a basic change in this nexus. Not many factories have so far been established in rural areas; nor has agriculture been mechanised to any considerable extent. Yet the institutions and cultural practices in villages have been changing rapidly for several decades. The part played by technological and economic factors is by no means negligible in this transformation of country-town nexus.

It is extremely significant that while the growth of industries in countries like U.K., U.S.A., and Japan induced people to give up agriculture in favour of industry, the consequence for rural India has been just the reverse. A look at the Census figures, from 1891 onwards would show that the percentage of total population dependent on agriculture has been increasing. Obviously, the pressure of population on land has been increasing all along. This is one of the results of change in the rural-urban relationship. Before the impact of modern socio-economic forces, Indian villages were marked by a balance between agriculture and industry. The urban centres were content to have from the villages a part of the surplus of agricultural produce chiefly in the form of taxes. There was no compelling inclination on the part of the pre-industrial city to sell its goods to the villagers. With the growth of industrialization in U.K. and other European countries, urban centres in India began to turn into supply centres of factory-made goods. Later on, some Indian urban centres also developed industries of their own. For the existence and steady growth of trade and industry in urban centres a growing demand for these goods in rural areas was vital. It was natural, therefore, that every effort was made by the urban centres to turn rural areas into true colonies. Villages were now expected to supply raw materials and labour to urban centres and provide an ever-increasing market for the goods of mass production. Thus a basic change was effected in the economic relationship between urban centres and rural India.

The change in this relationship inevitably meant that the traditional balance between agriculture and industry in villages received a rude shock. The village industries began to decline because of their inability to face the competition from cheap factory-made goods. The policy of the Government also tended to make the competition too hard for the village industries. Consequently, a large number of village craftsmen had to give up their traditional occupations and shift to agriculture. Thus the queer phenomenon of "de-industrialization" of Indian villages was only a consequence of the changed economic relationship between village and town. This change resulted into the decline not only of traditional cottage industry but also that of agriculture in village. It also meant that the occupational structure in rural areas underwent a radical change and many traditional crafts began to languish. This effected not only the economy but also the aesthetic aspect of village life.

Change in the occupational structure of rural India was however not the only consequence of the transformation of rural-urban economic relationship. Another important aspect, which is not altogether separable from the former, was the connection of village economy to the world-market. This meant that the village economy began to loose its subsistence character. It became more and more dependent on the world market. Thus the great depression of 1929-1931 broke the backbone of many village households by bringing down the prices of agricultural products to an extremely low level.

The weakening of the subsistence character of rural economy cannot but have a profound influence of the whole way of life. The basic motivations of work are different in a traditional subsistence economy from those of an acquisitive, competitive, market-economy. In the traditional village economy of India, use and not profit was the directing principle of production. An agriculturist household would usually try to grow in its own fields all types of eatables that it actually needed. Even when the products were not for the consumption of the household itself, they were meant usually for other neighbouring households which were bound with it through traditional jajmani bonds. Thus an agriculturist household would get throughout the year the services of traditional service-castes and craftsmen. And these latter in their turn would get a traditionally fixed part of the products of agriculture from the farmer at the time of harvest or during rites de passage and calanderic festivals.

The pattern of jajmani relationships was certainly based on reciprocity but neither work nor economic decisions were dictated by market forces. The division of labour was predominantly traditional. It was not governed by competition. Similarly, the exchange value or distribution were not determined by market mechanism, but by and large followed a traditional pattern. Thus, production for maximizing profit could not be the chief motive force of traditional rural economy.

The subsistence character of economy had deep implications for the pattern of social relationships and values. Cooperation and contentment rather than competition and desire for unlimited acquisition, marked the rural society. The material products too were characteristically different from the modern articles of mass production. Herbert Read has pointed out that in case of the modern culture the emphasis lies on marketability rather than on use and beauty.[3] In acquisitive, industrial societies, just as work gets alienated from life so also utility tends to get divorced from aesthetic considerations. In the traditional rural economy, however, even the commonest articles of everyday use combined beauty with utility. Moreover, because the craftsmen knew the person who was going to use the thing made by him, he would take special care not to be out of tune with the specific needs of the person and the occasion. The craftsman usually made a whole object, and thus the nature of his work was very different from that of an ordinary worker in a huge factory. He had the opportunity to be an artist as well as a worker. In traditional societies, as Anand Coomaraswamy and Eric Gill have put it, the artist is not a special kind of man, but every man is a special kind of artist.

The changed urban-rural relationship, however, began to erode this traditional character of rural economy and culture. With the decline of subsistence economy, money and profit motive are becoming more and more important as determinants of behaviour. The farmer is increasingly conscious of the market. In many areas there is understandably a swing in favour of cash crops. The transactions are more in terms of money. The incursion of machine-made products and modern attractions like cinema, enhance the thirst for cash. The increasing power of money in rural life often makes the villager more susceptible to exploitation by the moneylender.

Emigration from rural areas has been a very potent lever of socio-cultural change in recent decades. In India and other developing countries emigration from rural areas has certain features of its own. The people who go out of the villages are actually pushed out from there because of dire necessity, rather than being pulled by the attractions of city life. Agriculture in rural India is a very hazardous occupation indeed. Failure of crops due to drought or flood is a common event. In such an eventuality the villager is forced to leave the vollage in search of some employment in a city. Similarly when the debt to the moneylender becomes too heavy or a bullock dies, the villager has to go out in search of money. It is not often that the villager migrates to the city to enjoy urban life. He goes to the city to earn and accumulate some money to put his farm on a sound footing. He wishes to return to the village as early as possible. Even while the emigrant lives in an industrial city his outlook remains essentially rural.[4] He is not motivated to become in integrated part of the urban proletariat. This is responsible for many unwholesome aspects of contemporary urban life in India and is an obstacle in the way of the growth of healthy labour movement.

But the consequences of this migration for rural life and particularly rural social change are no less important. The emigrant usually leaves behind other members of his family such as his wife, minor children and elderly parents. This on the one hand results in an imbalance of sex ratio in urban centres and on the other it leads to many kinds of tension in rural life. Many folksongs describe with great pathos the plight of women whose husbands have gone away to Calcutta or Bombay for employment. When the emigrant is slack in sending money to his family tension in the family tends to mount. From the Bhojpuri speaking areas (eastern U.P. and western Bihar) this emigration has been going on for a long time. The Report of the United Provinces Banking Enquiry Committee of 1929-1930 says, "Twenty years ago it was commonly said that there was not a single family in Banaras division which had not at least one member in the provinces of Bengal, Assam or Bihar"[5]

The partial nature of emigration makes it even more effective as an instrument of socio-cultural change in rural areas. Since the emigrant leaves behind his family members, and himself intends to go back to the village finally, he becomes a living channel of communication between the modern urban centre and his village. His visits to the village are not infrequent. Whenever there is a marriage or some other celebration in the family, he goes to the village. During festivals and holidays also he likes to visit his home village. Through these visits he knowingly and unknowingly introduces many material and non-material elements of modern culture in the village. Apart from articles like flash torches and transistors, he brings with him new ideas and attitudes. A man who has lived for many years in an industrial city is not likely to remain too impressed with the local upper class and upper caste people. He often learns to resist discrimination and injustice through collective action. His ideas tend to spread quickly in the village also due to the prestige acquired by him through travel and stay in the city. If workers went to city for good, with their families, they could never have become such potent factors of social change in rural areas as they are when the nature of migration is predominantly partial.

The Politico-Legal Forces

The new politico-legal forces now at work in the Indian countryside are also the result of changed country-town nexus. In pre-modern days the villages were undoubtedly connected with the towns in a political sense. They were integral parts of kingdoms and empires which had their seats of government in towns. The villages regularly paid revenue to these governments, and the latter in turn were supposed to protect them from external invasion and internal disorder. In practice, however, the villages were quite independent in the management of their internal affairs. So long as they continued to pay the tax, and there was no violent rebellion, the kings and their representatives showed no eagerness to interfere in their internal affairs.

With the advent of the British rule, however, this situation began to change. The British were not satisfied with a portion of rural produce in the form of taxes. They wanted to exploit rural areas as suppliers of cheap raw materials and as markets for their factory products. The old political arrangement could, therefore, not suit them much. They felt an urge to do away with "medieval backwardness." They wished to push forward their judicial and administrative systems as far and deep as possible. In contrast to the earlier rulers, the British rulers did not accept the authority of village and caste panchayats. Otherwise also the form and content of the new legal system imposed by the British militated against the traditional functionaries and their power to inflict punishment. The rural people found the British administrative and legal system a force which had to be accepted as such. In due course the traditional organs of resolving conflict became too weak. What is more, the villagers seem to have lost faith in their capacity of self-goverment. A survey carried out[6] in rural areas of Rajasthan and eastern U.P. indicates that a high percentage of villagers in both these regions strongly felt that the State Government must exercise more strict control over the working of village panchayats. Of course, the panchayats in question are not the traditional ones but those introduced by the intitiative of various state governments after independence. This is in sharp contrast to the traditional self-government of villages and castes in pre-British time.

Perhaps the most potent ferment which the British rule introduced in rural India was the creation of private property in land. There is some controversy regarding the nature of land ownership in India in pre-British times. While Sir Henry Maine, Karl Marx, Radhakamal Mukerjee, and more recently Ramkrishna Mukherjee have held that land was communally owned by the traditional Indian village community. Other scholars like A.S. Altekar do not subscribed to this view. Whatever be the actual ownership pattern, there can hardly be any doubt that in pre-British times land was not a commodity freely sold and purchased in the market. It were the British who turned land into a marketable commodity.

The creation of private ownership in land means that the traditional socio-economic hierarchy in a village can be threatened by any individual or group which has sufficient money to purchase land. F.G. Bailey, in an interesting study[8] of social change in a village in Orissa has shown how an untouchable caste of liquor-sellers succedded in raising its status considerably through the gains made in liquor trade. It is also remarkable that the wind-fall profits made by this untouchable caste emanated primarily from the prohibition measures introduced by the government. The evidence furnished by Bailey indicates that it is usually governmental measures which make windfall profits possible and thus pave the way for changes in the socio-economic hierarchy of the village. It is also significant that Bailey regards extension of economic frontier as the chief source of change in the hierarchical structure of a village. These findings seem to underline further the need of scrutinising the changes in the country-town nexus.

For the last four decades or so, the administration is coming closer and closer to the villager for diverse reasons. The Second World War made the average villager familiar with administration through such measures as control and rationing. After independence various development programmes have taken administration almost to the doorsteps of the villager. Bringing about change in rural institutions and culture is the avowed objective of many of these programmes. It is not necessary to give here a detailed evaluation of the success of these programmes. It must be noted, however, that the effect of these programmes never remains confined to the aspects selected for change or the direction in which change is sought to be introduced. There are many unintended effects of programmes of induced social change. It is not impossible, for instance, that the establishment of an agricultural extension centre may lead more to adoption of modern dress and cosmetics than to that of modern techniques of agriculture.

In combination with the existing elements and processes in rural areas new social forces and movements often give rise to tendencies which are hardly intended. The most important case in point is that of the elections. Elections appear to be a normal feature of democratic life and their introduction could perhaps be expected to enrich democratic values. The introduction of elections, however, seems to have considerably enhanced casteism and factionalism. Caste is based on the principle of ascription and thus it appears to be essentially opposed to democracy, which is more in tune with the principle of achievement. Yet practice of democracy seems to have strengthened caste. A deeper analysis would, however, show that casteism is not the same thing as the caste system.

The Cultural-Ideological Forces

In the cultural-ideological aspect also the key to the nature of social change in rural areas seems to be provided by the changed nature of rural-urban relationship.[9] As mentioned above, in pre-modern times the culture in the non-industrial urban centres was based on fundamentally the same assumptions and values as those on which the culture was based. Whatever differences existed were those of degree of refinement and articulation. The two streams of culture could therefore co-exist without impairing each other. After the British impact, however, the culture and ideas in towns began to be transformed. A new worldview based essentially on Western ideas of individualism, competition, and achievement began to gain ground in urban centres. This worldview appears to be essentially opposed to the traditional worldview prevailing in rural areas. Naturally, as these ideas make intrusion in the village through modern education and modern means of communication, the very existence of the folk culture appears to be threatened. It will be noted that change is not a result of establishing contacts between rural and urban cultures for the first time. The contacts already existed, and perhaps on a deeper level than now. The difference lies in the changed nature of cultural ties.

With the spread of modern education in rural areas, the old balance of power in community, as well as in family, seems to be threatened. Formerly, almost all knowledge in the villages was derived through informal communication and personal experience. It was natural, therefore, to consider the older people as more knowledgeable. With the introduction of new sources of knowledge like books and newspapers, the greater knowledgeability of elders cannot remain unchallenged. In fact often the deviants from traditional norms are found to be more competent to tackling a new situation[10] Thus in many ways new cultural and ideological elements seem to be threatening the very existence of traditional rural culture.

It is interesting to note, however, that the peculiar circumstances of modernisation of traditional cultures of countries like India in the closing decades of the 20th century, may open up unforeseen possibilities of a synthesis between the traditional and the modern. A close look at the nature of contemporary social change in India and other newly developing countries would indicate the existence of such a possibility,[11] though it cannot be denied that a number of opposing forces are also at work and they may prove too strong for the emergence of such synthesis.

In the presence of certain economic-technological, legal-politico, and ideological-symbolic factors that have come into being by the middle of the 20th century, the folk-culture may be able to develop in such a way that its survival is not threatened. The technological, economic and ideological forces that existed in Europe in the early phase of industrialization (approximately between the last part of the 18th century and the close of the 19th century) threatened the folk-way of life more seriously than the corresponding forces that exist now.[12]

The technology of the earlier phase was marked by the large size of machines and the utter neglect of aesthetic considerations both in the makeup of machines and that of their products. Utility and cheapness were the watchwords. Considerations of beauty were looked upon with disdain. The folk products which displayed a balance between aesthetic and utilitarian aspects was considered backward. In this era[13] coal was the chief source of power. Transport of coal is too cumbersome and costly. Industries, therefore, concentrated around coal mines. There was little possibility of their dispersal. To provide adequate labour force to the industries it was imperative to disrupt settled life in folk-communities. The accent on low cost and marketability of products at the expense of quality and beauty made it impossible for the folk craftsmen to carry on his trade.

Today, we are in a different technological *era*.[14] The large size of machine is no more considered in itself a virtue. The trend is towards the reduction in its size. Small and portable but efficient machines are coming to the fore. New sources of power, petroleum and electricity, have made the dispersal of industry a practicable proposition. If electricity is carried to villages and small and medium size industries are set up in the countryside, it is not necessary to disrupt settled community life.

In the areas of economy, politics and ideology, forces are developing which may provide support to the folk mode of life. In the 18th and 19th centuries ideas of individualism, competition and achievement had reached the peak of their influence. These ideas were clearly antagonistic to folk values of corporate life, security and contentment. The elite during the first phase of the modern era was definitely harsh towards the folk norms and mentality. It was proud of its rationalism and efficiency, and looked down upon the folk as superstitious and lazy.

Today, these ideas have considerably mellowed down. The limitations of rationalism are widely recognised. Numerous ideological movements emphasise the value of cooperation and security. This is not to say that modern elite is going back to values of the folk communities. They, however, do not harbour the self-righteous indignation which impelled their predecessors to combat and suppress traditional rural culture. Under these changed material and ideological circumstances, it is not impossible that folk forms may find certain avenues of survival and growth.[15] Of course, they cannot hope to continue in the same form as they have been traditionally.

NOTES AND REFERENCES

1. J.N. Sinha, "Demographic Trends", *Economic History of India 1857-1956,* (ed.), V.B. Singh, Bombay: Allied Publishers, 1965, pp. 112-14. *There is some* divergence in the figures given in various sources but the basic trend of shift in population from industry to agriculture seems to be present. Some doubts have been expressed regarding the authenticity of census figures in this regard. It has also been said that the magnitude of shift from agriculture to industry indicates stagnation rather than decline of village industries. However, some regional studies undertaken on a limited scale seem to confirm that the decline in village industries was substantial.
2. Devendra Satyarthi, *Dhari Gati Hai,* Delhi: Rajkamal Prakashan, 1948, p. 1123.
3. Herbert Read, *To Hell with Culture,* London, 1941; *Art and Society,* London, 1936.
4. This is well demonstrated by Basant Dube. He found that all his respondents (emigrants from rural areas of eastern U.P.) were keen to go back to their villages. When he enquired about their low standard of living in Kanpur, even when their wages were not so low, they repeatedly said, "We have come here to earn, not to live." See Dube's "Emigrants from Eastern U.P. working as Factory Labourers in Kanpur, "Ph.D. Thesis Gorakhpur University, 1965.
5. *Report of the United Provinces Banking Enquiry Committee,* 1929-30, Vol. 1, p.30.
6. The survey was conducted under the direction of Indra Deva for the research project on Assessing the Degree and Depth of Acceptance of the System of Law in India in Terms of (i) Awareness, (ii) Value-Compatability, and (iii) Patterns of Adaptation, sponsored by the Indian Law Institute, New Delhi, 1966-67, pp. 169ff.
7. Ramkrishna Mukherjee, *Dynamics of a Rural Society,* Berlin, Akademie Verlag, 1957.
8. F.G. Bailey, *Caste and the Economic Frontier,* Oxford University Press, 1958.
9. This idea is adumbrated in a paper which appeared more than three decades ago. Cf. Indra Deva, 'Modern Social Forces in Indian Folk-songs", *Diogenes,* No. 15, UNESCO, Paris, 1956.

10. A very interesting illustration is provided by the short story "Panch-Light" by Phanishwer Nath Renu, in *Thumri*, Delhi, 1967, pp. 83-88.
11. Cf. Indra Deva, "Une Hypothese Sur 1' Evolution Sociale", *Diogenes*, No. 56, UNESCO, Paris, 1966, pp. 82-101.
12. How far folk—culture and folklore in Asian countries can continue to survive by striking a new balance with the contemporary socio-economic forces, has been analysed in some detail by Indra Deva in "Social Change in Asia and its Impact on Folk—Culture and Folklore", First Asian Folklore Conference, Indiana, Bloomington, 1966.
13. Lewis Mumford calls this era, the "paleotechnic" era. This phase according to him extends roughly from the middle of the eighteenth century to the close of the nineteenth century. Cf. Lewis Mumford, *Technics and Civilization*, London, George Routledge & Sons, 1947.
14. Mumford has designated this era as the "neotechnic" phase.
15. For a more detailed discussion of this aspect, see, Indra Deva, "The Future of Folklore", *Folklore in the Twentieth Century* (ed.) Venetia Newall ed., Boydell & Brewer in U.K. and Rowman & Littlefield in U.S.A., 1980.

CHAPTER 5

The Country-Town Nexus and Agrarian Mobilisation: Situating the Farmers' Movement in West U.P.

—Dipankar Gupta

This paper draws from two established streams of social science scholarship. One is the scholarship on rural urban interaction and change, and the other is the literature on peasant movements and agrarian mobilisations. While both these themes have been enriched by studies of different locales and periods, we shall in this paper limit ourselves primarily to the post Independence Indian context. Our principal concern here is to sketch a perspective which would be sensitive to the crucial specificities of contemporary agrarian mobilisations. In our opinion the problems that informed and lit the known approaches to rural urban interaction and change are not quite the problems that confront us today. If the specificity of our contemporary problems is not to be compromised by a tired and outmoded scheme we must begin to think afresh for an alternative frame of reference.

Historians and sociologists concur that the peasant movements of British India were quite different from the kinds of mobilisations we find today. While the rural urban context rarely entered as an active consideration in the studies of pre Independence peasant movements, it cannot be overlooked even in a cursory examination of contemporary agrarian mobilisations. Indeed many of these movements aggressively draw our attention to the altered nature of the rural urban nexus. In order to emphasis the reality of the altered circumstances and to invite sociological attention in this direction we feel that the term *"country town nexus*" would do better than either "rural urban continuum", or "rural urban interaction", or "great and little tradition." These latter phrases are better known but they connote a world which we have, by and large, left behind.

Rural-Urban Studies: The Significance of our Inheritance

Sociologists and anthropologists have been in the forefront of scholarly endeavors on rural urban relationships, particularly in the context of change. Indian studies have been particularly fortunate in this respect for some of the best scholars were attracted to this subject. M.N. Srinivas, Bernard Cohn, Milton Singer, Lloyd and Susanne Rudolph, E. Kathleen Gough, among several others, made sterling contributions in this field as well as in immediately contiguous ones.

The set of issues that motivated these social anthropologists had a 1950's flavour about it. India had just become Independent, survived the partition, and was setting out boldly to join the modern group of nation states under the charismatic leadership of Jawaharlal Nehru. There was of course the persistent drag in some circles that India would never change, not now nor ever. This variety of pessimism also had its advocates but the real issue of the fifties was how effectively India could modernise its traditional institutions and what kind of conservative reaction would such impulses to change invite. Economic, religious and kinship institutions were all subjected to intense scrutiny from a variety of value positions and the consequent literature is enormous and in general of a very high calibre.

It is not as if these scholars were only motivated by a purely empirical thirst to describe the various moments of change. They were also putting forward alternative frames of reference which were full of exciting possibilities. They encouraged concrete empirical research and at the same time challenged the hitherto regnant view that India was timelessly gripped by the "religious syndrome of backwardness"[1] . Vivid documentation of India's changing villages had far reaching theoretical implications though these implications were not always anticipated by the authors. Even so the effect was tremendous. One of the best known and perhaps the most widely read book of this genre is *Village India*[2] which was first published in the mid 1950's to an immediate furore of attention. The works of the best minds were represented in that book and it gave a lasting credibility to mainstream anthropological researches that set out to study social change in a hitherto traditional society.

In order to appreciate the breadth of the vista opened up by this variant of fifties scholarship one needs only to recall the vast quantities of works influenced by colonialism and Eurocentrism which only saw India as an unchanging and unchangeable monolith, strapped and bounded by inscrutable and unbending traditions and customs. Consequently it did not matter which age India was transported to by well meaning colonialists, it would essentially always remain the same. It was no mean task to challenge this view point especially as so many Indians were themselves voicing it from within with great fervour. It is also true that a variant of cultural nationalists reacting to British domination perhaps quite inadvertently legitimised this process. Their shrill chauvinism which harped only on the grandeur of Indian tradition encouraged an atavistic and revivalist outlook.

Our contemporary understanding of rural-urban interaction and change owes much to the social anthropological works of the fifties—to Srinivas, Cohn, Singer, etc.[3] Terms like rural-urban continuum, modernization of tradition, and westernisation, riveted argument to empirical detail in a highly persuasive manner. The elan and confidence of self government was matched by a desire in political circles to catch up with the industrialised countries. To this extent new policy schemes were introduced, new public industries and public works were set up, fresh investments opportunities were opened up all over the country, and there was no pronounced conservative reaction from anywhere amidst all this euphoria. Instead some of the dynamic trends which were faintly noticeable earlier deepened and became more manifest. New elites emerged, traditional institutions lost their famed grip, the joint family was holding on but under severe duress, and traditional customs and rites were being substantially modified. Castes too were organising and consolidating themselves in a most surprising way reflecting the changed nature of authority patterns in the society as a whole.

These studies may have had different universes to explore but they had a common focus, viz., the manner in which traditional institutions were reacting to *modern* economic and political pressures. Gough detailed in an early study how the much vaunted integrity and isolation of the village was a thing of the past.[4] Srinivas[5] dilated upon the modalities of modernisation in rural and urban settings. Singer[6] provided a schema for analysing the various stages of interaction between indigenous institutions and exogenous forces. Beals[7] and Scarlett Epstein[8] brought out the diverse impact of modern institutional inputs on differently endowed villages. These and other studies laid to rest the ghost of an unchanging India.

It is important to notice that in these studies the countryside is primarily a recipient of forces emanating from the town. This is wholly understandable as the effort then was to demonstrate that the rural regions, where the heart of India was locked in, was not intransigent and could be opened up to fresh impetuses from the metropolitan centres. By and large the process was in the direction of town to country.[9] The conceptual apparatus, while acknowledging a national disquiet and upsurge, could only operationalise itself on the ground by isolated studies of rural urban interaction. Unlike Srinivas's "sanskritisation"[10] whose central features have supralocal validity, the terms generated with respect to rural urban interaction had to be weighted (and vetted) afresh from locality to locality. But its most prominent contribution, as mentioned earlier, was to liberate the mainstream anthropological and sociological mind from the belief that Indian society was immutable.

Srinivas's contribution on the question of sanskritisation was not quite paralleled by his writings on modernisation/westernisation.[11] Sanskritisation is a deeper concept because one can draw postulates from its "existence statements" which can successfully condense variegated instances of caste mobility into a comprehensive framework. This framework has the advantage of allowing for still higher levels of generalisation (as for example with reference group theory), as well as the laying out of a proforma for investigation which is premised on a certain considered understanding of the caste system. Rural urban studies mentioned so far are different because they indicate very generally a direction of change but do not presume an understanding of the modalities of change. This is why there is little deliberate ratiocination upon this directionality of transformation, and in most cases the transition to modernity has been taken for granted. In the main these studies are most successful when they detail point by point the changes wrought by exogenous forces. If the changes are uneven or incommensurable there is no controlled and conscious framework of reference within which they can be understood.

Uneasiness with the Fifties Framework

The tendency to be dismissive of earlier scholarship is very tempting, but it cannot be done convincingly in this case. Without the empirical demonstrations of change and transformations in rural India which these earlier scholars provided, we would still be struggling today within the intellectual parameters set by colonialists and uncritical atavistic nationalists. Moreover even if actual studies of rural urban interaction were localised in their spread they spurred important developments in our understanding of the interaction between traditional institutions and modernity. Our appreciation today of the protean and malleable character of culture in general draws succour from the empirical data of rural urban studies.

By the end of the 1960's we were all fairly convinced that Indian society was open to change, that our culture was highly vulnerable to these change inducing forces, and that by and large there was no significant conservative reaction against the institutional deepening of the nodes of contemporary transformation. I believe that by the sixties and early seventies our understanding on these issues was settled and nothing new could be said. If such contributions sound *passe* today it is because they no longer charge the imagination like they used to earlier. To each epoch its own obsessions.

But what are our problems, our obsessions, today? I believe that while the rural urban studies which we inherited from the fifties sensitised us to the change potentials in society there was very little emphasis on the conflict and antagonisms that such changes generated. Nor does it seem that this inherited literature can help us much by way of elucidating the limits of development in a country like India. Scarlett Epstein had to return to her villages in the 1970's to realise that the first flush of post Independence euphoria had given way to a sense of despair and to a considerable mounting of tension. The Zamindari Abolition Act had run its course rather fitfully and ceased to hold any further liberating potential. Rural and urban poverty continued and in many cases worsened, and the altered circumstances of rural and urban life brought more agony than wonderment. The intellectual reflection on this state of affairs was not only manifested in self critical and self doubting scholarship, but also at the political level. The stately consolidation of Congress rule through the fifties and the sixties was severely jolted on a number of fronts. There also developed a wide variety of rural and urban movements whose presence was alien to our fifties inheritance.

It is not as if these features suddenly burst on the national scene. But it must be admitted that intellectually many of us were not ready to take stock of such phenomena.[12] Our rural elite had developed alright but was not exactly a replica of its urban counterpart. The urban sector too is hardly an encouraging sight. There is, in short, an absence of confidence and a conflict of ideals, and this is why the scholarship of the fifties on social change no longer resonates. The earlier brand of scholarship presumed a benevolent effect that the new forces of change would have on society. But the gradual unfolding of events took the shine off from an unilateral endorsement of change agents. Intellectuals and planners are groping today for an alternative perspective which would revive some measure of confidence in our vision of the future and in our analysis of the present.

Periodizing Peasant Movements

In the pages that follow I shall try and demonstrate the changed nature of rural agitation and mobilisation in contemporary India which will clarify why I believe that a new perspective is required for a comprehension of today's rural urban interaction. The stream of scholarship that I shall now draw upon relates to peasant movements and agrarian mobilisations in India. These studies have had a profound and deep impact in various social science disciplines. Historians, sociologists, anthropologists and economists, have all contributed in this field with rare inter-disciplinary verve.

The nature of peasant protest has not been the same in different historical periods and yet there has been a marked obduracy in retaining the term peasant while referring to the rural people of different historical periods and regions. There is perhaps good reason for that because agrarian people tended to group together in clusters in moments of crisis thus emphasising the overwhelming commonlity of their aspirations and goals. There have always been in the past other social classes in rural areas who lived off the land but were not called peasants. They were either seen as appropriators of "peasant" surplus, or as patrons of "peasant" households, depending upon one's point of view.

In British India the incidence of rural movements where the peasants by and large came together as a social category was widely noticed.[13] These movements were generally for lowering rents, or taxes, or for occupational tenure. It has also been recorded that these movements were local in their spread, and quite frequently (though not always) the enemy was the local overlord and not the government as such. In fact it was often believed by those who participated in such movements that if only word could be got to the Queen of England she would pull up her local representative as well as his native factotum and agent and all would be well.[14] Given the nature of the agrarian structure in British India it was not surprising that tenants, small farmers and middle farmers, could come together on occasion because of the many common interests that circumscribed their horizons.[15] It is often argued that peasant insecurity is a feature typical of colonial India and did not exist in this fashion, or to this extent, in pre British days. Even the image of an usurious money lender knocking on the door of an impoverished peasant is a colonial phenomenon.[16] The argument is that it was not in the interest of the elite in pre-British India to actualy dispossess peasants and resume their land. Usury was one way of binding them to a parcel of land, to a territory. In fact the landlords imposed heavy penalties on those who wished to escape. And yet the urge to migrate elsewhere to perhaps a less harsher regime took place extensively in Mughal India. This is how the peasants protested then. In British India, however, such a strategy would have meant certain destitution for the peasants and a perfect solution for the landlords.

To each period then not only its own kind of peasant movement, but also its own kind of elite behaviour. In Mughal India the landed overlords often led local revolts against Imperial authority[17], but in British India the members of the landed elite were known for their complete subservience and loyalty to the colonial powers. Not surprisingly the nature of the relationship between the governments of independent Indian and the rural elites has also undergone a change from the British days. This change could have been firmed up irrevocably and deepened had land reform measures been consistently and fully applied in independent India.

Our information on peasant movements and agrarian mobilisations after 1857 is rich both in empirical detail as well as in the theoretical processing of data. The post 1857 agrarian movements, or revolts, were largely caused by tenancy insecurity and usurious practices which were widespread throughout the country. These phenomena, historians seem to concur, were essentially the consequences of British colonial policies in India. As a result of these agrarian disturbances the British had to yield somewhat and issue certain compensatory edicts to pacify the rural poor. The Bengal Tenancy Act (1885), the Deccan Agricultural

Relief Act (1879), and the Punjab Land Alienation Bill (1900), are instances of such measures. But even so such respite came only to small and localised sections of the peasantry leaving the bulk of the rural masses by and large untouched. Throughout the first half of the twentieth century this process of struggle and concession continued with greater or lesser success.

The Congress government after Independence in 1947 legislated *zamindari* abolition which quickened the slow pace of change from what it was in pre British India. With *zamindari* abolition either some *zamindars* were ruined or were forced to change the style of their exactions from the rural poor. The ways in which the *zamindari* abolition acts have been perjured have been documented too well to bear repetition here.[18] In any case by the 1960's the movements for tenancy reform and for tenancy occupation were over. Overall too the phenomenon of tenancy cultivation had dropped very sharply.[19] A group of tenants with permanent tenure and large occupational holdings in their charge have emerged today more powerful than they ever were before. Most well-to-do landlords of yore either became capitalist farmers and evaded the land holdings ceilings by fictitious *benami* transactions and concealment, or sunk gradually into the middle and lower middle classes in urban India. Their world changed, and if they did not adapt with the times to take advantage of their headstart in land holdings, then they were gradually forced to either leave the village or live in it but under totally different conditions.

The poor predictably did not fare well. The small tenants who secured some land were constantly being pushed down by the weight of higher prices and by the fragmentation of holdings. The poorer tenants at will of pre-independence India in most cases became agricultural labourers with no rights to any land whatsoever. The number of agricultural labourers thus kept increasing in every census enumeration. Further, according to the Rural Labour Enquiry of 1974-75, as much as 30.3 per cent of all rural households were rural labour households. If one were to add to this another 14.7 per cent who own land but cannot depend on it for a principal source of livelihood then the picture gets really grim.[20] In a situation like this it is no wonder that the earlier issues which used to spark off agrarian movements are no longer as effective.

In India today we might say that there are primarily two types of agrarian mobilisations. One is of the poor agricultural labourers and other rural labour households. The other is of the richer farmers who produce a considerable marketed surplus. The very rich and sometimes "capitalist" farmers are generally with the richer farmers but more often than not they are also looked upon as exploiters by the agricultural labourers who work on their fields either as wage labourers or as share croppers. In other words, modernisation has come to rural India but without an all round roseate effect. Neither can it be said that this modernisation and such changes that have taken place in its wake in rural India are because of the effects of the urban world. The urban world exists, as does the national economy, but its effect on rural India is not a consequence of proximity but rather of a *nexus* which embraces country and town.

The Country-Town Nexus

The country town nexus of independent India took a while to gel. Rich peasants who became landed proprietors after independence were making their presence felt. But their assertion and aggression had to wait till the 1960's when irrigation works and HYV seeds came together. In Maharashtra, coastal Andhra, Punjab and Haryana, a large number of erstwhile well to do peasants became richer farmers and took to investing in agriculture and also outside the village. Though the preponderant drive was to buy more land there was also the desire to have a foothold in the city. [21] This new money from agricultural surplus was invested in grain trade, agro-industries, transportation, trawlers, rice mills, sugar mills, and so on.

The new spurt in agricultural prosperity actually affected most positively those who came out with large holdings after the *zamindri* abolition programme. It was these people again who benefitted most from the mechanical cum biological green revolution programmes that were intitiated by the government of India in the 1960's [22] Green revolution technology did not favour an altogether different category of rural people but those five per cent who owned 40 per cent of the land[23] and were thus well endowed. Irrigation and technology only furthered their hold. Today, even in prosperous Punjab, wealth and prosperity have not come to a large number of the rural poor. In fact the proportion of people living below the poverty line in Punjab has gone up from 18 per cent to 23 per cent between 1960 and 1970 .[24]

It is, therefore, a combination of several factors that has contributed to the contemporary country town nexus. We may cite first the development of native capitalism which found profitable lines of investment in independent India. This led to a considerable increase in capitalist development in general and to an expanding monetary frontier.[25] This also raised the demand for cash crops and at the same time enlarged the market for industrial consumer articles. The Green Revolution when it came made it feasible to operate on 2-3 acres of land provided one used HYV seeds[26], irrigation and fertilisers. While all this might have driven the poorer peasants to subsistence farming and caused a consumption squeeze[27] it propelled others to invest in machinery and capital assets.[28] Even small farmers in Punjab, as Dhanagare observes, were forced to invest a considerable portion of their resources in machinery for agricultural operations.[29]

This brings us to another crucial feature of the contemporary country town nexus. This nexus is all pervasive and it draws people of different classes into it. It is not possible to stay out of it and plough a lonely furrow. It is not a question then of whether one wants to or does not want to participate in the nexus. Regardless of one's individual choice everyone is brought within the ambit of the nexus. There can be a certain amount of resistance to it and even careful planning at an individual level but the nexus exists as a phenomenon which involves all sections, albeit differentially. There is an element of struggle, tussle and combat at different levels of interaction within this nexus. It does not have a flattened universal appeal, nor a steady incremental benevolence. This is how it can be distinguished from the interaction between "little and great tradition" where it is all a matter of giving a little and taking a little .[30]

It is difficult not to take the effects of this nexus into account when considering rural urban interaction. The leading factor of this nexus however is the character of capitalism that pervades the country as a whole. This capitalism in turn is also constrained and determined to some extent by the agrarian structure of the land. Unlike the kind of competitive capitalism that Adam Smith saw in England[31] we find in India a situation where the increase in agricultural marketed surplus has begun to taper off but industrial goods have only just reached a small section of the rural elite.[32] In Nadkarni's words India is in a "transitional fix."[33]

In the last several years the relationship between town and country in India has also changed more rapidly than it ever did in the past. The percentage share of agricultural income to national income has declined significantly from 49.6 per cent in 1961 to 36.4 per cent in 1981 (at current prices). But the work force has declined only marginally. This should help us appreciate further the difference between the picture of Adam Smith's England and contemporary India. The relative income for agricultural workers vis-a-vis industrial workers declined too.[34] This was further compounded when in the 1970's the "agricultural sector came out worse off in terms of prices..."[35] In the meantime the expenditure on fertilisers kept going up even though India's use of fertilisers is still among the lowest in the world.[36] The use of fertiliser consumption per hectare of gross cropped area has doubled from 16.1 kgs to 32.0 kgs between 1971-72 and 1980-81.[37]

The overall increase in fertiliser consumption too is very dramatic if we review the progress from 1960-61 onwards as Table 1 does below. Further the area under irrigation too has increased during these years

TABLE I

Fertiliser Production and Consumption

'000 tones of nutrients

	Nitrogenous		*Phosphatic*		*Potassic**
	Production	*Consumption*	*Production*	*Consumption*	*Consumption*
1960-61	98	212	52	53	29
1970-71	830	1,479	229	541	236
1980-81	2,164	3,678	842	1,214	624
1983-84	3,491	5,204	1,048	1,730	775
1984-85	3,917	5,486	1,264	1,886	839
1985-86	4,328	5,815	1,428	2,068	854
1986-87+	5,410	5,796	1,660	2,113	871

* There is no indigenous production.

\+ Provisonal.

Source: *Statistical Outline of India, 1988-89*. Tata Services Ltd., Dept. of Economics and Statistics, Bombay 1988; p. 58.

TABLE II

Cropped Area and Irrigated Area

	Net area sown	*Total cropped area**	*Net area irrigated*	*Gross area irrigated**	*Gross irrigated as % of cropped area*
			Mn. hectares		
1960-61	133.2	152.8	24.7	28.0	18.3
1970-71	140.8	165.8	31.2	38.2	23.0
1980-81	140.3	173.1	38.8	49.6	28.7
1982-83	140.8	173.4	39.9	52.0	30.0
1983-84	142.7	180.4	42.0	53.9	29.9
1986-87	143.0	175.0	44.0	57.3	32.7

Note: From 1982-83 onwards, figures are provisional.
* Including area sown/irrigated more than once.
Source: *Statistical Outline of India, 1988-89*. Tata Services Ltd., Dept. of Economics and Statistics, Bombay 1988; p. 58.

(Table II). There has also been a sensational rise in the number of electrical pumpsets. From a mere 21,000 in 1950-51 the number of pumpsets went up to 4 million in 1979-80.[38] In 1961-62 India manufactured 880 tractors and imported 3 thousand. The production of tractors too rose sharply and was at 81.5 thousand by 1981-82.[39] The increase in mechanisation also brought about a decrease in demand for wage labour in some sectors of the rural economy.

It is worthwhile to remember in this connection that it is not as if rural India was earlier completely cut off from extra rural influences. Infact most of the peasant movements in twentieth century India were influenced by the commercialisation of agriculture. But this commercialisation was not accompanied by a modernisation of agricultural inputs-whether chemical or mechanical. This is probably why these movements could afford to be *single pronged* and *remedial* in character. In contrast some agrarian mobilisations of Indian today are remedial, yes, but *multi pronged* and *prospective* too. One need only look at the Shetkari Sangathan led by Sharad Joshi, or the Bharatiya Kisan union led by Mahendra Singh Tikait, to be convinced of this. These movements look to the future by trying to influence national policies on prices, taxation structure, as also the basic approaches to economic planning and development. All this is quite new as far as agrarian movements in India are concerned.

Effects on Agarian Mobilization:
The Two Types of Rural Movements

We have stressed the effect of the nexus on rural India in particular because we believe it will lead us more directly to our stated interest in this paper, viz., agrarian mobilisations. As we said earlier there are two kinds of agrarian mobilisations in India today. One is the movement of poor peasants and agricultural labourers for higher wages and better working conditions. These movements are generally sponsored by the various rural wings of established political parties like the Kisan Sabhas, or the agricultural labourers unions of the CPI and the CPI(M), and by various fractions of the CPI(ML). This has led many observers to underline the sharp class basis of agrarian movements such as in Kerala where the poorer peasants and agricultural labourers are in the forefront.[41] The second type of rural movements are the farmer' (note, not peasants) movements such as the Bharatiya Kisan Union in west UP, Punjab and Haryana; the Shetkari Sangathan in Maharashtra; or the Karnataka Rajya Ryota Sangha in Karnataka. Here, apparently, the peasants present themselves as an undifferentiated phalanx as they often did during British India. But while saying this one should also bear in mind that these farmers' movements distinguish their interests quite clearly from the interests of the agricultural labourers and marginal peasants who are not net producers of surplus.

The class distinctions however do not end there. I think it is legitimate to argue that the two types of peasant movements in India today signify the manner in which the *country town nexus* has differentiated the countryside. Very often only one kind of movement is taken up for examination and not the other. When this is done it invariable presents an incomplete effect of the nexus. When studying the movements of poor peasants which are usually local in character (for they are principally against the local exploiter and his rapacious ways), the tendency usually is to avoid the set of circumstances which are supra-local in character but which impinge on the country side in determining wage labour and employer relations there. Paradoxically, while the demands of these poor peasants are taken up best by national parties their principal enemy is a visible one, viz., the local exploiter.

In the case of the farmers' movement the enemy is not in the village or in the vicinage. The government, either in the Centre or in the state, is targeted for attack. The demands put forward by these farmers invariably revolve around higher prices for agricultural produce, lowering of electricity, fertiliser and water charges and easier terms for loans for agricultural investment.[42] Such farmers' movements are often called *kulak* movements and are dismissively treated by many on account of the fact that they do not represent the interest of the vast number of farmers who are not net sellers of marketable surplus. According to V.K.R.V. Rao "only 21.4% of all operational holdings could be said to be contributing to marketed surplus and the bulk, viz., 78.6% of the holdings have no or negligible share in marketed output."[43] Further the land revenue as percentage of total revenue has fallen from 8.2% in 1950-51 to 2.5% in 1970-71. The rich farmers have been favoured by another criterion too. Agricultural tax as percentage of total tax has come down from 0.6% in 1950-51 to 0.16% in 1987-88.[44] And yet it is also true, as these farmers insist, that "total inputs as percentage of agricultural output have increased both in money and in real terms during the decade."[45] The rich farmers too then are victims of the nexus. Though we may argue that the agriculture sector is historically meant to feed and support a growing capitalist society, yet in terms of the here and now this argument is hardly going to persuade the bulk of rich farmers into a quiescent posture.[46]

The fact that the rich farmers movements have gained a lot of attention is because these farmers are more voluble and have greater staying power. They desist from merging with existing party formations, and the enthusiasm they generate is quite remarkable. This can be gauged from their membership figures. For example, the TNAA in Tamilnadu has a membership of three million while the Kisan Sabha of the CPI(M) has only 81 thousand members in the state.[47] While it is true that the rich farmers have a set of demands quite distinct from the poorer farmers it is only the very rich that seem to be quite confident of themselves. In the middle and lower tiers of the so called "rich" farmers there is considerable anguish as to how they will be able to protect themselves from the ravages of the country town nexus under which they are operating.

It is not at all surprising that national parties have not been able to project the demands of these rich farmers. Agricultural issues in each region are quite different in their specificities.[48] However the farmers' movements are quite content in staying outside national parties not because of their pre political nature, but because they have shrewdly calculated their effectiveness to be the greatest when they work as a pressure group outside established political structures.[49] This also gives them room to operate the more powerful levers of the government in their favour when movements of the poorer peasants antagonistically confront them. Such instances of switching political operations among rich farmers are common in almost all regions except perhaps for Haryana and west U.P. But in Punjab, Karnataka, Maharashtra and Tamilnadu, the facility with which rich farmers employ the weapons of the supra-local state on some occasions and the organisational organs of the more localised rich farmers movement on others should not be overlooked.

The reason for emphasisting these issues is because the farmers' movement has caused some confusion by its vociferous espousal of "Bharat" against "India." This has given rise to a false notion of a dichotomy between rural India (i.e. "Bharat") and urban India (i.e., "India"). It may have also led some to believe that the farmers are in fact rejecting India for an arcadian "Bharat." Such conceptions are easily corrected if we pay attention to the existence of the *nexus* which makes all these scenarios quite improbable. Additionally, it should also be remembered that the rich farmers' movement aggressively demands concessions from "India" and it manifests no desire to return to any untidy utopia of an idyllic and impoverished village republic. The rich farmers demand public investment on a large scale, but they are economically hurt because rural public investment is on the decline.[50] The farmers movement depends on cheaper and more abundant irrigation, power and fertilisers, for all of which the public sector is important. Our agricultural sector has broken from feudalism and from the so called "patron client relationship", but the industrial sector, public and private, cannot fully complement this transition. This is not so much because of the under development of the economy as it is due to the peculiar character of post colonial capitalism in India .[51]

Undoubtedly there will be different views as to why the industrial and agrarian sector do not fully complement each other. Ours may be a partial and incomplete one. But in this paper we are more interested in demonstrating the viability of operating with a frame of reference which keeps the country town nexus uppermost. This nexus, notwithstanding its many faults, self consciously returns to the structural relationship between rural and urban India. It goes beyond localities and regions and the manifestation of this nexus is replete with contradictions which cannot be wished away. The development of these contradictions will however depend on the particularity of the concrete and contingent conditions. For example, to go back to our original example, in some areas poor peasant agitations develop and grow whereas in other regions it may be the rich farmers lobby which is active. Wet regions as opposed to dry regions will also be affected differently by this nexus and will throw up a different mix of social and political options and demonstrate a different set of contradictions.

In west U.P. for instance the contradiction is not quite the same as it is in Maharashtra or even in other regions of U.P. This is why the Bharatiya Kisan Union (BKU) led by Mahendera Singh Tikait is different in many ways from the farmers' movements elsewhere. There are some broad similarities in the nature of the demands and also in its hostility to the government. The BKU too actively agitates for higher prices (it was sugarcane in the winter of 1987-88), lower electricity rates, and a reduction in the cost of other inputs. These, as we said earlier, have a certain basis and justification. The BKU's enemy too is the government and not a local despot or official. The difference is in the way the BKU in west U.P. projects itself as a community of *jat* peasants with an autonomous leadership principle which is based on community sanction and approbation. The interest of the farmers and the interest of the *jat* community are coterminous and this is what makes ideologies, even of the Sharad Pawar kind, seem quite redundant. Moreover the districtrs of west Uttar Pradesh, particularly Meerut, Muzzafarnagar, and Moradabad, are regions of *jat* dominated peasant proprietorship. The questions of wage labour are just not entertained by the dominant farmers in this region.[52]

The Bharatiya Kisan Union (BKU)

Though the BKU is strongest now in west Uttar Pradesh (U.P.) it actually began in the neighbouring province of Haryana. It was inspired by the late Charan Singh, the undisputed leader of the farmers in U.P. and Haryana. Some believe that when Charan Singh was dropped from the Janata cabinet in 1978 he set out to form the BKU, perhaps out of pique, but also to demonstrate his power base. The BKU was organisationally formed on August 13, 1978 and its first office bearers were from Haryana. Though units of the BKU were set up in Punjab and U.P., it somehow went under after the Janata Party's electoral debacle of 1980. It also suffered as a result of the manner in which Charan Singh squandered his charisma by his unabashed drive to be Prime Minister. When the Janata party lost the gerneral elections it was Charan Singh who was the Prime Minister. It was not till 1986 that the BKU stirred to life in U.P. The government of U.P. raised electricity rates in August that year from Rs. 22.50 per horse power to Rs. 30 per horse power. Much later Mahendra Singh Tikait, leader of the BKU today, paid a left handed compliment to the Chief Minister of U.P., when he said that it was the Chief Minister's incompetence that strengthened the BKU.[53]

Initially the leadership of the BKU in west U.P. was in the hands of Choudhury Sukhvir Singh, leader of the largest *khap* (loosely, clan) of west U.P. *jats*, and father-in-law of Tikait's daughter. But by January 1987 Tikait had out maneuvered Sukhvir Singh by organising a highly successful agitation at Shamli against the hike in power tariffs. The agitation continued till March 17. An estimated 5 lakh farmers *gheraoed* (sit in) the Karmu Khera sub station at Shamli. The government buckled under pressure and reduced the power rates from Rs. 30 to Rs. 25.[54] This immediately made Mahendra Singh Tikait into a national figure with various political parties vying to woo him with little success so far. Tikait is openly contemptuous and dismissive of all political leaders (with the exception of Devi Lal—Chief Minister of neighbouring Haryana).

**BKU and National Politics:
Against Parties but Inside Politics**

The BKU's distrust of national political parties has received wide coverage. Yet this does not place the BKU outside politics. Even though Tikait, the leader of the BKU, has steadfastedly stayed away from the major national and regional parties, he does not advocate a return to a mythical past. The BKU in no way evinces any desire to turn back from the modernising of agriculture but demands instead that modern agricultural inputs be made more easily accessible. It demands lower electricity rates, remunerative prices, assured irrigational facilities, and better terms of trade with urban industrial products. As a matter of fact in a private interview Tikait repeatedly said that if the terms of trade between agriculture and industry were to return to the 1950s level then the farmers in the BKU would give up their agitation. But he was also quick to add that as this could never happen the BKU must be ever vigilant in protecting the rights of honest farmers.[55] Even Tikait, rustic though he may be, has shrewdly realised the altered character of the post 1950s nexus. There is also the added realisation in Tikait that modernisation has not been uniform in bestowing its benefits on the Indian people.

The refusal of the BKU to make common cause with other political parties in no way signifies its reluctance to reach out to the cities to make its cause known. In January 1988, the BKU organised one of the most impressive political demonstrations in recent times in India in the city of Meerut, barely 40 minutes drive from Delhi and in the full view of urban India. Hundreds of thousands of farmers camped outside the District Collector's office in Meerut for 25 days. In all these days there was not one incident of unseemly mob behviour, violence, or even disorderliness. It was as if the BKU had also set out to win, or at least neutralise, the hearts of urban Indians who are so quick to find fault with their rural counterparts. They also, it seems, set out to teach urban India a few points on religious tolerance and inter-communal harmony. Less than a year before the BKU chose Meerut as its site for agitation the city had been engulfed by one of the worst communal carnages in recent memory. The enquiry into the communal killings of Muslims by the Hindus and also by the Provincial Armed Constabulary will perhaps never reveal the full story even when and if it is made public. The brutality of the carnage left a pall of gloom over the city and the atmosphere was surcharged with mutual suspicion and hostility. Muslims felt unsafe in non Muslim areas after dark and even during the day rarely strayed far from home. The peasants of the BKU changed all this: they opened Meerut up to its residents again by publicly avowing in their thousands to uphold inter- communal harmony.

This is an aspect of the BKU's activism that has gone unnoticed in most accounts I have read so far. Mahendra Singh Tikait indeed made a very special effort to both renew communal harmony in Meerut and also to preempt any attempt by opponents and detractors of the BKU to divide his organisation on communal grounds. When a BKU partisan died due to exposure or due to natural causes during the twenty day long agitation in Meerut, mortuary services from Hindu, Muslim, and Sikh traditions were performed simultaneously, though the religious faith of the deceased received ultimate priority. While the Meerut agitation was in progress Tikait used to deliver two speeches a day usually outside the Collector's office—the main site of the agitation. But the important issue is that it was customary for Tikait to end his speeches on every occasion with "*Allah ho Akbar*", followed by "*Har Har Mahadev*." On one occasion, on February 5, Tikait urged his men to call out "*Allah ho Akbar*", again, with more pasison. He chastised the gathering by saying: "This time you did not shout '*Allah ho Akbar*' as forcefully as you shouted '*Har Har Mahadev*." Surprisingly this aspect of the movement which is so novel and central to the BKU's ideology and political activism somehow escaped, to the best of my knowledge, the notice of most national journals and newspapers.

Neither can it be said that the desire for communal harmony exists only at the level of the leadership. This sentiment was expressed by a large number of the rank and life that had assembled in Meerut. In fact a small Hindu peasant from Moradabad said with some heat: "Why is the government raising the issue of Babri Masjid and Rama Janmabhoomi today, 40 years after Independence.[56] This is because the Congress has no other weapon in its armoury."[57] Very rarely does one hear such clear avowals of passionate secularism from urban Indians.

To a large extent the demographic character of west U.P. has a lot to do with BKU's secular charter on communal amity. The percentage of Muslims in west U.P. is much higher than what is either at the all India or at the all U.P. level. At the all India level Muslims constitute 11.3% of the population, and at the all U.P. level they make about 15.92% of the population. But in districts of west U.P., such as Meerut, Moradabad, Muzzafarpur, Bulandshahr, and Bijnor the Muslims constitute a bigger chunk of the total population.

The approximate percentages are as follows:

Muzzafarnagar	28.73%
Meerut	25.30%
Bulandshahr	19.37%
Moradabad	38.06%
Bijnor	39.45%

Source : Census of India, 1981 Series I Uttar Pradesh Household by Religion; pp. 2, 3, 14, 15, 644, 645, 650, 651, 656, 657, 674, 675.

While the percentage of Muslims is uniformly much higher in all these districts of west U.P. than the all India or the all U.P. figures, the proportion of Muslims in districts like Moradabad and Bijnor is really quite remarkable. It may be argued that the BKU has very real reasons for being so manifestly secular because a large chunk of its support structure consists of Muslims. In other words Tikait and the BKU are aware of the damage that communalists could do to the mass base of the BKU. Implicit in all this is the realisation that there are communalists outside who are willing and ready to cause such damage—the Meerut killers of 1987, for instance. For this reason BKU's espousal of secularism is not merely ethical but ideological and political as well.[57]

In other words Tikait and his followers are no ideological innocents. Tikait may abjure relations with political parties of all hues but this does not make him pre political or pre ideological. In fact Tikait is not really free from all political alliances. Time and time again as we mentioned earlier, he has come out in support of Devi Lal, the Chief Minister of neighbouring Haryana. Devi Lal gifted the farmers of west U.P., through the BKU, a sum of Rs. 2 lakhs and 20 electrical transformers. Surely this gift could not have gone any distance in alleviating the farmer's economic requirements, but even so Devi Lal's gesture was highly appreciated. It was seen as a gift "from the son of a *kisan* to Kisans."[58] At one time the BKU thought of raising a *kisan* army but Tikait abandoned that idea because he did not want the rest of the country to get a wrong impression of what the BKU stood for.[59] During the Meerut agitation there was news of violence from surrounding areas but the leaders, and Tikait in particular, were able to maintain calm and discipline among the agitationists assembled there. According to the *Indian Express* of 20th. May, 1988, Tikait on a later date also forbade his men from disrupting the Roorkee power house for this might again have upset people outside the movement. According to a BKU activist, and a close relation of Tikait: "We do not want to upset the routine of any city. We could have easily held up the milk supplies to Meerut, why even to Lucknow, but that is not our intention. After all the children of many *kisans* live in these cities."

The BKU is therefore aware of the non rural imperatives of conducting a farmers' movement. It is careful not to let any communal elements close to the union for this might rob it of its goodwill in the country as a whole. For the same reason the BKU scrupulously stays away from violence. This has led many observers to quip that Tikait wants to wear the mantle of Mahatma Gandhi[60]. Further though Tikait stays away from all major party, formations he believes that Devi Lal's party, the Lok Dal (B), which is in power in Haryana, is closest to their position and the BKU might even support it in case of an election.[61] But apart from this soft corner for Devi Lal Tikait elevates his distrust of political parties into a cardinal principle. At one time when the BKU was contemplating the formation of the *kisan* army it was felt that each recruit to this army should "swear by his mother not to join any political party."[62] Yet at the same time the motif of the BKU is *"jai jawan jai kisan."*[63] By the use of the word "jawan" (soldier in the Indian army) Tikait is once again reaching out beyond the rural districts of west U.P.

Though BKU's stance against parties binds the organization from making any direct dealings with political parties, it does not prohibit its members from voting in the national elections. A staunch supporter of

BKU remarked during the Meerut agitation: "the most important thing is to get the government to listen to us and to help us prosper. This Congress government does not seem to be interested at all: so why should we vote Congress? We'll vote for whoever supports us. May be the Janata Party, or Devi Lal, or whoever will be more attentive to our needs."[64] Tikait too said on one occasion that he would no longer vote for Congress but for Devi Lal's Lok Dal.[65] Though the BKU as such may not involve itself in national politics, its members are free to exercise their votes. In the words of a peasant supporter of BKU: "Who we vote for is our business. Our leaders cannot impose their political preferences on us. But the BKU as such should be out of politics."[66] Quite clearly the supporters of the BKU see great merit in strategic terms in keeping BKU independent of political parties. The BKU is, however, explicit about not supporting the Congress. In fact Capt. Bhopal Singh of BKU went to the extent of getting arrested for smashing the platform from which a Congress minister from U.P. was supposed to speak.[67] In such a situation open support for the Congres would be to invite trouble from the BKU.

The BKU Leadership and Peasant Proprietorship

The above will hopefully demonstrate that the BKU is far from being pre political or pre ideological though it is likely to convey such an impression to a quick observer. In districts such as Meerut, Moradabad, Muzzafarpur, and Bijnor, where the BKU is particularly strong, the legacy of the egalitarian *bhaichara* system still prevails. Peasant castes such as the *jats, rajputs,* and *tyagis* own and cultivate their own land in the main and consider themselves to be roughly equal in status. One could easily see this aspect of inter caste relations in Meerut. Food came to the agitators in the city from different villages every day and it was distributed freely without any considerations of caste. It was not like the 1920 peasant movement in Oudh where each caste and community ran its own kitchen during the course of movement.[68] This genre of egalitarianism among land holding peasants castes is quite in contrast to the ex-*zamindari* areas of east U.P. In these ex-*zamindari* regions both the land holding structure and social relations between different categories of landholders are very much more inegalitarian and stratified in character. Quite paradoxically, according to Jagpal Singh, a keen student of western U.P., members of low service castes (such as barbers, or smiths) are sometimes better off in the *zamindari* areas than in west U.P. In the latter regions because of *jat* dominance and the caste-occupation solidarity of the peasant castes, there is no room for manoeuverability for the landless service castes. If a dispute should arise between a barber and a poor *jat*, the *jats en masse* would sequeeze the barber out of his livelihood, if not out of his life. In eastern U.P., because of the presence of multiple castes, because there is no straight correlation between caste and land ownership, and also because of the criss-crossing of different systems of stratification, the poorer service castes can always hope for some measure of fair arbitration of disputes at the village level.

But the BKU is dominant in west U.P. and it is not at all surprising that Tikait's leadership is under constant surveillance by his men and followers who consider Tikait to be one of them. In a sense the members of the BKU are coparceners in the organisation. Tikait may be the leader but he is more like a first among equals. He may also be the leader of the Ballian *khap* (loosely, clan) but there are other powerful clans in west U.P. such as the Deshwal and Galliwara *khaps*. In fact Tikait's rival belongs to the Deshwal *khap*, a man who is his daughter's father-in-law. This fact alone tells us a great deal about the western U.P. kinship system for a daughter's father would in most other areas not dare to oppose the daughter's father-in-law.

Even during the days of the Meerut agitation when Mahendra Singh Tikait was the undisputed and high profile leader of the BKU, he was still not "charismatic". His followers were watching him closely and assessing his every move. As one peasant (with approximately 10 acres of land said): "If we find that Tikait is not listening to our problems we will replace him. We got rid of Charan Singh, didn't we?" The portion about Charan Singh was not strictly accurate, yet the assembled peasants in that gathering all demonstrably nodded their heads in approval. Though Tikait today is the leader of the BKU he is not and cannot be imperious in his actions. In this community of near equals Tikait (who owns about 15 acres of land) is watched closely. As a leader of a prestigious *khap* he has some family prestige but that is not a commodity that can be banked upon forever. His rival, Sukhvir Singh, is the head of the largest and most prestigious Deshwal *khap* but was ousted by Tikait, as mentioned earlier, from the leadership of the BKU. In addition, the peasants may choose someone like the late Charan Singh who did not belong to a dominant *khap* but who for more than forty years was the undisputed leader of the peasants of western U.P., and Haryana.

Soon after the Meerut agitation was called off there were some rumours that Tikait's position as leader was shaky and that he could be replaced any time. It was also said that Tikait's trusted lieutenant, Capt. Bhopal Singh, was ready to overthrow him. Bhopal Singh however refuted this allegation and said that he was still a staunch follower of Tikait.[69] Though Tikait had to call off the Meerut agitation without winning any concessions from the government he was not yet ready to go. In the first week of March 1988, Tikait organised a highly successful demonstration in Rajabpur (Moradabad district) and at Shamli (Muzzafarnagar) to protest against the police firing in Rajabpur on February 15 and 16 (i.e., when the Meerut agitation was on). It is reported that over one lakh assembled at Rajabpur for this protest demonstration.[70] As a matter of fact the BKU accused the government of engineering a communal situation on March 4 in Rajabpur so that the BKU's March 7 agitation against police firing would fizzle out.[71] Incidentally, March 4, 1988 was the day of the Holi festival when rowdyism often over takes the convivial bonhomie of the "festival of colours". Be that as it may this again indicates the BKU's sensitivity to the communal issue and its insistence on keeping communal elements out of the union. On April 22 again another demonstration was held by Tikait, but this time in Moradabad, demanding an enquiry into the Rajabpur firings.[72] This agitation was called a *jail bharo* (fill the jails) agitation when large numbers of BKU members voluntarily courted arrest. Here again one finds that Tikait and the BKU are quite tuned into the modes of protest followed by different national political parties and are not averse to using them in order to publicise their demands supra locally.

Tikait has been able to pull it off so far in spite of the resurfacing of his old rival, Sukhvir Singh, who publicly criticised Tikait's political acumen.[73] There are allegations too that Tikait is going soft on the Congress (I).[74] This is an old charge but so far there has been no substantiation of it. In some other quarters there is resentment that Tikait has not agaitated as much as he should have on the ban on the inter state movement of wheat.[75] On one occasion several members of the BKU held a meeting in a village in Muzzafarnagar district where some guarded criticism was made of Tikait. They also suggested that the BKU should not get highly bureaucratised and all posts barring that of the president and secretary should be done away with. Instead district level leaders should get more importance and five leaders from each district should be in the executive committee.[76] This again reaffirms the egalitarian structure that prevails among *jats* of west U.P., the context within which the question of Tikait's leadership should be understood.

Hyperlocalism and Political Indifference

The success of the BKU in west U.P. is almost directly related to its marginal influence in neighbouring regions. Neither do leaders of the BKU seem keen or eager to link up with other farmers outside. At the same time we have been reiterating in this paper that the BKU is not apolitical nor pre ideological. It believes that its interests can be put forwards best if it stays out of political parties and acts instead as a pressure group. This is a point on which most farmers movements in other parts of the country, for instance in Maharashtra or Karnataka, would concur. Sharad Joshi of the Shetkari Sangathan in Maharashtra has also come out in blasts against different political parties. Yet the vehemence with which Tikait and his men reject any dealings with political parties certainly surpasses Joshi's. Indeed on occasions it appears that Joshi is taking the cue in this matter from Tikait. For instance on April 18 of 1988 Sharad Joshi in a typical Tikait like flourish announced that the women partisans of his movement would prevent politicians from entering villages where the Shetkari Sangathan was strong, whether these villages be in Maharashtra, Gujarat or Madhya Pradesh .

The above statement reveals that Sharad Joshi's interests go beyond Maharashtra and are not confined to the problem of any one community. Tikait and the BKU are, however, clearly limited to western U.P. While their bases in neighbouring Haryana have all but gone their strongholds in west U.P. have become stronger. In fact the BKU leaders from Meerut, Bulandshahar, Muzzafarnagar, Bijnor and Moradabad, in meeting thought it would be wise to learn from the Gorkha movement in West Bengal and ask for a separate province of west U.P.[77] While Sharad Joshi is keen to set up an inter state corrdination committee to press for farmers' demands, Tikait seems to be quite content to cultivate his BKU in west U.P. This has angered Sharad Joshi who openly ridicules Tikait's obsession with not entering politics.[78] Tikait on his part considers Joshi to be a "political" creature who would have no objection to political wheelings and dealings. "He (Joshi) is of the same mould as the other politicans," Tikait argued in Meerut, "so why should we let him speak on our platform."[79] Tikait did not even allow the late Charan Singh's widow to speak from the

BKU platform in Meerut though the latter requested Tikait to be allowed to do so in full view and with folded hands. And this despite the fact that Charan Singh was the original inspiration behind the BKU and a great *jat* leader in his time. Not to mention that he was also the Prime Minister of the country during the last phase of Janata Party rule. Tikait is quite categorical that politicans do not have the interests of their constituncy at heart, but just their own selfish interests. Tikait and the current activists of the BKU are quite content to remain in west U.P. and not venture out to make common cause with cognate interest groups elsewhere. Tikait is proud of being a peasant and just that. He speaks in the *jat* dialect of west U.P. and proudly assertsed in 1988 that he has never gone to Delhi and has no desire to go there either .[80]

As we mentioned earlier the typicality of western U.P. perhaps allows and even encourages this hyperlocalism in BKU activism. Western U.P. is a region where the remnants of the *bhaichara* system among the peasant castes can still be seen. In this respect it is quite different from the ex-*zamindari* areas of even east U.P. In addition land in west U.P. is fertile and eminently arable. In Meerut district alone about 97 percent cultivable land has assured irrigation.[81] The peasants here have considerable confidence in themselves. Tikait for his part is not in the least overawed by city people and enjoys the discomfiture of urban scholars and journalists when they find it difficult to comprehend his round about and oblique answers to their persistent questions. The Meerut agitation may not have been a complete success in terms of forcing the government to raise the price of sugar cane, lower electricity rates, or to lift the ban on inter state movement of wheat. Yet the BKU has chalked up some successes. In villages where the BKU is strong no government officials can come anymore to disconnect tube wells for non payment of electricity bills.[82] In all likelihood, under BKU pressure the *kharif* crop prices for 1988 were also raised slightly by the government.[83] The electricity rates too were reduced from Rs. 30 per horse power to Rs. 22.50 per horse power.[84] The BKU however demanded that the rate should come down even lower to Rs. 17.[85]

The droughts of 1987-88 gave the BKU demands a ring of urgency. Though more sugar cane was crushed in 1988 than in the prevcious year (402 lakh quintals in 1988 as against 391 lakh quintals in 1987) the production of sugar fell to 32.65 quintals in 1988 from 36.91 quintals in 1987. This is because lack of rains brought down the sucrose content of the sugar cane so that the recovery rate average was only 8.12 percent in 1988 whereas it was 9.48 in 1987.[86] The farmers of west U.P. also know how important their agriculture is for the government of U.P. Of the 20 lakh tons that the government of U.P. intends to purchase in 1988 about 6 lakh tons will come from Meerut district alone.[87]

All this should not cloud the obverse reality that the farmers of west U.P. are tied to the market and cannot sever their ties with it. Their involvement with the market is not from a position of weakness but nevertheless there are strong elements of antagonism and tension. Yet, as we have been at pains to emphasise repeatedly, Tikait and the BKU do not think in terms of a moral economy of the peasant world but rather in terms of an agricultural sector fully enmeshed in the green revolution system of production. That the farmers of west U.P. are caught up with the contradictions of this process, much like the farmers elsewhere, make them only that much more determined to force the issue in their favour.[88] They want more fertilisers, mechanisation, irrigation and better terms of trade. As Tikait said: "The rural people should be proud of being farmers. We are the backbone of the economy. Why should the terms of trade between agriculture and industry get steadily worse for agriculture since 1951."[89]

CONCLUSION

While the BKU's hyperlocalism, its distance from political parties, and the undifferentiated nature of its peasant base, may make it appear similar to many pre-independence peasant movements, yet a closer look confirms that the altered nexus of contemporary India has left its imprint on Tikait's organisation too. The farmers' movements of today, whether in west U.P., or in Maharashtra, or in Karnataka, are also conscious of the changed character of their country town nexus and that is why the demands of these movements are never single pronged but multipronged, not just remedial but prospective too.

Finally it is worth reiterating that many perspectives and analytical opinions can contest for supremacy within the frame of reference of the country town nexus. This is the strength of this frame of reference. It comples us to think analytically as it draws attention to conflict, integration, struggle and change. It also reminds us that the issues of the fifties are over.

ACKNOWLEDGEMENTS

I am grateful to Gautam Navlakha and Jagpal Singh for their co-operation and advice. I alone, am, however, responsible for the errors and shortcomings of this paper.

NOTES AND REFERENCES

1. Milton Singer, 1972, When a Great Tradition Modernises, Delhi, Vikas, p. 40.
2. McKim Marriot (ed.), 1955, Village India: Studies in the Little Community, Chicago: University of Chicago Press.
3. Ibid.
4. E. Kathleen Gough, 1955, "The Social Structure of a Tanjore Village", in McKim Marriot (ed.), Village India: Studies in the Little Community, op. cit.
5. M.N. Srinivas, 1972, Social Change in Modern India, Bombay: Orient Longman.
6. Singer, op. cit.
7. Alan Beals, 1955, "Interplay Among Factors of Change in a Mysore Village", in McKim Marriot, ed., Village India: Studies in the Little Community, op. cit.
8. T. Scarlett Epstein, 1978, South India: Yesterday, Today and Tomorrow, London: English Language Book Society and Macmillan Press.
9. Studies in modernization of tradition and culture have a wider canvas. The direction of change in some studies like, for example, by Rudolph and Rudolph took the change agent to be the set of policy measures issued by the state relating particularly to universal adult franchise; see Lloyd I. Rudolph and Susanne H. Rudolph, 1967, *The Modernity of Tradition : Political Development in India*, Bombay : Orient Longman.
10. Srinivas, 1972, op. cit. pp. 1-45.
11. Ibid, pp. 46-88
12. A.R. Desai, 1979, "Introduction" in Peasant Struggles in India, Delhi: Oxford University Press, p. xiii.
13. D.N. Dhanagare, 1983, Peasant Movement in India : 1920-1950, Delhi: Oxford University Press, pp. 222-3
14. Ranajit Guha, 1983, Elementary Aspects of Peasant Insuragency in Colonial India, Delhi : Oxford university Press, p. 113.
15. Dipankar Gupta, 1986, "Continuous Hierarchies and Discrete Classes: Social Mobilization among peasants", in K.L. Sharma (ed.), Social Stratification in India, Delhi: Manohar.

16. Eric Meyer, 1983, "From Internal to External Debt", in Charles Malamoud (ed.), Debts and Debtors, New Delhi : Vikas, p. 162.
17. Dhanagare, 1983, op. cit., p. 27.
18. P.C. Joshi, 1975, Land Reforms in India : Trends and perspectives, Bombay, Allied, pp. 90-6. see also: Daniel Thorner, 1976, The Agrarian Prospect in India, Bombay: Allied.
19. M.V. Nadkarni, 1987, Farmers' Movements in India, Ahmedabad: Allied, p. 23.
20. Ibid.
21. Carol Boyack Upadhya, 1988, "The Farmer Capitalist of Coastal Andhra Pradesh", in Economic and Political Weekly, vol. 23, pp. 1376-82, 1433-42.
22. G.S. Bhalla, 1988, "Inaugural Address at Seminar Organized in Honour of Professor G. Parthasarthy" (Mimeo).
23. B.M., 1985, "Farmers' Agitations : Limits and Purposes", in Economic and Political Weekly, vol. 23, pp. 456-8.
24. D.N. Dhanagare, 1987, "Green Revolution and Social Inequalities in Rural India", in Economic and Political Weekly, vol. 22, (Annual Number), pp. AN. 143.
25. Amal Sanyal, 1988, "The Fiscal Crisis and the Monetary System", in Social Scientist, no. 179.
26. Nadkarni, op. cit. p. 23.
27. Epstein, op. cit., pp. 166-72.
28. Dhanagare, 1987, op. cit., pp. AN 138—AN 142; Nadkarni, op. cit., pp. 47-9.
29. Dhanagare, Ibid., p. AN 138.
30. McKim Marriot, 1955, "Little Communities in an Indigenous Civilization", in McKim Marriot, ed., Village India: Studies in the Little Community, op. cit.
31. Krishna Bharadwaj, 1987, Analytics of Agriculture-Industry Relation, Economic and Political Weekly, Vol. 22, Annual Number, pp. An. 17-AN. 20.
32. Ranjit Sau, 1972, "Indian Economic Growth : Constraints and Prospects", Economic and Political Weekly, vol. 7, (Special Number), pp. 249 60.
33. Nadkarni, op. cit., pp. 55-7.
34. Ibid., p. 43.
35. Ibid., p. 44.
36. Ibid., p. 48.
37. Ibid., p. 50.
38. Ibid., p. 48.
39. Ibid.
40. Dhanagare, 1983, op. cit., p. 224.

41. T.K. Oommen, 1985, From Mobilization to Institutionalization : The Dynamics of Agrarian Movements in Twentieth Century Kerala, Bombay: Popular Prakashan, pp. 16—102.
42. Terence J. Byres, 1988, "Charan Singh (1902-87) : An Assessment", Journal of Peasant Studies, vol. 15, pp. 139-89.
43. Nadkarni, op. cit., p. 32.
44. Navbharat Times, 11.2.88.
45. Nadkarni, op. cit., p. 52.
46. Terry Byres deals with some of the dilemmas facing left parties in the context of peasant mobilisations in the developing world. See Terence J. Byres, 1986, "Foreward : The Agrarian Question and the Differentiation of the Peasentry", in Aitur Rehman, *Peasants and Classes*, Delhi :" Oxford University Press. pp. xv-xviii.
47. Nadkarni, op. cit., p. 67.
48. Sharad Joshi, A leader of Shetkari Sangathan, said in a interview that "(e)ach product (agricultural-D.G.) requires a tailor-made approach", see Nadkarni, Ibid., p. 73.
49. Ibid. pp. 3, 76-7.
50. Nilakantha, Rath, 1988, "A Budget for Farmers", in Economic and Political Weekly, vol. 23, pp. 739-44.
51. Amiya Kumar Bagchi, 1988, "Colonialism and the Nature of Capitalist Enterprise in India", in Economic and Political Weekly, vol. 23, pp. PE. 38-50.
52. In Charan Singh's opinion a landless man is not a farmer (See Byres, 1988, p. 164). This point of view seems to orient the BKU's opinion even today. The BKU has nothing to say about the problems being faced by agricultural wage labourers. Sharad Joshi's Shetkari Sangathan, on the other hand, is often sensitive to issues concerning agricultural wage labourers (Tims of India, 19.4.88). While I came across several handloom weavers who would also benefit from a reduction in electricity rates. I did not come across a single agricultural wage labourer in Meerut during the course of the BKU's agitation in that city.
53. *Navbharat Times*, 8.2.88.
54. *Frontline*, 20.2.88, pp. 7-9.
55. Personal Interview.
56. Some Hindu organisations, principally the Vishwa Hindu Parishad, have been agitating for the closure of a 16th. century masjid (mosque) built by Babar, the founder of the Mughal Empire in India. The Hindu organisations contend that the site on which the mosque stands today was the original birth place of Rama, a supreme god/hero of Hindu mythology. The government has often been criticised for its weak kneed position on this issue which has been interpreted by many as covert support to the Hindu organisations.

57. It would be interesting to compare and contrast this aspect of the BKU with the 1920's peasant movement in Oudh, first under Baba Ramachandra and then under Madari Pasi see Majid Siddiqi, 1978, Agrarian unrest in North India, Delhi: Vikas.
58. Navbharat Times, 18.5.88.
59. Ibid.
60. In a personal interview in February 1988, Tikait said that violence at this stage of the movement's development would be unnecessary and counter-productive. But instead of rationalising his approach against violence in a Gandhian fashion, Tikait said, somewhat imperiously: "If we have to raise our hand we should raise it against someone worthwhile. What is the point of fighting against such lowly people who are agents of the government" (Personal Interview). See also Frontline, 20.2.85. p.5
61. The Indian Express, 20.5.88.
62. The Statesman, 27.4.88.
63. Ibid.
64. Personal Interview.
65. The *Indian Express*, 20.5.88.
66. Personal Interview.
67. *Indian Express*, 4.5.88.
68. Siddiqi, op. cit., p. 117.
69. Jansatta, 22.3.88.
70. The Times of India, 6.3.88.
71. The Indian Express, 11.3.88.
72. The Indian Express, 23.4.88.
73. Ibid.
74. The Indian Express, 11.6.88.
75. *Jansatta*, 10.6.88.
76. *Navbharat Times*, 23.4.88.
77. Ibid.
78. The Indian Express, 28.2.88.
79. Navbharat Times, 8.2.88.
80. Personal Interview.
81. Frontline, 20.2.88, p. 7.
82. The Indian Express, 7.5.88.
83. The Indian Express, 4.5.88.
84. The Indian Express, 23.4.88
85. The Times of India, 11.2.88.
86. The Times of India. 13.2.88.
87. Jansatta, 13.5.88.
88. Tikait remarked in Meerut on 7 February, 1988 : "We are not beggars that we should want things. We only demand what is just and that is why we are here". (Navbharat Times, 8.2.88).
89. Personal Interview.

CHAPTER 6

An Apoliticist Populism : A Case Study of B.K.U.

—D.N. Dhanagare

The Bharatiya Kisan Union (BKU) in Uttar Pradesh (U.P.), whose agitation in Meerut lasted for 25 days from 27 January to 20 February 1988, has created history. Since 1978, when it was first established, the BKU has been trying to mobilise farmers but could create only limited impact. The Meerut agitation-a part of that wider movement-however, turned out to be unique in more ways than one.

Earlier in 1984 the Punjab BKU under the leadership of Rajewal and Bhupinder Singh Mann had besieged the Punjab Raj Bhawan (Governor's residence) at Chandigarh. Thousands of Sikh farmers had then participated in the massive picketing of the Raj Bhawan and they were joined by leaders and activists of farmers' organisations from all over India.[1] But even that siege had not been as prolonged as the *dharna* of BKU supporters at the Commissioners's office in Meerut was.

The only parallel to the BKU *dharna* agitation in Meerut was Maharashtra-Shetkari Sanghatana's *rasta-roko* agitation in Nipani, as small town on the Karnataka Maharashtra border known for its tobacco cultivation and business, in March-April 1981. For 23 days the Sanghatana workers and supporters, under Sharad Joshi's leadership, had blocked the Bombay-Bangalore national highway paralysing traffic and communication on either side.[2] The Nipani agitation had a limited aim of drawing the government's attention to the grievances and plight of tobacco growers whom traders, middlemen and wholesalers fleeced by denying them a market price.

The similarities between the Nipani agitation seven years ago and the more recent agitation of BKU in Meerut are, however, more apparent than real. At Nipani the Shetkari Sanghatana's targets were fixed and its offensives were well planned like blocking the national highway for over three weeks which considerably affected market interests. In contrast the longest ever siege of a Commissionerate during the BKU agitation in Meerut was an innocuous symbolic protest as it harmed practically no one, neither traders or middlemen, nor any other classes, nor even the government of Uttar Pradesh. On the contrary, available reports suggest that shopkeepers in Meerut, petty traders, street vendors and itinerant peddlers had brisk sales. For them the BKU agitation was a blessing in disguise as it had brought to them new customers in large numbers and their inflow continued for nearly four weeks.

As for the U.P. Government, whose credibility under the then Chief Minister, Vir Bahadur Singh was at the lowest ebb, had little prestige to lose. In fact, somewhat unintentionally, it gained a bit of it when the BKU leader Mahendra Singh Tikait lifted the *dharana* unconditionally since neither the Rajiv Gandhi government at the centre nor V.B. Singh's in the state was in any way willing to give in to the BKU pressure. They had their own reasons to sit tight on BKU demands and not to get worked up by the siege.

The Meerut siege was a massive agitation not only in terms of the numbers but also in terms of the tenacity demonstrated by the hundreds of thousands of farmers who arrived in Meerut to join the stir.[3] By any standards the performance of Tikait's BKU was remarkable as it managed to keep the agitators peaceful and restrained throughout the 25 day siege. The Nipani agitation of the Shetkari Sanghatana, in contrast, was marred by police firing in which *satyagrahis* became martyrs and about 100 were wounded on the last day of the stir when the Karnataka police arrived on the scene to arrest the Sanghatana leaders. But the BKU supporters displayed striking patience, courage and discipline. Nowhere was there any symptom of panic, frenzy, pandemonium, melee or a show of wanton destruction—often associated with a crowd psyche. All the agitators who came across long distances settled in the sprawling grounds of the Controller of Defence Accounts (CDA) or squatted on any open space they could find during the biting cold of the north Indian winter at its peak.

The BKU workers and volunteers functioned in a most orderly manner. The supply of food was arranged from neighbouring villages and it was served daily to all the camping agitators. The efficient organisation of the agitation in Meerut by BKU was reminiscent of the organisastion of the Bardoli *satyagraha* by Sardar Patel some sixty years ago in South Gujarat.[4] The communication of commands and instructions from the top to the rank and file of the BKU was unfaltering. This would not have been possible without the farmers' fraternal solidarity, commitment to a cause and above all without their unflinching loyalty to their new leader Mahendra Singh Tikait. Such a noticeably peaceful protest (*dharana*) unruffled by minor provocations from either police or administration, has been a rather rare phenomenon in the annals of the history of peasant struggles in India.

When the *dharana* was first started in the CDA compound in Meerut, the BKU had prepared an 11 point charter of demands. Later the demands increased to 27 when a memorandum was placed before the Meerut Commissioner. Subsequently the full list of demands, added upto 35, in which many of the earlier demands were repeated. The major demands of the BKU were:

(i) Raising the price of sugarcane from Rs. 27 to Rs. 35 a quintal.

(ii) Arrears on account of electricity bills of the previous year be written off; the excess amounts collected from those farmers, who had paid the bills at the increased rates, be refunded to them.

(iii) No penalty be imposed for non-payment of electricity bills, and a facility be made available to pay the bills at the nearest substation of the Electricity Board.

(iv) Fixed power tarrif in relation to the depth of the ground-water level.

(v) An uninterrupted power supply for 12 hours a day for agricultural/farm connections where pump-set and bore-wells are in use.

(vi) Prompt attendance to all complaints from power consumers and immediate repairs of defective transformers in several villages.

(vii) An immediate withdrawal of all false criminal cases implicating some BKU activists after the protracted Shamli agitation (in Muzaffarnagar district) in 1986-87.

(viii) Tax relief for all farmers on account of the unprecedented drought in the country; and

(ix) Substantial reduction in canal water charges, as well as in land revenue (tax).[5]

There were other minor demands which included: improved educational facilities and reservation of seats in government jobs for children of farmers; pension for farmers above 55 years of age; a CBI inquiry into the killing of Rajkumar Ballian-an advocate turned BKU worker by the U.P. police; and an urgent completion of the canal constrution work under the Krishna Hiddan Doab project as well as its immediate linking to Kallarpur through the Deobandh branch of the Ganga canal.[6]

Some of these demands are highly local but genuine for the agitating farmers. However, most of the demands, particularly those pertaining to remunerative prices for sugarcane, reduction in electricity/canal water charges and the like are the same raised by the Punjab BKU, the Shetkari Sanghatana in Maharashtra or by the Karnataka Rajya Rayatha Sangh—since the mid-1970s. Both the major demands (which are all pan Indian in nature) or the minor ones (which ventilate local grievances of farmers in U.P.), all draw attention to the urgency of narrowing the yawning gap between standards of living and civic amenities in cities and towns on the one hand and in the villages on the other.

The treatment meted out to needy farmers by government officials is yet another source of resentment and anguish. This is even doubly true of farmers in western U.P. where 'they have often ended up paying more in bribes to corrupt officials of the U.P. Electricity Board, State Irrigation Department and the like than they did in legitimate government dues'.[7] In fact the BKU leader Tikait himself complained about political graft and corruption in U.P. since 'on an average a farmer has to pay anything from 5,000 rupees to 8,000 rupees to get his son a job in the police and about 15,000 rupees for a job in the army'.[8]

It is evident then that most of the BKU's demands and grievances centre around 'power supply, irregularities in electricity bills and the electricity department's failure to ensure and restore a steady power supply to farmers', besides of course remunerative prices for sugarcane or wheat and so on. These issues had not cropped up overnight. The BKU movement had in a way gathered momentum in U.P. with its 18 month long protest agitation staged at Karmo Kheri village near Shamli in Muzaffarnagar district since 1986. It was here that attention was first focussed on 'electricity issues' by over one lakh farmers of the BKU who offered *satyagraha* and courted arrest in March 1987. In this agitation BKU supporters clashed with the police and three villagers were killed in the firing that followed.

When the gravity of the situation dawned on the U.P. state administration, three state ministers were sent to the venue of the agitation to hold parleys with farmers' representatives, but the latter kept on the pressure by refusing to cremate the bodies of the three martyrs until the government conceded their demands. It was then that

10 out of 11 demands of the BKU were instantly met while the matter of power (electricity) rates was referred to the cabinet.[9]

The Meerut siege in January-February 1988 was therefore a continuation of the same prolonged agitation near Shamli. It was staged as a renewed stir partly to augment pressure on the government for reducing electricity rates and also partly for enlarging the scope of the farmers' general demands. Growing wiser from the past unhappy experience, the U.P. government first evolved a compromise formula according to which a 25 per cent concession was to be offered to all those farmers who paid their electricity dues on time and the sugarcane price was to be fixed on the basis of recovery.

These compromise terms were offered to the BKU leaders on the 15th day of their siege in Meerut.[10] They turned them down without realising that to sustain a farmers'movement beyond a certain point is rather difficult. An astute leader like Sharad Joshi of Maharashtra's Shetkari Sanghatana would have terminated the protest siege right at that point and would have turned the agitation into at least a partial success instead of letting it flop into an unconditional retreat ten days later as it actually did under Tikait's leadership. After the Meerut *dharana* which ended in a fiasco, BKU supporters must have marched back their villages in utter frustration, despondency and with resentiment.[11]

At the end of the Meerut agitation what remains is a paradoxical situation. Whereas the BKU led farmers' movement as such suffered reverses, maybe temporary ones, the personal popularity of Mahendra Singh Tikait seemed to be rising. This semi-literate typical *kisan* of a medium sized landholding emerged as an enigma who is now being revered by his BKU followers almost with the same veneration tinged with hysteria that the indigo cultivating tenantry of Bettaih and Motihari subdivisions had showered on Mahatma Gandhi when he visited Champaran distirict (in Bihar) at the time of the legendary Champaran *satyagraha* in 1917.[12] But to consider Tikait as a replica of the Mahatma, as most of the agitating farmers in Meerut did , is to blow his stature out of all proportions.[13] Any attempt to attribute charismatic qualities to Tikait would undoubtedly make Max Weber turn in his grave!

Why did the BKU siege in Meerut snowball and burst like a soapwater bubble? The answer to this question has to be sought in the approach of Tikait's BKU to politics and in its attitude to other sister organisations of farmers in other parts of the country.

Not too surprisingly, Tikait's and his BKU's attitude towards political parties and power politics is ambivalent. Sometimes it is even marked by hostility. Like all other farmers' organisations in other parts - such as Punjab, Maharashtra, Karnatka, Tamil Nadu and so on, the BKU in Uttar Pradesh too has proudly declared itself to be a purely non-political forum. In Maharashtra, Sharad Joshi has in fact argued time and again that the rise of his Shetkari Sanghatana is a total defeat of the party system and that some parties have even tried to divide the farmers' movements.[14] But whereas on the one hand Sharad Joshi believes that regardless of which party comes to power it is going to perpetuate the policy of starving farmers, on the other hand he has perhaps been the most tactful in using political parties for selectively entering into alliances.

Though Tikaits' BKU shares Sharad Joshi's scepticism about political parties, its overt gestures to parties and political leaders clearly suggest that it lacks the tactfulness with which the Sanghatana has handled them in Maharashtra. Tikait forgets conveniently that BKU's founder President, the late Choudhary Charan Singh, was a politician of no small stature. In fact it was only when Charan Singh was dropped from the Janata ministry in 1978 that he found it necessary to reassert his *kisan* identity by setting up the BKU. Charan Singh himself never overstressed the 'nonpolitical' character of the new forum. For him it was no more than one of the weapons in his political armoury - an instrument of power politics. To that end BKU did organise a massive farmers rally in Delhi on 28 December 1978 to coincide with his birthday.

In Charan Singh's time the BKU's purpose was rather limited. It did not seriously engage itself in any sustained mobilisation of farmers on any major issue as the BKU's counterparts did in other states from 1978 to 1986. Moreover, the election reverses of Charan Singh's party, the Lok Dal, suffered in 1980 and 1984 had conclusively proved that his BKU was hardly a political force to reckon with. He had failed to transform the BKU into a political instrument of the Lok Dal as he had originally intended. It was only when Mahendra Singh Tikait revived it that the BKU acquired some political significance particularly in the western districts of Uttar Pradesh. But quite paradoxically Tikait started insulating it from political parties and power poltics instead of building bridges with them tactfully.

In utter disregard for his mentor, the late Charan Singh, Tikait thus started treating politics as a dirty arena mired by the vilest interests and machinations of unscrupulous power brokers. And this perception set the revived BKU's tone towards political parties including the opposition. Throughout the 25 day *(dharna)* agitation in Meerut, the BKU's indifference, often with streaks of suppressed hostility towards political parties, was visible. It was a complete turn around, because Tikait had earlier associated himself with the opposition parties during their conclave convened by the Haryana Chief Minister Devi Lal at Surajkund. But then Tikait suddenly changed his stance and strategy. At the Meerut siege Tikait's speeches as well as conduct clearly suggested that he was rather over anxious to keep the BKU movement 'uncontaminated' by the intrigues of opposition leaders. And in this he spared no one. Neither V.P. Singh of the Jan Morcha nor Gayatri Devi (widow of Charan Singh), Ajit Singh of the Lok Dal (A) - now merged with the Janata Party, nor Chandra Shekhar, President of the Janata Party, was allowed to use the BKU platform to address the agitators in Meerut.

Apart from Tikait's contempt for opposition parties, even more baffling is his attitude to other sister organisations of farmers. For example, soon after the siege started in Meerut, Sharad Joshi of Maharashtra's Shetkari Sanghatana rushed to Meerut to express solidarity with the BKU and its cause for which the siege agitation had been launched. But even Sharad Joshi was not given access to the BKU platform. It is very likely that by associating V.P. Singh with the Sanghatana's massive rallies in Latur, Satara and Nagpur (all in quick succession in the second half of 1987) Joshi had antagonised Tikait whose displeasure with V.P. Singh is now an open secret.

Initially Mahendra Singh Tikait was so enamoured by V.P.Singh's honesty, uprightness and integrity that he had invited him to attend the BKU rally at Shamli (on April 1, 1987). V.P. Singh who was then still in the Congress (I), could not attend for some reason. Later, when the opposition parties organised a joint rally in Muzaffarnagar which was attended by representatives of most of the farmers' organisations from other parts, Tikait stayed away. Apparently he disliked the presence of V.P Singh at the rally. By that time V.P. Singh had been ousted from the Congress (I). This incident further widened the gulf between Tikait's BKU and other farmers' organisations as well as opposition parties.

Althought Sharad Joshi and others of their Inter-State Coordination Committee wanted to rope in Tikait by offering him its convenorship, Tikait simply rebuffed them to make known his displeasure over their continued intrigues with V.P. Singh. In fact, from a meeting of different farmers' organisations held in Delhi in September 1987 (covened for planning the organisation of a mass rally in Delhi in October) Tikait left in a huff. The differences over inviting V.P. Singh to participate in the rally finally turned out to be irreconcilable.[15] With these turn of events the Congress(I) circles must have had the last laugh for they had every reason to receive with delight Tikait's estrangement from opposition as well as from other *kisan* movements.

The BKU's apoliticism under Tikait's leldership was neither naive nor a matter of conviction. It was quite selective. Tikait was shrewd enough to allow Maulana A. Bukhari, the Shahi Imam of Jama Masjid (Delhi), to address the agitating farmers in Meerut. The preponderance of Muslims among the cultivating classes in the Meerut-Saharanpur belt had made it politically expedient for Tikait to compromise with his policy of keeping the BKU aloof from politicians and political parties. Although the Maulana does not belong to any party, the political significance of his presence at the Meerut agitation cannot be overlooked. After all the solidarity of agitating farmers from different religious communities had to be maintained at any cost in a city like Meerut which is perpetually riot-stricken. Hence, however much a political novice the uneducated Tikait might appear, his sailing it alone in the Meerut siege was a clear indication that he did not lack political wisdom and sagacity.

But, how wise was it for the BKU in U.P. to have distanced itself from all political forces in general, and from similar other farmers' organisation, in particular, when their broader demands are the same? Renumerative prices for agricultural produce, reduction in electricity tariffs and in irrigation water rates, moratorium on farmers' loans and increased subsidy on inputs are the main items on the agendas of almost all farmers' organisation today and the BKU in U.P. is no exception. Therefore, joining hands with sister organisations would have averted the BKU's political isolation.

It is equally difficult to identify Tikait's allies as well as enemies, and his attitude to the Congress (I) is no less puzzling. Throughout the BKU agitation in Meerut, for example, Tikait chose to be vague in his attacks on the Congress (I) governments in the state and at the centre. He had antagonised, and once even insulted the then U.P Chief Minister V.B. Singh. When the latter had come to Muzaffarnagar for talks with Tikait (after the massive agitation in Shamli, 1987, in which three BKU activists had become martyrs in the police firing) none of Tikait's workers had cared to follow any protocol or even the normal courtesies of receiving the Chief Minister appropriately. Even during the 25 days siege of the Commissionerate in Meerut two U.P. ministers, Saidull Hassan and Hukam Singh and a Union Minister of state Rajesh Pilot, who were deputed to mediate but did not succeed, were treated by Tikait rather curtly. This was quite evident in Tikait's addresses to the rally every evening.[16]

Under these circumstances the state government would have normally followed its impulse to use repression and to prevent the Meerut agitation from materialising. But it did not do so. Despite all anticipations, caravans of bullock carts full of BKU supporters moved towards Meerut from the 26th of January 1988 were not stopped. No force nor police repression was let loose on the agitators although they kept the Commissioners's office beleaguered for nearly four weeks. Tikaits's indifference to the opposition, particularly to V.P. Singh and to all other farmers organisations must have relieved the Congress (I) circles which explains why the U.P. government went out of the way to provide water and helped maintain law and order

For obvious reasons the U.P. government was not keen to smash the BKU stir because the Congress (I) higher-ups must have felt that neither the Meerut siege nor the farmers' movement in general would make the party lose sympathy and political support more than what it has already lost in the Jat dominated area which is known for its hostility to the Congress (I). On the contrary, factional infighting was enough to weaken the predominantly Jat farmers organisation - the BKU. Given the political ancestry of Tikait's BKU such calculations on the part of the ruling party were not wide off the mark.

It is well known that Meerut, Muzaffarnagar, Bijnor and Saharanpur districts of western Uttar Pradesh, where Jats comprise roughly 40 per cent of the population, are the traditional strongholds of the late Charan Singh. By virtue of their numerical concentration as well as their control over sizeable proportion of cultivable land, the Jats dominate both the politics and economy of this region. After his ouster from the Janata ministry at the centre, Charan Singh did revive the Lok Dal party of the pre-Janata merger days. But this resurrected party had done little for the peasants who have been its main support base for years. Organising *kisan* rallies had fetched little tangible gains to the farmers who suffered both appropriation by market forces and oppression by a corrupt local bureaucrcy. Paradoxically a predominantly *kisan* party like the Lok Dal in U.P. had rendered itself redundant by alienating the Jat peasants at the grassroots level.

During Charan Singh's prolonged illness itself the faction formation process was gathering momentum in the Lok Dal. It did not take too long to crystallize into two camps. These camps were not based on ideological differences but on the personal ambitions of factional leaders. One of the Lok Dal factions was led by Ajit Singh (Charan Singh's son); it has now merged with the Janata Party. The other faction led by H.N. Bahuguna, a former Chief Minister who has completed several circles of moving from one party to another. But the latter faction has gained some respectability in the Hindi speaking belt, particularly in Haryana where it won a landslide victory in the assembly poll in an alliance with the Bharatiya Janata Party leading to the formation of the Devi Lal ministry.

Both the Lok Dal factions were fast losing touch with the reality at the grassroots and had become oblivious to the need to mobilise farmers - their main support base—on issues dear to them. This is precisely where the new BKU leader Mahendra Singh Tikait filled the gap. He did not of course openly renounce his Charan Singh-Lok Dal heritage but focussed his attention on mobilising *kisans* and turning them into a political force, though, quite ironically, insulating them from all other political forces. With the emergence of Tikait there were now three heirs of Charan Singh instead of two. Naturally these developments were by no means unwelcome to the Congress(I).

Even when the BKU was in the midst of the Meerut agitation, internal factional tussles kept surfacing. Not all *khap* leaders supported Tikait. For example, his strategies and tactics were not endorsed by Choudhary Sukhvir Singh, Vice President of the BKU whom Tikait had displaced from leadership. In a meeting of all members of *desh khap*, held in Meerut on 27 January, Sukhvir Singh disapproved of the *gherao* as a real solution to *kisans'* problems. He was supported by Shyam Singh (from Vamnoli) and Saar Singh (from Lohata). But this anti Tikait drive was countered immediately by another BKU unit leader Anup Singh. Opponents of Tikait favoured more militant action - such as an open rebellion or an insurgency against the state instead of a harmless siege.[17] Though Tikait was not averse to militancy including violence, quite surprisingly he refrained from using the idiom of insurgency throughout the 25 day siege. A subdued approach to the BKU agitation by the Vir Bahadur Singh government was in a sense a reciprocation; it avoided any precipitate action which could have provoked large scale violence. The BKU agitators and their leader

Tikait having failed to achieive any positive outcome in the 25 day long ordeal, finally saw through the wisdom of lifting the siege unconditionally as the only face saving device before the movement started petering out. The ruling party thus won the battle of nerves by exhausting the patience of Tikait and his BKU supporters.

Are we therefore to interpret the unconditional retreat and withdrawal of the stir and lifting of the Meerut siege as a major setbck to, if not an outright failure of, the BKU movement in U.P.? Jumping to such a conclusion would be rather misleading, for it would detract us from the real social forces that lay beneath the peasant ferment in India in the 1980s in general and particularly those which explain the rise of Tikait, his growing popularity and an effective organisation of the BKU in Uttar Pradesh.

What are these social forces? It is generally believed that rich farmers and the better off peasants constitute the sheet anchor and are also the main participants of the farmers' movements that have gathered momentum all over India since about 1978-79 on the question of remunerative prices and other linked issues affecting the farm sector. Some observers have argued that having a vested interest in preserving the existing property relations in land, rich land owning groups have always tended to abjure violence as a means of protest and have often opted for liberal-reformist constitutional agitations, including passive resistance (*satyagraha* and the like).[18] Barring stray incidents of violence in *rasta-roko* or *rail-roko* agitations in certain parts, the contemporary farmers' movements have confined themselves by and large to peaceful protests. The BKU's *dharna* in Meerut was no exception to this general pattern. It can be argued therefore that the peaceful assertion of peasant power through mass mobilisation in a way defines its class character.[19] This argument is basically deductive in format though not totally untenable empirically.

The relationship between the emergence of the rich peasantry as a class and the new *kisan andolans* in the 1980s should neither be doubted nor accepted as an axiomatic one, but needs to be qualified and stated more explicitly. The green revolution has unquestionably contributed to the rise of rich farmers as a class with definite class interests as well as a distinct political identity. The state policy and sponsored rural development programmes have been chiefly responsible for the rise of such an opulent class.

Through the green revolution strategy, important inputs such as high yielding varieties of seeds (particularly paddy and wheat), fertilizers and pesticides as well as energised well, canal and lift irrigation facilities were brought to the door-step of the cultivating households in rural India.[20] To promote agricultural growth, the basic productivity of the primary producer had to be augmented without necessarily draining his already fragile resources. This meant that the inputs had to be supplied at heavily subsidised rates. However, notwithstanding such subsidies, most of the inputs for modernisation of farm production required large capital investments which were, and are even now, beyond the means of small and marginal farmers who constitute an overwhelming majority in rural India.[21]

What is true of farm inputs is even doubly true of agricultural credit. A great bulk of institutional credit was grabbed by rich farmers through their political linkages, patronage and protection. Though the nationalisation of major commercial banks in 1969—a progressive measure no doubt—had eased the situation slightly for the poor and marginal sections, rural credit sources continued to be as inaccessible as before. Consequently, only a tiny class of rich farmers became the principal beneficiaries of development. In fact the policy and practice of rural development differed widely as agricultural development was reduced to an euphemism for using public funds to serve the private interests of a handful of rich farmers.[22] True the green revolution resulted in growth on the one hand, but on the other hand it also increased socio-economic inequatities in rural India.[23]

Naturally, a class of farmers developed a vested interest in preserving and sustaining such a developmental strategy which was bound to produce its own contradictions. The rich farmers' interests clashed with interest outside the farm sector—particularly those of urban-industrial and market forces. The agrarian economy linked to the wider political economy via the market could not have possibly escaped certain contradictions—particularly between those who want raw materials and food produced in farms supplied at cheap rates to urban industries and consumers, and those of farmers who want remunerative prices for their produce as to cover their production costs and leave them some margin of profit. It is primarily in these contradictions that lie the genesis of the farmers' movements in the 1980s.

Two more fascinating dimensions of India's rural development need to be mentioned here. First, although agricultural growth is visible in terms of food production rising from about 45 to 50 million tons in the pregreen revolution days to about 150 million tons today, farm prices have not kept pace with agricultural production.[24] In sharp contrast with increasing industrial prices almost without any limit, the relative stagnation in prices of farm produce was felt by farmers from the mid-1970s onwards. The declining agricultural profitability is then the major issue which was cogently articulated by ideologues of the farm lobby; often referred to as the *kulak* lobby. They argue that farm prices not linked to production costs are non-remunerative and adversely affect not just the rich farmers but also the small and middle farmers who grow cash crops.

The second dimension is usually emphasized by critics of the farm lobby. To them the other side of the story is that the contribution of the agricultural sector to the national economy as a whole has steadily declined. For example, in the total tax revenue of the state it has dropped dramatically from 8.8 per cent in 1950-51 to 1.1 per cent in the budget estimates for 1987-88; and the share of agriculture to national income has dropped from 69 per cent in 1950-51 to around 30 per cent in 1987-88.[25]

Leaders and ideologues of the present day farmers movements shrewldy ingnore this nose diving role of agriculture in the national economy; instead they focus their attention primarily on the growing disparties between the rural-agrarian *Bharat* and urban-indusrial *India*. There could not have been a more captivating and appealing dichotomy to bring forth the ethos of what is basically the 'terms of trade' issue in the Indian context. The credit for conceptualising the issue of the yawning gap between the rural and the urban India in the simplest possible phraseology—*Bharat* versus *India* —must go to the leader of Maharashtra Shethari Sanghatana—Sharad Joshi.[26] Mahendra Singh Tikait's BKU in U.P., that launched the Meerut agitation, raised demands in conformity with the assertions of the same 'Bharat versus India' ideology although Tikait lacks both the rigour of thought and the sophistication of articulation that characterise Sharad Joshi. In fact in ideological formulations the latter is far ahead of his peers from other sister organisations.

Critics of Tikait and Joshi dismiss the catchy 'Bharat versus India' formulation and counter argue that some gap between the agricultural and industrial prices is not only unavoidable but is also desirable to promote more balanced growth, to ensure that the national economy develops into a self-sustaining and a self-regulating one, and also to check inflationary tendencies that any increase in farm prices unleash, adding to the burden of the rural and urban poor. Moreover, a government that provides distribution of essential goods through fair price shops and simultaneously offers inputs to famers at heavily subsidised rates cannot possibly go on conceding to farmers' demands indiscriminately.[27]

Such an economistic critique of the farmers' movements is founded on the assumption that these movements are largely the making of rich farmers and that medium and small farmers are not in the least affected by relatively stable farm prices. Such fallacious and hence untenable assumptions are accepted now only by those who allow themselves to be carried away by stereotypes of rural India. A number of studies have shown that even small and medium farmers endeavour to use modern inputs, and turn to cash crops to agument their income and to improve their standard of living. So the small and middle level farmers too are being drawn into the vortex of the market. The issue of remunerative farm prices is, therefore, no longer confined to the interests of the rich farmers; rather it is of even greater concern for the small and medium holders who have started producing for the market, though partially, but still lack the capacity to hold on to their produce till favourable prices are offered in the market. If the usurpation of all farmers at the hands of market forces is to be prevented, then truly there is no substitute to a support price linked to cost of production, argue the ideologues of the farmers' movements.

The green revolution leading to the paradox of growth in productivity but decline in profitability, disparties in the incomes of different strata of society and the growing imbalances between the city and the countryside thus constitutes the background of the emergence of the farmers' movements in the 1980s, including the BKU movement in western Uttar Pradesh.

Building solidarity among all farmers and uniting them vertically is by no means an easy task. The organisational strength of the BKU and the sources of Tikaits' undiminished popularity even after the Meerut retreat[28] remain to be explained. Here the role of caste and clan must be stressed. The caste solidarity of the Jats is undoubtedly the backbone of the BKU in U.P. It is also significant that the BKU has little following in eastern U.P. It's strength and impact are more visible in the western U.P. districts which are dominated by the Jats who also happen to be the prime beneficiaries of the green revolution. But even there the internal structure of the Jats has proved to be quite functional to the BKU.

Among the Jats there are a total of 365 *khaps* (equivalent of *gotras*), referred to earlier, of which 18 *khaps* which claim large membership are concentrated in the western districts of U.P. Based on a belief in common ancestry, the *khap*-clan organisation has engendered fraternal feelings (*bhaichara*) rigidly observed by the Jats.[29] Though originally launched in 1978 the BKU could truly take off only in 1985 when it was reorganised on the basis of *khaps* whose Choudharies now comprise the subordinate leadership of the BKU. The clan heads have now acquired a new recognition as heads of their respective BKU units. This new quasi-political role has given the *khap* leaders a share in organisational power and has provided the grassroots an opportunity to participate in the decision making process.[30]

The organisational change proved beneficial to Tikait in first acquiring leadership and later in sustaining it. Tikait, himself the hereditary Choudhary of Baliyan *khap* in a sense usurped the BKU leadership from his brother-in-law and also Chaudhary of Deshwal *khap* whom Tikait named to head the BKU unit of the *khap*. This change took place at the time of the massive rally in Shamli in April 1987 in which Tikait obviously outmanoeuvred all other claimants to the BKU leadership and still could manage to restore balance among the different *khap* based factions by recognising their respective Choudharies as the BKU-unit heads.[31]

Those inclined to explain the contemporary farmers' movements in terms of the interface between primordial loyalties and newly emerging class structure in rural society tend to over-state the role that the reorganisation of the BKU on the cast *khap* basis played. The caste-clan formations among the Jats have certainly facilitated vertical solidarity and have helped the BKU in bringing poor Jat farmers closer to their more fortunate bretheren. But what about the non-Jat poor famers who too rallied under the banner of the BKU in support of the economic demands knowing that the Jat dominated BKU's demands would benefit rich farmers more than the poor in the same region? The present day farmers' movements, including BKU in U.P. cannot therefore be reduced to pure 'class' forces or 'caste-clan' or similar primordial forces. In doing so we assume that ideologies necessarily are class or caste ideologies.

A restricted epiphenomenal view of a movement's ideology (in the present discussion the BKU ideology) as a function exclusively of the class position would still leave the question unresolved as to why poor and middle farmers too get drawn within the ideological ambit dominated by the rich not belonging to their affilial ties. To argue that class and political action necessarily correspond with each other is to repeat economistic canons of orthodox Marxism in a deterministic fashion. The contemporary mobilisation of farmers is fast acquiring properties of a populist movement in which there is a growing disjunction between class and ideology on the one hand and between them and the scope of political action they arouse on the other.

In this context Gramsci's approach to ideology and political action should help us solve this conundrum. To him, the subjets of political action need not be identified within a social class exclusively; they are in fact the 'collective wills' which obey specifically formed laws of their own but again in an indeterminate manner. Subjects who exist as a 'class' at the economic level are not necessarily duplicated at the political level. Hence, political action initated by a populist movement draws into it inter-class subjects whose hegemony transcends simple class alliance, and their superior unity is realised through ideology.[32] As Ernesto Laclau would put it: in the case of populist movements the reductionist equation between the 'people' and 'classes' simply does not work.[33]

It is this kind of fusion of inter-class subjects which is being achieved with an ever increasing success by the ideology of the farmers' movements in the 1980s. In the BKU's Meerut agitation, which is a part of the same phenomenon Mahendra Singh Tikait's adroit handling of primordial affinities of caste and *khap* reinforced that inter-class unity. It is only when we recognise that populist movements of this nature act primarily as a source of delineation for the masses at large, that their specific nature and role at a given moment in history becomes comprehensible.

The economic and political compulsions of a farmers' movement of the populist nature seldom go hand in hand. But with a more pragmatic outlook and deft management the two can be held in perfect balance at least for some time by an astute leader. For example, Sharad Joshi of Shetkari Sanghatana was quick in adopting the demand for 220 rupees as a minimum wage for agricultural labour. This was a studied move to demonstrate that the farmers' movement is not against agricultural labourers.[34] Tikait's approach is too inelastic to accommodate such compulsions for tactical reasons, at least. Otherwise he would have been more discreet in his public utterances.

Some of the other demands he occasionally aired during the 25 day siege in Meerut—such as 'scrapping of the Land Ceiling Acts, and

Minimum Wage Acts' and also seeking 'permission for farmers to cut their own trees' certainly do not project him as a progressive leader. Impropriety of this kind is likely to cost him allies and win him more enemies. Once the implications of such status quoist demands seep down to the rank and file through political education, it would not take long to wreck the inter-class unity of the movement. Tikait has therefore a long way to go in mastering the art and politics of social movements.

The rise of farmers' movements, no doubt, would call for some political realigments in India in the immediate future. However, will Mahendra Singh Tikait and his BKU be able to manage the political compulsions and turn its populism into a transformative movement in the long run so that a proper balance between the town and the countryside in India gets restored? It is almost certain that Tikait's apoliticism in general and his indifference to other sister organisations of farmers in other states would insulate the BKU. His obduracy and stubbornness may be seen as personal virtue of a *khap* leader among the Jats. However, these can and do become stumbling blocks for a movement whose ideology visualises total social transformation. BKU's present charter of demands hardly comes close to such a sophisticated ideological formulation.

With his present stance Tikait may become the Jat leader in importance second only to the late Charan Singh and at this rate he would perhaps end up eventually either as a leader of a pressure-group at best or a naive power-broker or agitator without an ideology at worst. If he fails to overcome both his obsessions and his self-imposed political insularity, it is anybody's gues that Tikait may not succeed in building a mass movement for broader social transformation in the long run.

NOTES

1. Sharad Joshi, 'Farmsers' view of Punjab', *Indian Express* (Bombay), August 2, 1984; p.8
2. For Details see, Vijay Parulekar, *Yoddha Shetkari* (in Marathi). Pune: Rajhans Prakashan, 1982.
3. Several investigative reports on the BKU stir in Meerut are available now. For example, see P.K. Roy, 'Farmer Power', *Frontline (5)* 4 (February 20-March 4,1988), pp. 4-14

4. See, D.N., Dhanagare, *Peasant Movement in India, 1920-1950.* Delhi: Oxford University Press, 1983. Chapt. IV.
5. Details of demands are available in: *Amar Ujala* (Hindi daily-Meerut), January 27, 1988, p.10; also see Nirmal Mitra and Kuldeep Kumar, 'Peasant Power', *Sunday* (15)4, (February 23-March 3. 1988), pp. 35-41.
6. 'Honour in retreat' (Special feature), *India Today* (13)5, March 1-15, 1988, pp. 84-86; *also Amar Ujala,* Janaury 27, 1988, p. 10.
7. N.S. Saksena, 'Politics of law and order',*Times of India (Bombay), April 13, 1988, p.8.*
8. *India Today, op.cit..p.*86.
9. For details see Roy, *op.cti.*, pp.8-9 and 'Peasant Power', *Sunday, op. cit.*, pp.38-39.
10. See *Times of India* (Bombay), February 11, 1988, p.1.
11. The term 'resentiment', as used by R.K. Merton, implies 'a feeling of hostility, but coupled with a sense of powerlessness and therefore a continual reexperiencing of impotent hostility', See his *Social Thoery and Social Structure (1968 enlarged ed.).* Indian ed., New Delhi: Amerind 1975, pp. 209-10.
12. D.N. Dhanagare, *Agrarian Movements and Gandhian Politics.* Agra: Institute of Social Sciences, 1975, Chapt.II.
13. Girilal Jain, 'Peasant agitation in Meerut', *Times* of India (Bombay), February 10, 1988, p. 8.
14. See Sharad Joshi,*Bharat Speaks Out.* Bombay: BUILD Documentation Centre (Occasional Papers No.3), N.D., pp. 8-9.
15. Roy, *op.cit.*, pp. 9-10
16. These details have been taken from the daily reports on the Meerut Siege and rally that appeared in *Amar Ujala.* (Hindi daily, Meerut) from January 28 to February 20, 1988.
17. *Amar Ujala,* January 28, 1988, p. 10.
18. I too have argued this position in my earlier study (1983: Chapters V and IX).
19. Jain, *op. cit.*, p. 8.
20. See, A.R. Desai, *Changing Profile of Rural Society in India.* Bombay: C.G. Shah Memorial Trust, 1985.
21. G.S. Bhalla and G.K. Chadha, *Green Revolution and the Small Peasant.* New Delhi: Concept, 1983, pp. 47-49.
22. See Satya Dev, 'The National Seed Project in India', *The Journal of Administration Overseas,* (19)4, (October). pp. 262-69.
23. D.N Dhangare, 'Green and Social inequalities in rural India', *Economic and Political Weekly* (annual number-1987) (22) 19-21, pp. AN 137-44.
24. Pradip Bose, 'Farmer agitations', *Seminar* 267 (Peasants and Prices), November 1981, pp. 58-62.

25. In a pre-budget survey many leading Indian economists therefore favoured introduction of agricultural income tax. See *Times of India* (Bombay), February 11, 1988, p. 17.
26. See 'Farmers' movements in India' by Sharad Joshi, in his *op. cit.* (n.d.), pp. 72-81
27. For such critics, see M.V. Nadkarni, Farmers' *Movements in India.* Delhi. Allied, 1987; particularly see the foreword to this book by C.H. Hanumantha Rao.
28. Dev Dutt, 'Sowing for Power', *The Week* (6)11, March 6-12, 1988, pp. 17-19.
29. For details see M.C. Pradhan, *The Political System of the Jats of Northern India.* Bombay: Oxford University Press, 1966, pp. 57-59. Also see, Richard G. Fox, *Kin, Clan, Raja and Rule*. Bombay: Oxford Universitsy Press, 1971, pp. 17-26.
30. *Times of India* (Bombay), February 19, 1988,p. 9.
31. Roy. *op. cit., p.*7.
32. See A. Gramsci, *Selections From Prison Note-Books.* London: Lawrence and Wishart, 1971. For an excellent summary of Gramsci's position see also C. Mouffe (ed.), *Gramsci and Marxist Theory*. London: Routledge and Kegan Paul, 1979 , pp. 188-95.
33. E. Laclau, *Politics and Ideology in Marxist Theory,* London: Verso, 1977, pp. 12-13.
34. See the press note issued by the Inter-State Coordination committee of farmers' organisations at Jalgaon on 18 April, 1988.

CHAPTER 7

Transformation of Class Structure in Contemporary Rural India

—Pradip Kumar Bose

1. Problems of Transition

A correct understanding of the transformation of class structure in contemporary India is dependent on the resolution of two theoretical problems: the capital labour relation and the conceptualisation of classes. For the class structure of any society, a transition from one formation to another signifies the collapse of old classes and the birth of new ones; in other words, this period simultaneously involves the process of class decomposition, class transformation and class formation. In recent years, the literature on peasants in complex societies has dealt extensively with the nature of the articulation of capitalist with non-capitalist modes of production. Most authors[1] seem to agree that capitalist expansion and its penetration in the rural areas of the third world has not been universally successful, nor even smooth and irreversible but rather a convergence of contradictory forces. Complex forms of articulation involving both persistence and destruction reflect a continuous dialectic between capitalism and the previous social formation: class formation, class disintegration and class conflict are important elements in this proces. They will be shaped both by the changes brought about by capitalism and by the specific dynamics of the pre-existing social formations.

The classical conception of the agrarian class-structure implies increasing polarisation where the petty commodity producer will tend to disappear, a capitalist relation of production will develop involving an agrarian bourgeoise and a rural proletariat. This notion posits a class of capitalist farmers who will run their big estates with machinery and capital intensive methods of production and employ landless labourers. The polarization of the rural class structure will arise via differentiation of the peasantry. This argument on the characterisation of petty commodity production as a 'transitional' stage of development and petty commodity producers as a 'transitional' class followed from the analysis of the tendency towards class differentiation within this stratum. Since petty commodity production is defined in terms of the untiy of labour and capital in contrast to capitalist production which is predicated on the separation of labour and capital, eventual class polarisation is assumed in capitalist agriculture. However contemporary India presents a much more complex picture and warrants a more ingenious analysis of the transformation of class-structure. The view that petty commodity production was structurally unstable due to its inherent tendency towards class differention is shared by many, however there are others who would argue that family-labour farms have persisted in the countryside and there are limitations to the generalisation of capitalist relations of production in agriculture. Without entering into this debate we can point out that like in other third world countries Indian evidence also suggests the partial, and incomplete nature of 'agrarian transition', that is in terms of the real subsumption of labour by capital, and the formation of a rural capitalist class and a rural proletariat of wage labourers completely separated from the means of production.

However there are other models like the Frank-Wallersteins[2] conceptualisation of capitalism. This model rejects the 'classical model' of agrarian transition wherein the process of internal class differentiation of pre-capitalist agriculture brings into being rural wage workers and capitalist farmers. The decisive criterion in this case is the exchange relations that pertain in the world economy. Their main concern is with relations of surplus appropriation *between* economic systems. Here wage labour, sharecropping or tenancy become alternative modes best suited for a particular type of production as capitalism is defined only on the basis of exchange relations. But the problem with this type of analysis is that it neglects the effects of the development of commodity relations at the level of production and fails to demonstrate how an insertion in to the capitalist world economy transforms the societies and determines the emergence of new class structures. Others bring out the important distinction between the formal and real subsumption of labour under capital, not developed in

Frank-Wallerstein 'trade centered' analysis of production relations, and point out that capital can exert control over the production process without fully expropriating the direct producers. Capitalist exchange relations can be mediated through non-capitalist forms of production, such as family labour or peasant agriculture. In short, various theoretical positions challenge the notion of the 'classical model' as universal and indicate that this model of capitalist differentiation, with the expropriation of direct producers and their real subsumption by capital as free wage labour, describes a particular case or variant of the process and not 'its sole or necessary form of development.' General or universal formulations of agrarian transition and rural class differentiation are thus open to question. For instance Bernstein[3] reminds us that Lenin did not restrict his attention solely to the 'classical model' as outlined in this paper. Lenin also considered conditions in which the movement of capital incorporate the peasantry by a process of 'vertical concentration' with forms of capital attempting to regulate production without undertaking its direct organization. This he characterized as the subsumption of simple commodity producers by capital in peripheral social formations. Here, however, the question remains: how is one to characterize small commodity producers when their real subsumption to capital is incomplete.

The recent debate on the mode of production in Indian agriculture also attempted to explore the 'point of domination' of capitalist social relation in agrarian structures where the development of commodity relations occurred under colonialism. However this debate still remains open since "none of the authors give the criteria for deciding when commodity production has ceased to be a peripheral activity within a mode of production and becomes instead the general form of production."[4] The generalization of commodity production if taken as the necessary and sufficient condition for the development of capitalist relations will mean that labour power and the means of production be separated and circulate as commodities. But the development towards generalised commodity production can be seen as a historical process towards a continuum. This presents major difficulties in characterizing agrarian transition because the point at which conditions of capitalist production come into existence is not easy to locate. One suggested way out of this impasse is to determine the 'point of domination' by analysing the process of social differentiation and the development of the home market.

2. Problems of Class Analysis

The process of differentiation has two aspects: historical and sociological. Sociologically coherent analysis of agrarian class formation in India is still uncommon. A clear analytical distinction in the sociological sense must derive indicators of inequality from a problematic in which 'social class' is constituted in terms of differentiation which poses class in terms of the social relations of production. However in India the use of a variety of criteria to define agrarian classes frustrate any comparative study of regional variation and of change through time. Though it is true that every local class structure is the product of its unique history yet the questions of ownership, of control over land and its product, and the questions of domination and power over people and their labour power are answerable only with reference to culturally constituted systems of meanings and values. Difficulties however are exacerbated by a failure to agree on what kinds of criteria are most important in the definition of agrarian classes.

One can delineate at least three distinct approaches to the definition of agrarian classes. The first approach focuses on categories indigenous to the society being studied. While the appeal to the indigenous categories derives its strength from the assumption that they are indeed "the categories in terms of which he (the villager) thinks and acts",[5] the problem arises because of the ideological nature of the people's images of their society which often distort the underlying structure of thier relations. The other two approaches can be distinguished as the *distributional* and the *structural* approaches towards the definition of classes. In the distributional approach people are assigned to diferent classes depending on the association between people and things and on the basis of quantitative differences in the distribution of things. Since classification remains arbitrary and *ad hoc* in this approach it does not contain within itself any explicit directives for the historical analysis of class dynamics.

Structural studies on the other hand focus on relations between different groups of people i.e., on social relations, particularly as these relations are themselves related to differential control of the means of production. Along with landed property, labour contribution is the other basic feature that structuralist use to differentiate agrarian classes. Their theoretical orientation also assumes that major classes are opposed to one another in a relationship of conflict. In empirical terms class distinctions are made in terms of hiring-in and hiring-out labour relative to self-employment along with the criteria of possession of means of production and economic viability.[6] On the basis of such criteria generally five classes, viz., landlord, rich peasant, middle peasant, poor peasant and agricultural labourer are proposed. However in some cases the structural distinctions are used not to analyse relations within and between classes, but as descriptive labels for strata that are in fact separated by distributional criteria, specifically by the amount of land held[7] or by occupational classification. Some on the other hand even though use the five class scheme they define them in terms of the combination of one or more occupational statuses. This analytic tactic of substitution subordinates the theoretical holism of the structural approach to the conveniences of empirical description, and confines the analysis within an essentially stratigraphic and atomistic framework. In any case to assess the nature of transformation at an all-India level we have to refer to all the studies which analyse the agrarian structure in terms of classes. It is obvious that no two definitions of classes are the same and this makes comparative analyses difficult but they can still signify at a crude level the broad distinctions of classes and their transformation, which can be useful , at least, as a heuristic device.

3. Transformation of Class Structure

While writing in the 1950s Daniel Thorner noted: "Some parts of India, as for example Andhra, Tamil Nadu and Bihar, have to this day large absentee landlords, whose holdings are let out to tenants. In Bengal there are known to be several layers of tenants and subtenants between the zamindars and the men who actually till the soil. The former princely states still contain a great variety of *jagirdars*, *inamdars*, and other holders of large estates under especially privileged tenures."[8] He described India as having a 'unique agrarian structure' which represented a blending of remanants from the pre-British economic order together with the modern western concepts of private property. He divided rural India into three main classes: the maliks or proprietors, the kisans or working peasants and the mazdur or agricultural labourer. The key to this division was the amount of actual labour contributed to the production process and the share in the product. He however averred that the primary aim of all classes was not to increase their income by adopting more efficient methods, but to rise in social prestige by abstaining in so far as possible from physical labour. This complex of legal, economic and social relations he characterised as the 'built-in depressor' uniquely typical of Indian countryside. In the 1960s he revised his earlier characterization of the rural scene and noted 'the distinct emergence of a nation-wide class of capitalist producers.'[9] In between Zamindary Abolition Acts were passed in various states in the 1950s. Though these acts did not give land to the landless or land poor, nor they were intended to, they at least deprived the big landlords to a large degree of their village power, and turned them to farming through greater use of hired labour. This laid a basis for the richer peasants to come to power in the villages and develop as capitalist farmers. Not only was a "new" economic class created but there was also a fresh impetus for mobility among the intermediate castes as well.

The spread of co-operative credit societies, land development banks, sugar co-operatives, government's assurance of substantial price support for farm products, subsidized inputs like water, power, fertilizer, diesel, tractors, etc. and institutional credit helped the consolidation of the rich farming class. That the rich farmers were able to claim an increasing share of government reasources for itself especially after 1965 is shown by a number of studies.[10] Though empirical identification of the class of rich farmers is arbitrary, estimates show that large-size farm households cultivating holdings above 4 hectares constitute about 19 per cent of agricultural population and account for 60 per cent of cultivated area and 53 per cent of crop output.[11] Since the statistics on the development of forces of production which shaped the rise of this class is well documented, we would rather concentrate on the sociological characteristics of the classes.

The class of rich farmers includes the upwardly mobile peasant farmers with a long history of direct cultivation. They are now expanding through buying and leasing-in land from absentee or small landowners. The erstwhile non-cultivating landlords have converted themselves into active farmers with the help of new technology and active government support in terms of low taxation, high support prices, liberal provision of credits and subsidized inputs. They have now found cultivation a more profitable proposition than rack renting. Byres[12] suggests it was the medium to smaller landlords who as a result of tenancy abolition were encouraged to become direct cultivators. This involved an ejection of tenants and their replacement by wage labour. He however mentions that these tendencies within the landlord class were nowhere on a scale sufficient to suggest the possibility of widespread 'capitalism from above.' The rich peasants on the other hand were stabilised as independent proprietors in the wake of land reforms and were on their way to becoming the new dominant class in the emerging agrarian structure. There was an increase in more purely commercial as opposed to 'feudal' tenancy, and in the 1960s there was a rise in the amount of land rented in by rich peasants, who as a result gained control of a larger proportion of the tenanted area.[13]

These tendencies were more marked in *ryotwari* and *mahalwari* areas. In these regions at least the rich peasants were on their way to becoming the dominant class of the countryside. And since these were the locations of the largest concentration of marketed surpluses the rich peasants had a growing influence in the polity. They showed themselves to be eminently capable of exercising political power, not only in the village, but also at the level of district, state and centre. Many of the rich peasants also branched out into trading, transport, and other businesses and services. The establishment of tiny transport companies, flour mills, oil mills, brick kilns, cold-strorages were all part of this process. With the formation of sugar cooperatives they transformed some of their wealth into capital to generete one of India's biggest industries. A typical capitalist farmer today has a competent younger generation and he systematically seeks to diversify economic activities by placing some in service, some in business, leaving one or two to manage the land. Some are even employed to take care of political pressures as well. Diversification of interests represents the investments of accumulated agricultural surplus outside agriculture; it is also a protection against the risks of pure cultivation.

While agricultural profits are invested in small business, often business profits are re-invested in agriculture and land. Inspite of such tendencies, the farmer-capitalists have remained confined to small business and trade and so far have not entered the ranks of industrial capitalists. A recent study of capitalist farmers of Andhra Pradesh points out certain tendencies which are to a large extent true of other parts of India. The study notes that:

> "the new technology has led to a sharp increase in the number of rural business-cum-agricultural households as well as to a diversification in the type of investments made by them. With the spread of green revolution technology, opportunities were created for rich farmers to become dealers of fertilisers, pesticides, and agricultural machinery, a type of trade that is qualitatively different from the traditional trade in agricultural produce. Some of these who were able to get distibutorships and dealerships from the manufacturing companies (mostly located in towns) prospered

> and expanded into other types of urban business. Contracting is another activity in which a cultivator can engage part time; if he is successful he may grow into a large-scale full-time contractor based in a town. New types of agro-industry and other rural-based small industries, cinema halls, and speculation in urban real estate are other 'modern' avenues of investment for the rural rich. While wealthy farmers who diversify into rural-based business may continue to be primarily cultivators, there are many others who are drawn into urban enterprises and who eventually give up agriculture."[14]

The process indicates a rural-urban connexion, rural-urban kin ties and the interpenetration of business and agriculture and rural urban property interests within this class. Rural-ruban migration is not only a function of economic diversification but also of the high value that is placed on education. The switch to non-agricultural occupation and urban migration by educated children is the outcome of the high premium placed on modern education.

The Andhra study also points out that "practically every medium and large landowning family in these villages (and some with small holdings), have highly educated and/or urban based members. As a result, there is a complex well of ties between rural and urban society, particularly within the elite, which has produced (or reinforced) an urban-oriented culture among the rural rich. This culture in turn reproduces the pattern of out-migration because town life and urban occupations are more highly valued by the rural elite than are rural life and cultivation. Wealthy families seem to have one foot alredy out the door, and they were awaiting an opportunity to make the move to town, an opportunity that will come to their sons and daughters if not to themselves.[15] In south Gujarat Breman[16] also describes the process of rural industrialisation nourished by a dynamic having its origins in the recent modernization of agriculture. Kathlenn Gough[17] in her study of Tanjore villages characterizes as medium bourgeoise thosewith landed estates producing for the market, owners of smaller mills, local transport, operators, urban real estate dealers, local trading and retail merchants. Her study shows that from the 1950s and 1980s, this class became more closely tied to imperial capital through loans and subsidies or through serving as agents for foreign, or mixed Indian and foreign, corporations and profited from its links to foreign capital.

A sizeable section of the rich farmers belong to the intermediate castes who have a long history of direct cultivation. Their attempt to establish hegemony coincided with the rise of discontent among the labouring classes. On the one hand by demanding higher crop prices they have unleashed their offensive to bring other classes into their fold, and on the other hand various incidents of atrocities and repression against the labouring classes also point towards their offensive against the rural poor. Their attitude can be characterised as anti-labour and their mentality as social-Darwinist on account of their brutal indifference towards those classed as being socially lower.

The middle peasants are distinguished by the fact that they are relatively little involved in the production for the market. As Alavi has pointed out, both Lenin and Mao described two distinct structures of agrarian social relations both of which were characterized by a master-subordinate relationship; and a 'sector of independent peasants':

Landlords - sharecroppers (poor peasants)
Independent smallholders - (middle peasants)
Capitalist farmers - agricultural proletariat

Alavi's argument is that "middle peasants...do not stand between the rich peasants and the poor peasants; they belong to a different sector of the rural economy."[19] If 'a different sector of rural economy' means a different mode of production, the problem is that of relationship of this mode with the social formation. On the other hand other analyses suggest that the situation of the middle peasantry is essentially precarious. So that they eventually join the ranks of 'the exploiters' or 'the exploited.' In other words they are quite intrinsic to the dynamics of differentiation. As Harriss in his study of northern Tamil Nadu noted, "Investigation of the process of production in Randam has ...shown that there is a group of independent producers which is highly 'mobile' in the sense that some of its members are significant 'exploiters' who may be on their way to becoming 'rural capitalists', whilst others are rather 'exploited.' So it might appear that in Randam the 'extreme groups' are on their way to being developed at the expense of 'the middle."[20] He however cautions that there can be questions as to whether the mobility which is observed results in polarization, or whether there is not simply a great deal of movement around a rather stable median position.

There are some who claim that this class of independent producers is extremely small or non-existent in India.[21] However Bardhan's estimate for West Bengal is that they make about 30 per cent of all agricultural households. On the basis of data reported by the Farm Management Survey he concludes that this class is relatively small in South India but quite substantial in North and North-West India. According to Bardhan in West Bengal the region where agricultural productivity is low the importance of this class is highest which suggest an inverse relation between agricultural progress and proportional importance of this class. He however gives two contrary examples which are significant in the context of rural-urban nexus. He writes: "But the cases of two other districts, Howrah and particularly 24 Parganas, point to another significant factor. These two are among the agriculturally most stagnant districts in West Bengal, and yet the proportional importance of poor peasants and landless labourers is among the highest in the state, and that of family farmers relatively low. This may have to do with the proximity of these two districts to the urban agglomeration of Calcutta, which may have accelerated commercialization of labour transactions in agriculture even without any substantial development of the productive forces on the farm."[22]

The process of rural proletarianization is more problematic. Byres after discussing a number of studies draws up the balance sheet as follows: "I would interpret the foregoing as, indeed, signifying the operation of a process of proletarianization of the peasantry, or depeasantization: one that is complex, but as yet partial in its impact. The 'new technology' has produced conditions in which, by a variety of means, the poor peasantry has lost an increasing share of the operated area to rich peasants. Not only that, but the poor peasantry is, in different ways, being transformed more and more into a rural proletariat."[23] The incomplete proletarianization that Byres describes boils down to the fact that increasingly more small owners surrender the working of their properties to larger farmers without giving up their own rights in them. Other studies qualifies the relationship by indicating that in high-rainfall, naturally fertile, areas where population density is high, the proportion of landless or near landless is large and wage labour is cheaper to hire. The extent of proletarianization is relatively high, even though these areas are not necessarily technologically progressive. Bardhan writes: "These are historically areas of relatively secure wet agriculture where the mounting population is absorbed with an astonishing elasticity (a process described by Geertz as one of 'agricultural involution') with continuous subdivision and multiplication of rights on land leading to elaborate hierarchies with the actual manual work of cultivation done only by those who are at the bottom of the heap."[24] The situation is not the same in sparsely populated regions remotely connected with centres of commercialization. Here the extent of use of wage labour is rather low. In other words the extent of proletarianization is dependent, among other things, upon ecological, demographic, and institutional factors. The general indications, however, points to an increase in the use of hired labour over time along with economic growth. To the extent the increase in the number of agricultural labourers are from the eviction of erstwhile tenants, it might indicate the change in the composition of rural workers rather than proletarianization. On the other hand joining the ranks of rural workers from the class of middle and poor peasants would definitely indicate the extent of proletrarianization. The statistics on small farms show that households with ownership holdings of less of than one hectare have considerably improved their number - between 1970-71 and 1976-77 the percentage of holdings below one hectares increased from 50.9 to 54.7.[25] This has led some to suggest that as the logic of household economy is determined by the needs of simple reproduction, its economic 'behaviour' is different from that of a capitalist economy which operates on the logic of accumulation regulated by the mechanism of price of production.[26] For instance falling prices deteriorates the terms of exchange for commodities produced relative to comodities needed for reproduction which compel such households either to reduce consumption or intensify commodity production or both simultaneously. This has been termed as simple reproduction 'squeeze.' Verogopoulos has argued that "family farming is the most successful form of production for putting the maximum volume of surplus labour at the disposal of urban capitalism. It also constitutes the most efficient way of restraining the prices of agricultural products."[27] He has argued that the family labour farms persist because they do not have to finance profits and rents. Others have emphasized the efficiency of small producers, while still others have suggested explanations in terms of the divergence between labour time and the production time inherent in natural qualities of the object being produced. Excess of production time over labour time results in the inefficient use of constant capital, lower rate of profit, labour recruitment problems and complications in the smooth realization of value in the sphere of circulation.[28] That the small producers continue to reproduce themselves is without question. New technology, because of the larger demands for agricultural inputs, has increased their dependence on bureaucracy and traders.

The class of rural workers is further internally stratified, with those with land at the top and those who are totally landless at the bottom. Political factors also influence the determinants of class positions. As Bardhan points out the class position of the tenant for instance, depends on tenurial security. Political process plays' an important part in the imposition of this security such that two regions with two different kinds of politifal attitudes would have two different kinds of class structure. He writes: 'A landless tenant in Kerala could have belonged to the class of 'family farmers', but were he located in Bihar, would be indistinguishable from a landless wage labour."[29] Though India has a very large agricultural labourer population, they operate under a large number of restrictions and to that extent are not 'free.' As Rudra[30] has shown, the 'market' for the sellers of labour is confined to their village and neighbourhood. Marx pointed out that the buyer of labour power does not get its value immediately after the conclusion of the contract, but he has to incur some cost in harnessing it in the process of production. Therefore 'dependability' of the worker becomes an important consideration and as Rudra has shown in many instances labour from the immediate neighbourhood is preferred even when wages are somewhat lower outside. Loyalty of the worker is ensured through regular credit and sometimes with emergency help and thus the employer is able to maintain and consolidate his social control over the labour process. So far as the rural workers are in possession of their labour power they constitute the other axis of this unequal power-nexus. This also implies that the social boundaries of a village community may significantly circumscribe the process of transfer of surplus value and thus class formation gets territorially segmented.

In other parts, however, the territorial segmentation is often broken by the capitalist farmers by importing labour from more backward areas to keep wages down. It is generally argued that the determinants of migration are the factors like increased labour intensity of the new cropping pattern, absorption of the landless labour force into expanding non-agricultural employment and unsatisfactory performance of local labourers, etc. Breman, on the other hand, shows that in the developed regions of Gujarat, labour from elsewhere is rendered mobile not for these reasons but in order to create a surplus labour force.[31] The supply of migrant labourers results in cost cutting because of its depressive effect on local wages, and thus the bargaining position of the local landless is weakened, which also weakens his relative power. The employer can also exercise far greater control over the migrants who work in a strange environment and are not familiar with local usages. By breaking territorial segmentation the capitalist farmers have achieved two things: firstly, they are able to keep wages low and, secondly, the strong opposition of interests between the two segments of workers becomes a weapon in the hands of capitalist farmers to counter the growing consciousness of the landlesss workers thus preventing this section from breaking out of their dependence.

4. Ideology and Class

The profit in capitalist agriculture can be derived from three sources: a) greater productivity of land: b) a protected market and c) a depressed wage-level which can originate from surplus wage labour or from a sizeable poor peasantry. Since India can be characterized in terms of the last alternative, the development along classical lines is to that extent complicated. Further complications are introduced by the fact that the agrarian ownership structure can be controlled and manipulated politically. The possibility of reproducing these conditions for capitalist development depends, then, on the political representation of the agrarian bourgeoisie, and its alliances with other classes.[32]

When capitalism expands and penetrates into rural areas, the dominant classes will attempt to establish the political, legal, and ideological forms necessary for its functioning and stability. In this process they will encounter ideological practices which originated in social relations now subordinate to capitalism. To explain this situation some have introduced the concept of 'ideological articulation' which allows for a dynamic and historical analysis because it does not assume that the diappearance of non-capitalist ideological practices is a pre-condition for modernisation. In India capitalism has not yet successfully incorporated nor effectively eliminated all pre-capitalist ideological practices. Furthermore, it can be argued that all these ideological practices do not necessarily have to be eliminated in order for capitalism to be successful. Ideology of caste still remains a dominant constituent in the system of meanings through which rural people interpret the world, and this seems to give coherence to the totality of relationships. In this sense ideology cannot be excluded from the understanding of the process of class formation. The explanation of forms of symbolic domination, 'how people participate in their own repression', is necessary if one is to comprehend the constitution of class formation in India. In other words both economic and ideological aspects of the articulation of the peasantry and capitalism is called for because the problems of 'tradition' and consciousness is very much linked with the problem of the analysis and transfonnation of class structure. As Raymond Williams once suggested: "what we have to see is not just 'a tradition' but a *selective traditon*: an intentionally selective version of a shaping past and pre-shaped present, which is then powerfully operative in the process of social and cultural definition and identification."

REFERENCES

1. See Barbara Bradley, "The Destruction of Natural Economy." *Economy and Society*, 4(2), 1975; Ernesto Laclau, "Feudalism and Capitalism in Latin America", *New Left Review*, 67, 1971; C. Meillassoux, 'From Reproduction to Production : A Marxist Approach to Economic Anthropology', *Economy and Society*, 1(1), 1972; William Roseberry, "Rent, Differentiation, and the Development of Capitalism among Peasants", *American Anthropologist*, 78(1), 1976.
2. A.G. Frank, *Capitalism and Underdeverlopment in Latin America*, (New York: Monthly Review press, 1967); I. Wallerstein, *The Modern World System* (New York:Academic Press, 1974).
3. H. Bernstein, "Notes on Capital and Peasantry", *Review of African Political Economy*, No. 10, 1977.
4. D. McEachern, "The Mode of Production in India", *Journal of Contemporary Asia*, Vol.6, 1976, p. 446.
5. Andre Beteille, *Studies in Agrarian Social Structure*, (Delhi, Oxford University Press, 1974), p. 49.
6. See Utsa Patnaik, "Class Differentiation within the Peasantry: An Approach to the Analysis of Indian Agriculture", *Economic and Political Weekly*, 11(39), 1976; P.K. Bardhan, 'Agrarian Class Formation in India', *Journal of Peasant Studies*, October 1982; P.K. Bose *Classes in a Rural Society* (New Delhi, Ajanta, 1984); Joan Mencher, "Problems in Analysing Rural Class Structutre", *Economic and Political Weekly*, 9(35), 1974.
7. See, for instance, Joan Mencher, *Agriculture and Social Formation in Tamil Nadu* (New Delhi: Allied, 1978).
8. Daniel Thorner, *The Agrarian Prospect in India* (New Delhi, Allied, 1976) pp. 8-9.
9. *ibid.*, p. 2
10. See Ashok Mody, "Resource Flows between Agriculture and Non-Agriculture in India, 1950-1970", *Economic and Political Weekly, 16 (10-12), 1981;* Ashok Mitra, *Terms of Trade and Class Relations* (Calcutta, Rupa, 1979).

11. P.K. Bardhan, *The Political Economy of Development in India* (Delhi, Oxford University Press, 1984), p. 46.
12. T.J. Byres, "The New Technology, Class Formation and Class Action in the Indian Countryside", *The Journal of Peasant Studies*, 8(4), 1981.
13. Kalpana Bardhan, "Rural Employment, Wages and Labour Market in India: A Survey of Research - 1", *Economic and Political Weekly*, 12(26), 1977, p. A 83.
14. Carol Boyack Upadhya, "The Farmer-capitalist of Coastal Andhra Pradesh", *Economic and Political Weekly*, 23(27), 1988, p. 1381.
15. *ibid.*, p. 1381.
16. Jan Breman, *Of Peasants, Migrants and Paupers*, (Delhi, Oxford University Press, 1985), pp. 42ff.
17. Kathleen Gough, "Socio-Economic Change in Southeast India, 1950s to 1980s", *Journal of Contemporary Asia*, 17(3), 1987.
18. H. Alavi, "Peasants and Revolution", *Socialist Register*, 1965.
19. *ibid.*, p. 244.
20. John Harriss, *Capitalism and Peasant Farming* (Bombay: Oxford University Press, 1982), p. 200.
21. K. Gough, "Peasant Resistance and Revolt in South India", in A.R. Desai (ed.) *Peasant Struggles in India* (Delhi: Oxford University Press, 1979); Ashok Rudra, ',Class Relations in Indian Agriculture", *Economic and Political Weekly*, 13(22-24), 1978.
22. P.K. Bardhan, "Agrarian Class Formation...", p. 83, op. cit.
23. T.J. Byres, "the New Technology..", p. 430, op. cit.
24. P.K. Bardhan, "Agrarian Class Formation..." p. 85, op. cit.
25. *Data on Agricultural Land Holdings: 1976-77* (Bombay: CMIE, 1981)
26. H. Bernstein, "Notes on Capital and Peasantry."
27. K. Vergopoulos, "Capitalism and Peasant Productivity" *The Journal of Peasant Studies*, 5(4), 1978, p. 446.
28. S. Mann and J.M. Dickinson, "Obstacles to the Development of a Capitalist Agriculture", *The Journal of Peasant Studies*, 5(4), 1978.
29. P.K. Bardhan, "Agrarian Class Formation....", p. 79, op. cit.
30. Ashok Rudra, "the self-contained Village Society", *Frontier*, 13(19-21), 1981.
31. Jan Breman, *Of Peasants, Migrants and Paupers, op. cit.*
32. See Ashok Mitra, *Terms of Trade and Class Relations, op. cit.*

CHAPTER 8

Education, Migration and Social Change in India: A Preliminary Analysis

—*Mahendra K Premi*

The literature on urbanisation and migration has generally focussed attention on the analysis of rural-to-urban migration. Economists have suggested various models to explain the volume and direction of labour mobility. They have generally assumed that developing countries have experienced mostly rural-to-urban and possibly some urban-to-urban migration. Micro-level studies have also been conducted to increase understanding of the behavioral patterns of the migrants and the dominant factors responsible for the decision to migrate. Most of these studies have concentrated on the primate cities of the developing countries and cities of the more developed world. (For an inter disciplinary review of macro and micro approaches to migration decision making, see De Jong and Gardner 1981).

It is not the primate city alone of a country that attracts migrants from rural and other urban areas. Other cities, which may be termed as intermediate cities, also attract large numbers of migrants. Together with the primate and other metropolitan cities, they form a system in which most of the country's economic cultural, political, and administrative activities take place. A useful way to study urbanisation and migration, particularly migration, therefore, is to consider the set of cities as a system that is different from rural or non-city urban areas in its functions. Moreover, these cities in India accounted for about two-thirds of the total urbanward migration during the seventies. Consequently, a study of internal migration, particularly focusing on the educational attainment of the migrants becomes quite important and meaningful.

Drawing on migration data from the 1971 population census for the 147 class I cities (with population 100,000 and above) this paper examines the differentials with respect to educational attainments of the migrants and their occupational placement in comparison to the nonmigrants[1]. It then discusses the role of education of the migrant in the country–town nexus and in bringing social change among the people in the country.

Earlier Studies

The Research Programmes Committee of India's Planning Commission sponsored city surveys during the 1950s and 1960s that described the growth of the selected cities during the first half of this century, the pattern of inmigration to them, and the characteristics of the inmigrants vis-a-vis those of nonmigrants (for example, Sovani et al. 1956; Malkani 1957; Iyengar 1957; Mishra 1959; Sen 1960; Dhekney 1960; D'Souza 1969). Comparing nine of those surveys covering the cities of Baroda, Gorakhpur, Hubli, Hyderabad-Secunderabad, Jamshedpur, Kanpur, Lucknow, Poona and Surat, Bulsara (1964) concluded that industrial cities attracted a larger proportion of inmigrants than did nonindustrial cities. Although rural migrants moved largely within the same district, or to a nearby metropolitan city, urban migrants travelled further in search of employment and most of them were literate, some with primary, and some with middle and high school education.

Zachariah's study of the migrants to Greater Bombay, besides indicating their selectivity in age, sex, marital status, and family status, showed that their educational attainment was much higher than that of the populations of the states of origin but lower than that of nonmigrants in Bombay. The over-representation of the migrants in blue-collar and unskilled manual occupations, and of nonmigrants in white-collar occupations, was due mainly to the difference in educational attainment (Zachariah 1968:340-42).

Analysing the 1961 census data on migrants to large cities (those with population of 100,000 or more inhabitants) Mitra (1967) in contrast to Zachariah's findings, found that the ratios of the literates and educated was consistently higher among inmigrants than among the total population of those cities. In their analysis of the pattern of inmigration to 101 class I cities during 1961-71, Mitra et al. (1980) concluded that about 40 to 50 percent of the male migrants were illiterate or semi-literate (having upto 5 years of schooling). With few skills or little education or training, most of them were engaged in low-grade production activities, indigenous means of transport (e.g. rickshaws, handcarts, horse-drawn carriages), or lowgrade services; some worked in petty trade and personal services, only few had found employment in administrative, technical, professional, or kindred services.

Reviewing the research findings on social change and internal migration from Africa, Asia, and Latin America, Simmons et al. found that people who migrate are not the "dregs of society" or the vast pool of illiterate labour, which classical models might predict, but more educated than those they leave behind because of greater employment opportunities for the educated and the greater amount of information available to them (Simmons et al. 1977:55-58).

A growing body of evidence in the Asian and Pacific region indicates that the migrants tend to come from better educated segments of their original populations. The continuing high attraction of primate cities seems to be due to their offering the greatest array of occupations for persons at all levels of skill and particularly for those without "urban" skills (United Nations, ESCAP 1977:5). The concentration of educational institutions, particularly those of higher learning, in big cities means that persons desiring more education must locate themselves where the facilities exist, consequently "more education" becomes a reason for migration (United Nations, ESCAP 1977:5).

In summary, almost all studies reviewed above indicated that migrants were better educated than those whom they left behind, but there was little evidence of their being better educated than people in the places of destination. Desire for more education was found to be a reason for migration. Some studies concluded that migrants were over-represented in blue-collar occupations or the urban informal sector and only a few had managed to find white-collar jobs. Those studies have generally compared recent migrant workers with total workers. But migrants, being young, are largely in their first or second jobs, whereas other workers belong to all ages and many of them might have changed their jobs several times, thus being upwardly more mobile. Moreover, some studies have studied only those migrants who were found living in slums, bustees, or resettlement colonies. Hence, such comparisons are not particularly valid. Cities send their highly qualified and trained workers to other cities, to noncity urban areas, and sometimes to rural areas. Consequently, we are of the view that migrants generally possess higher levels of education and skill than nonmigrants and that they are likely to be engaged in white-collar jobs in greater proportions than the nonmigrants.

Data Base and Its Limitations

As indicated earlier, this paper examines the differentials in educational attainment of the inmigrants to all the class I cities in comparison to the nonmigrants. the basic data were obtained from the following two tables of the 1971 census:

1. Migrants to cities classified by sex, broad age groups, educational level, and, in case of workers, occupational division.
2. Workers and nonworkers according to main activity, classified by place of last residence.

It is noteworthy here that while the census tables provide the educational attainment and occupational distribution of migrants, no such information was available for the total population of each city. To compare educational attainment and occupational placement of the migrant and nonmigrant workers it was necessary to obtain information on educational attainment of all workers and their occupational distribution by level of education at least for some cities. That information was, however, published for each district separately by rural and urban residence. For making the desired comparison we selected those districts where the population of the main city constituted at least 85 percent[2] of the total urban population of the district in which the city was located. We then assumed that the educational and occupational distribution of workers in the urban populations of the selected districts represented the educational and occupational distribution of the workers of the cities situated in them. We could find 24 such cities in the country. There were certain inconsistencies, however, in the published data for four districts and cities. Excluding those four cities, information available for twenty cities was used for the proposed analysis-eight of them with population of one million plus, six with population between one-half million and one million, and the remaining six with 100,000-499,000 inhabitants (Annex 1).

In order to understand the pattern of inmigration to cities and the differentials in the characteristics of the inmigrants more clearly, the cities were classified into different groups according to their size, growth rate, functional specialization, age as a class I city, and regional location. (For more details, see Premi and Tom 1985:15-20).

TABLE 8.1

Literacy Rates of Nonmigrants, Migrants (Classified by Migration Stream), and Migrant Workers by City Characteristics: India, 1971

City characteristics and sex of population group	Cities (N)	Nonmigratns	Total migrants	Migrants with last residence in India: Total	Elsewhere in the district	In other districts of the same state	In other states	Migrant workers
All cities								
Both sexes	147	48.2	61.6	61.3	54.2	66.2	66.1	71.8
Males	147	55.4	74.3	73.9	71.3	76.7	74.4	75.7
Females	147	39.6	48.5	48.4	38.6	55.2	56.4	41.7
City size								
1,000,000+	9	54.8	64.3	62.8	57.4	64.8	65.7	72.3
500,000-999,999	10	48.2	62.5	62.1	46.7	66.4	71.5	73.5
200,000—499,999	54	48.8	62.9	62.6	54.2	67.5	67.7	72.5
100,000—199,999	74	47.0	60.2	60.0	55.0	65.5	64.3	71.0
Growth rate								
High	68	49.0	62.7	62.4	56.6	66.8	64.7	71.8
Medium	51	47.6	61.1	60.7	51.9	66.2	68.1	71.7
Low	26	48.1	60.1	60.0	54.1	65.1	66.4	72.9
Functional specialization								
Manufacturing	68	48.1	60.1	59.8	53.0	64.3	65.1	70.6
Trade and transport	58	48.5	62.3	61.9	56.3	67.4	65.8	72.1
Service	21	48.0	64.3	64.2	52.8	69.7	70.4	75.0

Length of existence as class I city								
Before 1901	25	49.9	62.7	61.9	50.3	64.9	68.6	72.7
1901-41	24	49.2	62.6	62.5	53.6	69.1	69.1	73.3
After 1941	87	48.6	60.9	60.7	56.1	65.7	65.2	71.2
New cities	10	37.7	61.3	61.3	49.0	65.2	60.9	71.1
Regional type								
Himalayan	6	51.3	63.5	63.8	55.5	70.4	69.0	70.4
Upper Ganga plains	24	44.4	58.1	57.7	48.6	60.9	65.1	70.9
Middle and lower Ganga plains	21	43.3	59.1	58.1	47.9	66.6	67.2	71.4
Central plateau	27	46.3	61.0	60.6	49.7	63.8	64.8	71.3
Deccan plateau	35	49.2	61.0	61.0	56.9	66.7	63.4	70.6
Coastal plains	34	53.9	66.2	66.1	63.2	70.2	69.6	74.7

Literacy and Educational Attainment of the Migrants

As described earlier, studies conducted in India show that migrants to the cities generally have lower educational attainment than nonmigrants and are placed in low paid urban occupations. We have hypothesized that migrants to cities (including both from rural as well as other urban areas) generally possess higher level of education than do nonmigrants. When educational attainment is controlled, migrants are found in higher proportions in white collar jobs than are nonmigrants.

Further, we hypothesized that the longer the distance travelled, the better educated the migrants would be; specifically, that the educational levels of the interstate migrants would be higher than those of intradistrict or interdistrict migrants.

A comparison of the literacy rates of the non-migrants and the migrants by city characteristics, migrants being further classified by migration streams (Table 8.1) indicated much higher literacy rates of migrants than those of nonmigrants. This was probably because of variations in the age composition of the two subpopulations.[3] The differences were greater for males than for females.

Literacy rates of intradistrict migrants were consistently lower than of interdistrict or interstate migrants in all city categories classified according to city characteristics. This finding implies that illiterate migrants generally travel short distances because (1) they tend to be poor, have almost no entrepreneurial skills, and do not have the resources to go further ahead; (2) they do not receive much information as the literates do about job-opportunities of far-off places; and (3) as unskilled workers, they do not believe that they would receive higher wages by travelling long distances. Therefore, illiterate migrants prefer to move to the nearest city, which generally is only of local economic importance. No significant literacy rate differences were found among interdistrict and interstate migrants in most categories when the migrants were classified according to city characteristics.

The distribution of male, female, and total migrants by levels of education (Table 8.2) shows that a little more than one-fifth of the total migrants were educated at least to the high school level. The proportion was three-tenths among males and a little more then one-tenth among females.

As for educational levels of migrants in different streams, we expected that longer the distance migrants travelled, the better educated they would be. In the absence of data on actual distances travelled by migrants from last residence to the current one, we assumed that the interestate migration stream represented long distance movement, interdistrict the medium distance, and intradistrict the short distance movement. The educational levels of interestate migrants should, therefore, be higher than those of interdistrict migrants, and their educational levels, in turn, should be higher than those of intradistrict migrants. Our data indicate that the proportions of interdistrict and interestate migrants in higher educational categories were larger than those of intradistrict migrants. The differences became statistically significant with middle or higher levels of education. Further, the differences were sharper in the case of females (Table 8.2).

For the two sexes combined there was hardly any difference between the distribution of interdistrict and interstate migrants (the index of dissimilarity[4] being equal to one). This may indicate that migrants in the two streams travelled similar distances in moving to their current destinations, or that distances beyond a certain range did not make any differene in the educational attainment of the migrants. When a comparison is made by sex, however, the proportions of male migrants with high school and with graduate and above levels of education were much higher among interdistrict migrants than among interstate migrants, the differences being statistically significant. In contrast, among females the proportion of high school completers, diploma holders, and with graduate and post-graduate degrees was significantly higher among the interstate migrants than interdistrict migrants (Table 8.2).

Thus, while the finding for males negates our hypothesis, the finding for females does not. As an explanation for the particular pattern for males, we suspect that in cities located near state borders, there is substantial interstate migration between bordering districts. Although hard data are not available to confirm this theory, we find that of the 24 cities with high proportions of migrants in the interstate stream, six were in border districts and three were union territories.

The analysis of literacy rates and educational attainment of lifetime migrant and nonmigrant workers in the 20 cities for which relevant data are available (Table 8.3) shows that there was no significant difference between the proportions of literates (76.2 percent among male migrant workers and 74.0 percent among male nonmigrant workers) when the comparison is made using the eight million plus cities (all except Calcutta). The difference in the proportion of literates (77.6 percent among migrant and 67.6 percent among non-migrant workers),

TABLE 8.2

Percentage Distributions of Migrants in Different Migration Streams and of Migrant Workers of each Sex by Education: India, 1971

Migration stream and sex	*Cities (N)*	*Education Level*						
		Illiterate	*Literate without formal education*	*Up to primary level*	*Primary to middle level (8th grade)*	*High school and diploma*	*Graduate and above*	*All levels*
Total migrants								
Both sexes	147	38.43	12.59	15.27	13.03	16.09	4.59	100.00
Males	147	25.66	13.17	15.89	15.28	22.95	7.05	100.00
Females	147	51.54	12.06	14.70	10.75	8.95	2.00	100.00
Last residence in India								
Both sexes	147	38.73	12.60	15.13	12.93	15.99	4.62	100.00
Males	147	26.11	13.18	15.72	15.11	22.77	7.12	100.01
Females	147	51.60	12.06	14.59	10.74	9.00	2.02	100.00
Last residence elsewhere in district of enumeration								
Both sexes	144	45.75	12.34	14.63	11.66	12.75	2.87	100.00
Males	144	28.72	13.73	16.20	15.45	20.77	5.12	99.99
Females	144	61.43	11.16	13.24	8.19	5.22	0.77	100.01
Last residence in other districts of the state								
Both sexes	145	33.76	12.78	15.18	13.92	18.38	5.99	100.01
Males	145	23.28	12.75	14.71	14.82	25.25	9.22	100.03
Females	145	44.78	12.90	15.71	13.01	11.06	2.54	100.00

Last residence in other states								
Both sexes	147	33.87	13.03	15.75	13.99	18.06	5.30	100.00
Males	147	25.65	13.42	16.20	15.02	22.59	7.12	100.00
Females	147	43.55	12.62	15.22	12.59	12.79	3.23	100.00
Migrant workers								
Both sexes	147	28.19	10.48	15.52	14.42	22.75	8.64	100.00
Males	147	24.27	11.19	16.89	15.52	23.41	8.72	100.00
Females	147	58.29	4.41	4.90	5.44	17.55	9.42	100.01

however, becomes significant when the comparison is made with all 20 cities. The situation was similar for female workers.

Moreover, with respect to educational attainment, the proportion of male migrant workers with high school and other diplomas and in graduate and above categories was significantly higher than the proportion of nonmigrant workers (Table 8.3), whether we make the comparison using eight metropolises or all 20 cities. Among women, although the proportion of migrant workers in both these educational categories was higher than that of nonmigrant workers, the differences were significant only when all 20 cities were considered together. Our finding implies that migrants, particularly males, move to the cities because they are mainly attracted by better job opportunities there, and not because of poor conditions in rural areas. The finding that migrants are not the "dregs of society" (Simmons et. al. 1977:55) is further confirmed.

Occupational Classification of Migrant and Nonmigrant Workers

Since data on occupational classification of all workers (similar to data on migrant workers) are not available for each city from the 1971 census tables; it was not possible to compare the occupational placement of migrant and nonmigrant workers of all 147 cities. However, a comparison has been made in Table 4 on the basis of data for 20 selected cities. The analysis of the occupational distribution of migrant and nonmigrant workers (other than cultivators and agricultural labourers), both for males and females shows that a significantly higher proportion of migrants than nonmigrants of both sexes was engaged in professional, technical, administrative, executive, and managerial jobs. The proportion of male migrant workers in clerical and related activities was also significantly higher than of nonmigrants. A significantly higher proportion of male migrants worked in service occupations than did nonmigrants, but the opposite was true for females. The proportion of nonmigrant workers of both sexes was, however, significantly higher in production activities.

An analysis of data for the eight metropolises shows that among male workers a significantly higher proportion of migrants than of nonmigrants worked in prestigious white-collar jobs - professional, technical, administrative, executive managerial and related categories (divisions 0-2). Significantly more nonmigrants worked in the sales category. They also worked in greater proportions as production process workers but, the difference between nonmigrants and migrants was not

TABLE 8.3

Percentage distributions of male and female migrant and nonmigrant workers by education: 20 selected cities of India, 1971.

	All 20 cities				*8Metropolises*			
	Males		*Females*		*Males*		*Females*	
Educational level	*Migrant*	*Nonmigrant*	*Migrant*	*Nonmigrant*	*Migrant*	*Nonmigrant*	*Migrant*	*Nonmigrant*
Literate and educated	77.6	67.6	54.1	43.6	76.2	74.0	52.4	52.6
Literate without formal education	11.3	12.7	3.9	5.2	10.3	11.0	3.6	4.6
Up to primary level	15.4	17.7	4.2	5.2	16.7	19.1	5.0	6.8
Primary to middle level	14.9	15.0	6.1	5.6	15.1	17.9	5.8	7.1
High school and diploma	25.6	17.3	25.0	17.6	24.7	20.5	25.6	23.5
Graduate and above	10.4	5.0	15.0	9.9	9.3	5.5	12.5	10.6

Notes: Table excludes cultivators and agricultural laborers, if any. Here, the percentage of migrant workers of a particular sex with a specific level of educational attainment equals the number of migrant workers of that sex having the given level of educational attainment divided by the total number of migrant workers of that sex, multiplied by 100. The percentage of nonmigrant workers of a particular sex with a specific level of educational attainment equals the number of district urban workers of that sex having the particular educational attainment minus the number of migrant workers of that sex and educational attainment divided by the number of district urban workers of that sex minus the number of migrant workers of that sex, multiplied by 100.

significant, Consequently, it may be concluded that migrant workers possess higher levels of education and skills and are more frequently engaged in white-collar jobs than nonmigrants.

To gain a better understanding of the differentials in the occupational placement of the migrant and nonmigrant workers, we compared the occupational distribution of male migrant and nonmigrant workers in the 20 cities by controlling for educational attainment. No significant differences were observed in their proportions in division 0-1 (professional, technical, and related workers) and division 3 (clerical and related workers) for different levels of education. Migrant workers were, however, significantly more numerous in division 2 (executive, administrative, and managerial workers) and division 5 (service workers), but significantly larger proportions of the nonmigrants were in division 4 (sales and other related workers). Since a large majority of sales workers in India are in the unorganised sector, it seems that nonmigrants form a large share of the urban informal sector. A significantly higher proportion of nonmigrant than the migrant male workers were also found in production process work (division 7-9) for different educational levels.

The above analysis contradicts the findings of Zachariah (1968) and Mitra et al. (1980) regarding the occupational placement of migrant and nonmigrant workers in Indian cities. The present data establish that migrants go to cities because of better job opportunities there, and not because they are unwanted at their places of origin.

It is noteworthy here that 38 percent of the total population of the class I cities in India was migrant population, the proportion among males being 37 percent and among females 40 percent. Migrants from rural areas comprised 53 percent of the total migrants and those from urban areas accounted for 41 percent of the migrants, the remaining 6 percent came to the cities from other countries. There were 4 migrant workers for every 3 nonmigrant workers, the ratio was slightly higher among females than among males. The proportion of migrant workers was specially high in the comparatively new cities (3 migrant workers for every nonmigrant worker), cities in the Himalayan region (7 migrant workers for every three nonmigrant workers), and in service cities (3 migrant workers for every two nonmigrant workers). In such cities migrant workers dominated their economy and also determined their functional specialisation to a great extent.

Consequences of Migration and Social Change

The consequences of migration on the communities of origin and destination can be classified under demographic, economic, social, political and other consequences. The social consequences largely relate to the integration and acculturation of migrants at destination; changes in the ethnic or religious composition of the population of receiving areas; impact of remittances on living conditions in the places of origin; and the resultant social changes in both the sending and receiving areas.

From the social point of view, migrants are regarded as a "bridge" between the traditional culture and modernizing societies and forebearers of social change in the communities of origin since, when these people return back either for good after a successful career or for short vacations, they carry with them new ideas in the form of new techniques of production, new style of living, and rationality of behaviour, etc. Further, various types of consumer durables including clothing which these migrants take with them serve to demonstrate their successful career at destinations. In a way, this encourages the young adults to outmigrate from those villages to destinations where these return migrants had worked in the past or where the visitors are currently working.

From the viewpoint of the receiving communities, particularly the primate or metropolitan cities, the studies have generally emphasized the negative consequences, such as unplanned and haphazard growth of cities and some of the worst slums. Rural poverty carried to the cities through rural-urban migration is most visible in slum and squatter settlements, environmental deterioration, sub-standard housing, and low levels of health and nutrition (de Souza 1978:xv). The spontaneous settlements of the urban poor, however, are not merely aggregations of shacks and huts but communities of fellow migrants, many of them being literate and educated. Each of these communities is based on a network of primary affinities of language religion, village, caste or kin, which enables the migrants to become socialised and acculturated in the complex and diversified environment of a metropolitan city (Majumdar 1978). Moreover, the literate and educated migrants act as catalytic agents in changing the social outlook of their brethren, specially in enthusing them with ambitions and entrepreneurship.

While analysing the consequences of migration on the communities of origin, (Connell et al.) indications are that at the individual household or village level, certain groups clearly benefit from

TABLE 8.4

Percentage Distributions of male and famale migrant and nonmigrant workers by occupational division: 20 selected cities of India, 1971

Occupational divisions	*All 20 cities*				*8Metropolises*			
	Males		*Females*		*Males*		*Females*	
	Migrant	*Nonmigrant*	*Migrant*	*Nonmigrant*	*Migrant*	*Nonmigrant*	*Migrant*	*Nonmigrant*
0–1 Professional, technical, and related Workers	8.82	5.87	37.36	25.36	7.17	5.32	28.58	24.75
2 Aministrative, executive, managerial, and related workers	6.66	2.43	0.90	0.48	7.62	2.48	0.96	0.47
3 Clerical and related workers	17.94	13.44	8.66	8.50	15.88	14.49	12.59	13.41
4 Sales workers	13.06	16.54	6.13	8.32	13.44	17.13	6.73	8.98
5 service workers	12.23	8.67	19.75	24.06	10.54	8.32	21.45	22.29
6 Farmers, fishers, hunters, loggers, and related workers	1.11	1.63	0.90	1.19	1.01	1.50	0.91	1.34
7-9 Craftspersons, production process workers, and labourers not elsewhere classified	37.59	49.37	25.33	30.36	42.54	48.92	27.43	27.56
X Workers not classifiable by occupation	2.58	2.05	0.98	1.72	1.78	1.84	1.34	1.21

migration, and remittances act as a potent means of social mobility. If the remittances are substantial and sustained over a period of time, they are used in several villages to develop the productivity or agricultural base of the village. It is, however, noteworthy that usually migration, particularly of educated people, brings major net remittances only to those households who can afford the foregone income and the initial costs involved in sending outmigrants. In contrast, the poorest households in most of the villages having families with no migrants and, hence, no remittances, are the worst sufferers. This may result in greater inequality among the different sections of the village society and in new and more extreme social differentiation in the village (Connell et al. 1976:103).

A negative impact of continuous outmigration of literate and educated persons from the village and small towns is that it leaves those communities devoid of their skills and intelligence, and hampers the growth of those areas over time.

Opening of hitherto isolated areas either because of their strategic importance (as of Ladakh), or for social and economic development (as the tribal areas in the central India belt) has brought very important social change. Taking the case of Ladakh, after the Chinese war in 1962, and war with Pakistan in 1965 and 1971, it became necessary to establish army units in that area on a permanent basis and to build roads for their movement into different areas. This also helped opening of Ladakh (Kargil, Leh, and other places) for the tourists and other persons including businessmen. This movement of the people into the isolated areas has brought very substantial social change among the Ladakhis. They are now entering into modern sector jobs in larger and larger numbers and the parents are sending their children to school for acquiring education and certain skills. The army has played a positive role in boosting the economy of these areas by providing medical aid, and by helping educational institutions as and when it became necessary.

A recent survey in three villages of Kargil and Ladakh districts (during June-July 1988) indicated that the villagers recognise the changes which have come in their villages over the past ten years or so and are now demanding more facilities in terms of road connectivity, establishment of school and medical facilities, and even availability of electricity.

NOTES AND REFERENCES

1. Such data have not been tabulated for all the Class I cities of the 1981 census. Certain information has only recently become available for the 12 metropolitan cities with one million plus population. The analysis of these data will take some time.
2. The cut-off point at 85 percent was purely arbitrary, but it provided a sufficient number of cities for which data on migrants could be compared with data on the district urban population. A smaller percentage would have allowed us to include several more cities in the analysis, but by definition that would have meant inclusion of a larger component of populations of other urban areas of the districts in the category of nonmigrants even though a fair proportion of those populations were of migrants.
3. The proportion of children below the age of 15 was much higher among the non-migrants than among migrants. But one expects almost all children above the age of 7 to 8 in the cities to be literate. This, along with higher sex ratio (males per 100 females) of non-migrants in higher age groups, should lead to higher literacy rates. On this assumption we compared the literacy rates of the nonmigrant and the migrant subpopulations of class I cities.
4. The index of dissimilarity is defined as half the sum of the absolute differences (without regard to signs) of two percentage distributions relating to the same or similar items.

Jal F. Bulsara, (1964) *Problems of Rapid Urbanisation in India.* Bombay: Popular Prakashan.

John Caonnell, Biplab Dasgupta, Roy Laishley, and Michael Lipton (1976). *Migration from Rural Areas: The Evidence from Village Studies.* Delhi, Oxford University Press.

Gordon F. De Jong, and Robert W. Gardner (eds.) (1981). *Migration Decision Making*, New York: Pergamon Press.

B.R. Dhekney, (1960). *Hubli City: A Study in Urban Economic Life.* Dhar war: Karnataka University.

Alfred De Souza, (ed.) (1978). *The Indian City.* New Delhi: Manohar Publications.

Victor S.D'Souza, (1968). *Social Structure of a Planned City: Chandigarh.* New Delhi : Orient Longmans Limited.

S. Keshav Iyengar, (1957). *A Socio-Economic Survey of Hyderabad—Secunderabad City Area.* Hyderabad: Indian Institute of Economics.

Tapan K. Majumdar, (1978). 'The urban poor and social change: a study of squatter settlements in Delhi' in Alfred de Souza (ed.) *The Indian City.* New Delhi: Manohar Publications.

H.C. Malkani, (1957). *A Socio-Economic Survey of Baroda City*. Baroda: Maharaja Sayajirao University of Baroda.

B.R. Mishra, (1959). *Report of the Socio-Economic Survey of Jamshedpur City*. Patna: Department of Applied Economics and Commerce, Patna University.

Asok Mitra, (1967). 'Internal migration and urbanization in India, 1961'. *In International Union for the Scientific Study of Population: Contributed Papers*. Sydney Conference.

Asok Mitra, Mukherji Shekhar and Bose Ranendranath (1980). *Indian Cities: Their Industrial Structure, Inmigration and Capital Investment, 1961-71*. New Delhi:Abhinav Publication.

Premi, K. Mahendra and Judith Ann L. Tom (1985). *City Characteristics, Migration, and Urban Development Policies in India,* Papers of the East-West Population Institute, No.92, Honolulu: East-West Center.

S.N. Sen, (1960). *The City of Calcutta,* Calcutta; Bookland Private Ltd..

Simmons, Alan, Sargio Diaz Brignets, and Aprodicio A. Laquaian (1977). *Social Change and Internal Migration*. Ottawa: International Development Research Centre.

N.V. Sovani, D.P. Apte, ad R.G. Pendse (1956). *Poona: A Resurvey: The Changing Pattern of Employment and Earnings*. Publication No. 34, Poona: Gokhle Institute of Politics and Economics.

United Nations, Economic and Social Commission for Asia and The Pacific (ESCAP) (1977). *Report of the Expert Group Meeting on Migration and Human Settlements*. Asian Population Studies Series, No. 38. Bangkok.

K.C. Zachariah, (1968). *Migrants in Greater Bombay*. Bombay: Asia Publishing House.

ANNEXURE I

Cities for whch selected characteristics of migrants and nonmigrants have been compared.

1. Greater Bombay
2. Delhi
3. Madras
4. Hydrabad
5. Ahmedabad
6. Bangalore
7. Kanpur
8. Poona
9. Nagpur
10. Lucknow
11. Jaipur
12. Agra
13. Indore
14. Allahabad
15. Gwalior
16. Jodhpur
17. Gorakhpur
18. Rampur
19. Agartala
20. Pondichery

CHAPTER 9

Social Composition of Industrial Workers: Rural-Urban Links of Workers at Bokaro Steel Plant

—*Sharit Kumar Bhowmik*

This paper attempts to present and analyse some of the findings of a survey of workers employed in the Bokaro Steel Plant (BSP). This survey was conducted a decade ago but the results have been analysed only recently. The workers who were studied here are those engaged in modern heavy industries. These workers are presumably different from the traditional workers engaged in jute, textiles, plantations etc, who constitute the bulk of industrial workers. The level of education, salaries and facilities of these workers are higher than those of traditional workers. Some managerial "experts" have even labelled them as high wage islands. At the same time, it cannot be denied that these workers form the advanced section of the working class. This raises a question: how different are these workers from traditional workers? There is a need therefore to understand this new worker, his socio-economic background and his rural links. This is the objective of this exercise.

The Bokaro Steel Plant is a public sector undertaking (known as Bokaro Steel Limited) under the Steel Authority of India. The plant is situated in Bokaro Steel City (BSC) in Dhanbad district of Bihar. BSC is an industrial town which was created in the early 1960s when the steel plant was commissioned. BSP is obviously the major employer here and another public sector undertaking, Hindustan Steel Construction Ltd. comes second. Besides these, there are a number of small industries which provide employment to a few thousand workers.

The survey covered workers engaged in the different industries in BSC; but in this paper we have taken only workers employed at BSP.

The survey was conducted in August-September 1978. Data was collected through a fairly elaborate questionnaire which was administered to individual workers. A total of 250 workers were covered in this manner. These workers were randomly selected but care was taken to ensure that all sections were covered. We tried to ensure that proper weightage was given to different levels of skills and to the various shops in the plant.

Profile of the Workers

Of the 250 workers covered, 94 were skilled, 100 semiskilled and 56 unskilled. Grouping of workers into these three categories was based on their responses. We thought it more convenient to group workers in this manner rather than according to the specific posts they occupy. There would have been too many occupational categories in that case and it would have been more difficult to cross tabulate the data. The total number of workers covered in each category more or less reflects the proportion of workers in these categories in the plant. Around one fifth of the workers at BSP are unskilled and the proportion of semi-skilled and skilled workers are equal.

For 99 of the workers covered, this was their first employment. The rest had been previously employed in other industries. An overwhelming majority of these workers, 242 of them, were born in rural areas while only 8 were from urban areas. This indicates that the rural linkes of the workers were fairly high.

On going through the places of origin of the workers we found that though most of them were from Bihar (232), very few were from the district or from contiguous districts. This is of course the trend in all public sector undertakings (with the possible exception of the BHEL plant at Ranipur, Hardwar) which are established in backward areas. The local people rarely find employment in these industries. In BSP too we find that only 19 workers were from Dhanbad district. The other districts of Chotanagpur were also poorly represented. There were 12 workers from Giridih, 6 from Hazaribagh, three from Palamau and one from Ranchi. The workers in the sample were drawn from 30 districts of the state. The bulk of them were from Patna, Mongyr, Rohtas, Bhojpur, Sivan and Nalanda districts. There were 13 workers from Uttar pradesh of whom 4 were from Balia, one from Jaunpur, and Azamgarh and Gazipur had 3 each. The other 5 workers were from other states, namely, Punjab (Amritsar), Madhya Pradesh (Jabalpur), Kerala (Palghat), West Bengal (Midnapur) and Maharashtra (Dhulia).

The employment pattern shows two features. Firstly, a majority of the workers have previous experience and secondly, very few were from the region. As noted earlier, the latter feature is common to most public sector undertakings in backward areas. Advanced industries such as BSP require workers who have some amount of skill and a fair level of education. They prefer workers who have experience in working with machinery. This is why we find that a majority of the workers covered had previous experience. Regions like Dhanbad and its adjoining districts are backward and, prior to the establishment of BSP, had hardly any industries. One cannot expect the local population to have the experience that BSP was seeking while recruiting workers. The old workers told us that previous employment was essential for getting employment in the initial phase, even for unskilled work. This had even led to a thriving racket of providing fake employment certificates to job seekers at a price.

Occupational Background

In order to understand the social background of the workers, their father's and grandfather's occupations were noted. This would help in understanding intergenerational mobility in occupations. We found that only one workers's father had been an industrial worker. Hence for the remaining 249 workers there had been a change of occupation from the previous generation. We have placed the occupations of the father and grandfather in six categories. These categories are, peasant, agricultural workers, industrial workers, service, white collar workers, and self employed. These categories were based on the response of each worker. Workers who had given their father's and/or their grandfather's occupation as *krishak, krishi karya, kheti, kissan* were placed in the category of peasants. It is not possible to draw a distinction between different sections of the peasantry, i.e., marginal, small, middle, large etc. because data on the landholdings of parent's or grand parent's were not noted. However, details of the land holdings of the workers were taken and these will be discussed in a later section.

The categories, agricultural workers, industrial worker and white collar worker comprised single occupations. The two other categories, service and self employed, comprised more than one occupation. Fathers and grandfathers who held jobs other than white collar ones were placed in service category. These people had been employed in class IV service as peons or something similar or had been employees at the village level. There were two types of occupations in the self-employed category, viz., those of the shopkeeper and petty trader.

The information on fathers' occupation shows that peasants form the largest group. There were 173 workers, accounting for 69.2% of the total, whose fathers were peasants. The service category came next with 28 (11.2%). There were 17 workers whose fathers were agricultural workers (6.8%) and only one worker's father had been an industrial worker. There were 16 fathers in the self-employed category while 15 were white collar workers.

On comparing the occupations of the grandfathers with those of the fathers we find that 197 had common occupations. Here again peasants formed the largest group. There were 167 workers whose fathers and grandfathers were peasants. All 17 workers whose fathers were agricultural labourers had their grandfathers in the same occupation. In the service and self-employed categories there were 6 and 7 workers respectively, whose fathers and grandfathers had common occupations. The occupations of the grandfathers of the 15 workers whose fathers were white collar workers were different from those of their sons and grandsons. In fact we find a three generational occupational mobility in this group. Thirteen of these grandfathers were peasants and two were self-employed.

We can see from the above data on occupations of the two previous generations that there has not been any significant occupational mobility over the generations. There were changes in occupations of father and grandfather in only 53 cases (i.e., 21.2% of the sample). This is possibly because a majority of the earlier generations were engaged in agricultural activities, either as peasants or agricultural workers. Of the 173 workers whose fathers were peasants, 167 of them (i.e., 96.5%) had their earlier generation in the same occupation. In the case of workers coming from families of agricultural workers there was no occupational change over two generations.

Level of Education

The workers have been divided into nine groups on the basis of their educational achievements. The first group consists of workers who have had no education. There are 9 workers in this group. The second group comprises workers who have had primary education. These number 35. Those who had studied upto high school but did not pass their matric (or Higher Secondary) form the third group. There are 48

TABLE 9.1

Level of Skill and Level of Education

Skill	*Level of Education**									
	1	*2*	*3*	*4*	*5*	*6*	*7*	*8*	*9*	*Total*
Skilled	-	-	-	12	37	11	17	16	1	94
Semiskilled	-	7	33	24	23	8	-	5	-	100
Unskilled	9	28	15	4	-	-	-	-	-	56
Total	9	35	48	40	60	19	17	21	1	250
(%)	(3.6)	(1.4)	(19.2)	(1.6)	(2.4)	(7.6)	(6.3)	(8.4)	(0.4)	(100)

TABLE 9.2

Comparison of Father's Occupation and Level of Education

Father's Occupation	*Level of Education**										
	1	*2*	*3*	*4*	*5*	*6*	*7*	*8*	*9*	*Total*[1]	
Peasant	5	21	35	27	47	13	12	12	1	173	(69.2)
Service[2]	-	7	5	5	6	1	2	2	-	28	(11.2)
White Col.	-	-	-	3	1	3	2	6	-	15	(06.0)
Self Emp.[3]	-	-	5	3	4	2	1	1	-	16	(06.4)
Agril. Lab.	4	7	3	1	2	-	-	-	-	17	(06.8)
Worker	-	-	-	1	-	-	-	-	-	1	(00.4)
Total	9	35	48	40	60	19	17	21	1	250	(100.0)

1. Figures in brackets indicate percentage
2. Non-white collar jobs, mainly class IV. category
3. Shopkeepers, or petty traders.

*Columns for Level of Education indicate: 1. No. education, 2. Primary 3. Middle school 4. Matric/S.S.C. 5. Matric + technical 6. Undergraduate 7. Undergraudate+technical 8. Graduate 9. Graduate+technical.

in this group. These three groups together represent workers who were non-matric, i.e., those who have not completed high school. They collectively constituted 36.8% of the total workers covered. We can hence see that a majority of the workers have completed their high school or had attained higher qualifications.

The fourth group comprises those who had passed their matric and in the fifth group are those who had technical qualifications in addition. These people had certificates or diplomas in technical education from ITIs or government sponsored apprenticeships in industry. There are 100 workers in this group. The sixth group comprises those who had studied upto the college level but did not graduate, and those who had a technical certificate or an apprenticeship in addition form the seventh group. These two groups have 36 workers. The last two groups comprise graduates and graduates with additional technical qualification. There is only one worker in the last group and the eighth group has 21 workers, making the total number of graduate workers 22.

Table 9.1 gives a comparison of the level of skill and the level of education. All 9 workers who had no education were unskilled workers. The educational levels of this category of workers is lower than those of the other two categories. We find that only 4 workers have passed their matriculation and the rest are in the first three groups. The educational levels of the skilled workers are expectedly higher. All workers here are matriculates or more. The qualifications of semi-skilled workers are distributed more widely than the skilled or unskilled workers. It is interesting to note that there are 5 graduates working as semi-skilled workers.

The general educational levels of the workers at BSP indicate a change in the composition of industrial workers in modern heavy industries. We find the workers in these industries are more educated than their counterparts in traditional industries. We see matriculates working here as unskilled workers and graduates as semi-skilled workers. The wages, service conditions and other facilities offered in public sector industries seem to have encouraged educated people into joining the ranks of the working class. In order to understand the social background of the workers we compared their father's occupation with their level of education in Table 9.2. This will give us an indication of the relationship between father's occupation and the son's educational level. We find that the largest group, namely, peasant, has workers in all levels of education. There are five workers with no education, but the lone graduate with additional technical qualification is also from this group. There are 21 who have completed primary school and 35 have studied upto high school. Workers with matric and post-matric qualifications constitute the majority in this group (112 out of 173, i.e., 64.7%).

A more detailed analysis of the distribution of educational levels among workers whose fathers were peasants could be possible if these people had been differentiated by the size of their land holdings. We could then determine whether there is any relationship between size of holdings and level of son's education among the peasants. Unfortunately, information on the land holdings of the previous generations were not noted. However, we have compared the land holdings of the workers with their educational qualifications and level of skill in a later section. The land holdings of the workers give some indication of the holdings of the previous generation as in most cases land has been inherited.

We find there is some relationship between the father's occupation and the son's educational level in the other occupations. For instance, sons of white collar workers all have matric or post-matric qualifications with 6 of them being graduates. On the other hand we find that the educational levels of the sons of agricultural workers are lower. Only 3 of the 17 workers are matriculates or have post-matric technical qualification, whereas there are 4 who have no education and 7 with primary eduction. The lone industrial worker's son is a matriculate. In the service category the distribution is more or less even, with a slight weightage towards higher studies. There are 12 workers who have studied till the primary or post primary levels and there are 14 workers who have studied to the matric and post-matric levels.

Ownership of land

One of the most important indications of the rural links of the workers is with respect to the ownership of cultivable land. The respondents were asked how much land they owned individually. If the land was jointly held by the worker's family he was asked what his share was. The data thus collected showed that 191 owned land in their villages. Of the 59 who did not own land, 8 were urban based and 7 had stated that they had no connection with their villages. The 17 workers whose forefathers were agricultural workers too did not own any land.

TABLE 9.3

Land Holding and Level of Education

Land holding (in acres)	Level of Education 1	2	3	4	5	6	7	8	9	Total	(%)
Nil	3	14	13	6	14	3	2	4	-	59*	(23.6)
Below 1 ac	3	4	7	6	8	1	1	-	-	30	(12.0)
1 - 2.5 ac	2	12	11	12	14	9	5	5	-	70	(28.0)
2.6 - 5 ac	1	5	9	7	11	4	4	2	-	43	(17.2)
5.1 - 10 ac	-	-	2	8	10	2	2	6	1	31	(12.4)
Above 10 ac	-	-	6	1	3	-	3	4	-	17	(06.8)
Total	9	35	48	40	60	19	17	21	1	250	(100)

* Of these, 8 workers were urban based and 7 had no connection with their villages.

TABLE 9.4

Size of Holding and Level of Skill

Land Holding (in acres)	Skilled	Semiskilled	Unskilled	Total
Nil	22	21	16	59
Below 1 ac.	5	16	9	30
1 - 2.5 ac.	29	23	18	70
2.6 - 5 ac.	15	19	9	43
5.1 - 10 ac.	14	16	1	31
Above 10 ac.	9	5	3	17
Total	94	100	56	250

The land holdings varied from those owning less than an acre to those owning more than 10 acres. The data on land holdings is given in Table 9.3 and 9.4. We have grouped the workers according to the size of their holdings, into 6 groups. The first comprises those with no land and the second with those with less than an acre. These two groups together comprise 89 workers or 35.6% of the total. The third comprises workers holding between one and 2.5 acres. This is the largest single group with 70 workers here (i.e. 28%). The fourth group has 43 workers (17.2%) with holdings between 2.6 and 5 acres.

We can see that as far individual holdings go, most workers would fall in the marginal or small farmer category. There are 143 workers with holdings ranging from less than half an acre to 5 acres. They account for 57.2% of the total and 74.9% of the land holders. However one has to keep in mind that these are individual holdings of the workers. The total holdings of their extended families in the villages will possibly be much more.

In the last two groups we have workers with holdings of between 5.1 and 10 acres and above 10 acres, respectively. There are 17 workers who had holdings of more than 10 acres and 31 workers had holdings ranging from 5.1 to 10 acres. These two groups account for 19.2% of the workers and 25.1% of those owning land.

Table 9.3 gives a comparison of the level of education of the workers with their land holdings. We find that there is a positive relationship between the two. As size of holdings increase the level of education also increases. For instance, 8 of the 9 workers with no education are in the land holdings groups of 0 to 2.5 acres. Similarly, 30 of the 35 workers with primary education also fall in the same three groups. If we take the total number of workers who have either no education or have studied upto middle school we find that 75% of them are in these three land holding groups.

On the other hand the proportion of workers who have completed their matriculation or have studied beyond it, tends to increase with the increase in land holdings. In the zero land holding group the percentage of workers with matric or post-matric qualifications is 49.1. This increases to 53.3% for the group with holdings of less than an acre, and to 64.3% in the next group (1 to 2.5 acres). The group representing workers with holdings between 2.6 and 5 acres has 65.1% in this category, and the next group (5.1 to 10 acres) has 92.5%. At the same time, the percentage for the last group (above 10 acres) falls to 64.7%.

Trips to Village

The connection workers have with their village is an indicator of their rural links. We have tried to find out how often workers, who still have contacts with their villages, go there. The number of times each worker went to his village annually is shown in Table 9.5. There were seven workers who had no contact with their villages, apart from the eight workers who were urban-based. There were 12 workers who lived in their villages and commuted daily to their place of work. There were therefore 223 workers who lived away from their villages but maintained contact with.

The last column of Table 7.5 (i.e. Total) gives the number of times the workers visited their villages. We find that 159 workers (rows 4+5+6) visited their respective villages more than once a year. In other words, 63.6% of the total sample of 71.3 per cent of those maintaining contact with their villages but living away from them, visited their villages more than once a year. This is another indicator that the rural links of the workers were strong because most workers did not come from contiguous districts of Dhanbad. Their villages were therefore not very close to their place of work.

Table 9.5 also gives a comparison of the size of landholdings of the workers and trips to their villages. This will help us in determining whether the size of holdings have any bearing on the worker's trips to his village. The data presented in this table shows that there is some connection. Those with larger holdings made more trips to their villages. Of the 17 workers who possessed more than 10 acres, one lived in his village and the others all visited their villages more than once a year.

On the other hand, we find that workers with no land make less frequent trips to their villages. There were 59 workers who did not possess any land. Of these seven had no connection with their villages and eight were urban based. Therefore, there were 40 workers who lived away from their villages but maintained contact with them. There were 26 workers (65%) who went to their villages once a year or less, while 14 (35%) visited their villages more than once a year.

The next group is made up of those workers with less than one acre of land. There were 30 workers in this category one of whom lived in his village. We find that visits to their villages by these workers were more frequent, as 20 of the 29 workers (i.e. 69%) went to their villáges more than once a year. In the next group, i.e. those possessing between

TABLE 9.5

Size of Land Holdings and Trips to Village

Trips to Village	*Land Holdings (Acres)* NIL	*1*	*1 - 2.5*	*2.6 - 5*	*5.1 - 10*	*10+*	*Total*
1. No Connection	7	-	-	-	-	-	7
2. Less than once a Yr.	12	-	3	2	-	-	17
3. Once a Yr.	14	9	12	9	3	-	47
4. 2 to 3 times	10	13	32	20	11	7	93
5. 3 to 5 times	3	6	12	8	11	8	48
6. More than 5	1	1	8	3	4	1	18
7. Lives in Village	4	1	3	1	2	1	12
8. Urban Based	8	-	-	-	-	-	8
Total	59	30	70	43	31	17	250

TABLE 9.6

Trips to Village and Cultivation of Land

Trips to Village (annual)	*Does not Cultivate* 1	*Cultivates Own Land* 2	*Others land* 3	*Own & Others* 4	*Total* 5
1. No Connection	-	-	-	-	7
2. Less than once	17	-	-	-	17
3. Once a yr.	33	8	6	-	47
4. 2 - 3 times	49	39	4	1	93
5. 3 - 5 times	31	16	-	1	48
6. More than 5	9	9	-	-	18
7. Lives in village	4	4	4	-	12
8. Urban Based	-	-	-	-	8
Total	143	76	14	2	250

TABLE 9.7

Size of Holdings and Workers' Involvement in Cultivation

Participation in Cultivation	*Size of Holdings (acres)* NIL	*1*	*1-2.5*	*2.6-5*	*5.1-10*	*10+*	*Total*
Does not Cultivate	33	17	43	25	16	9	143
Cultivates Own Land	-	9	26	18	15	8	76
Cultivates Others Land	11	-	-	-	-	-	11
Cultivates Own and Others	-	4	1	-	-	-	5
No Connection	7	-	-	-	-	-	7
Urban Based	8	-	-	-	-	-	8
Total	59	30	70	43	31	17	250

TABLE 9.8

Remittances

Remittances	*Size of Holdings (acres)* Nil	*1 ac.*	*1-2.5*	*2.6-5*	*5.1-10*	*10+*	*Total*
1. Lives in Vill.	4	1	3	1	2	1	12
2. Gets and Sends	-	2	12	16	11	6	47
3. Does not Get or Send	8	-	12	6	7	2	35
4. Sends, does not get	32	27	39	17	5	6	126
5. Get, does not send	-	-	4	3	6	2	15
6. No connection	7	-	-	-	-	-	7
7. Urban Based	8	-	-	-	-	-	8
Total	59	30	70	43	31	17	250

one and 2.5 acres, the percentage of workers visiting their villages more than once a year was 77.6. For workers possessing between 2.6 and 5 acres the percentage fell to 73.8 but it was still higher than the first two groups. In the fifth group, comprising workers owning between 5.1 and 10 acres, we find that 89.6% visited their villages more than once a year. In fact 15 of them (52%) visited their villages more than three times a year. Hence we can see that ownership of land is an important factor which binds the worker to his village.

Cultivation of Land

One can presume that since workers went to their villages often their involvement in cultivation must be high. The fact that workers with land visit their villages more often than those without land reenforces this belief. One would presume that workers owing land went to their villages more often because they personally cultivated land. We had asked the workers whether they went to their villages during the agricultural season and whether they cultivated land. In case they cultivated land they were asked whether they cultivated their own land or other people's lands as well. We found that most workers did in fact prefer to go to their villages during agricultural season. The data on the involvement of workers in cultivation is given in Tables 9.6 and 9.7. Table 9.6 compares the number of trips to the villages with cultivation of land and Table 9.7 relates the size of holdings of the workers with their involvement in cultivation.

We can see from Table 6 that most of the workers did not infact cultivate land. There were 143 workers, out of 235 workers (60.9%) who maintained contact with their villages, but did not cultivate land. We also found that 89 of these workers (62.2%) went to their villages more than once a year, with 40 of them (28%) having been to their villages more than thrice a year. We can see from the table that out of 159 workers in the sample who went to their villages more than once a year, 89 of them (56%) did not take part in cultivation. These workers may have gone to their villages to supervise agricultural operations or they may have wanted to take time off from factory work. Workers who went to their villages less frequently, i.e. once a year or less, were even less inclined towards cultivation. Only 14 of the 64 workers in these two groups cultivated land in their villages.

There were 76 workers who cultivated their own lands. We can see that the proportion of workers cultivating their own land increases with the frequency of their trips to their villages. Only eight of the 47 workers (17%) who went to their villages annually cultivated their lands (cols. 2+4). There were 17 workers (35.4%) who made 4 to 5 trips a year to their villages and half of them made more than five trips, who cultivated their own land.

Apart from the 76 workers who cultivated their own land, there were five who cultivated their own as well as others lands. This brings the total of those who cultivated land to 81 which is 39.8% of the landholders. This means that 60.2% of the workers owing land did not cultivate their lands when they went to their villages.

An interesting feature here is that though most of the workers did not take part in cultivation there were 16 workers who cultivated other people's lands when they went to their villages. Five of them did so in addition to cultivating their own lands. We can see from Table 7 that the 11 workers who only cultivated others land did not have land of their own. Of the five who cultivated their own as well as others land, four of them possessed less than one acre each and one had between 1 and 2.5 acres. However, what is significant here is that 33 out of the 44 workers (i.e. 75%) who did not posses land but maintained contact with their villages did not cultivate land.

Table 9.7 gives the relation between size of holdings and workers' participation in cultivation. The figures show that more than half the workers in each of the five land holding categories did not take part in cultivation. The proportion of non-cultivators was higher among those with smaller holdings. There were 143 workers who possessed five acres or less (excluding those who did not posses land). Of these 58, i.e. 40.6%, cultivated their own lands. On the other hand, out of the 48 workers who held more than five acres each, 23 i.e. 48%, participated in cultivating their lands.

It is quite evident that by and large workers at Bokaro did not work on land. This is inspite of their rural links being strong, if one is to judge from the frequency of their trips to their villages. Though one cannot offer a detailed analysis of this phenomenon at this stage, interviews with some of the workers revealed that they considered agriculture as an inferior activity. They felt that since they were occupying fairly well paid jobs as industrial workers they need not engage in cultivation. They therefore preferred to supervise agricultural activities when they went to their villages.

From the data collected we find that there are mainly four reasons which determine the frequency of trips to the villages. Firstly, the workers' families live there and they go to visit them and also give them money. Secondly, to ensure a fair share of the produce in cases where land was jointly held by other members of the family. Thirdly, to supervise agricultural activities, and fourthly, to bring back a part of their produce, in kind or cash. Though quite a few workers sent remittances to their villages, there was a sizable section which received goods or cash from their villages. We shall discus this in the next section.

Remittances

Table 8 give a break up of remittances of the workers in relation to their holdings. We found that remittances operated both ways. Workers sent money to their villages but many of them also received remittance or goods from their villages. They either brought food grains or cash from the sale of their crops. We have grouped the workers into seven categories. Three of these, namely, those living in their villages, those with no connection, and those who were urban based, need not be considered in our analysis. The other four categories are, workers who sent remittances to their villages and also received cash or goods from their villages, workers did not send or get remittances, those sent remittance but did not receive anything and, finally those who only got remittances or goods from their villages but did not send anything.

From the totals in Table 9.8 (last column) we can see that 126 workers sent money to their villages without receiving anything. This is just over half of the total sample and comprises 56.5% of those who did not live in their villages but maintained contact with them. The proportion of workers sending only money to their villages is higher among those with no land or with small holdings. There were 40 workers with no land but who maintained contact with their villages. Among those 32 sent remittances and 8 did not send anything. In all these eight cases we found that the workers lived with their wives and children in Bokaro but had other members of their families in their villages. Their trips to their villages were less frequent. There were 29 workers holding less than an acre each who lived away from their villages and all of them sent remittance. Two of them also got occassional remittances from their villages. In the next landholding group (1 to 2.5 acres) there were 67 workers living away from their villages and 39 of them (58.2%) sent remittances while 12 obtained goods or cash as well from their villages. There were 12 who did not get or send anything, while four recieved remittances or foodgrains from their villages but they did not send anything to their villages. We can see that the total number of workers sending remittances to their villages is higher among workers holding 2.5 acres or less. These workers numbered 98 out of the 126 who sent remittances, i.e. they account for 77.8% of those sending remittances.

An interesting feature here is that there was a small group of workers, numbering 15, who only received goods or remittances from their villages without sending anything there. Most of them had holdings of above 2.5 acres. If we add this to the 47 workers who got as well as sent remittances we have a total of 62 workers who received cash or kind from their villages. This means that a little more than one-fourth (27.8%) of the 223 workers who lived away from their villages but maintained contact with them received remittance or goods from their villages. We also find that just as the proportion of workers sending remittances was higher among those with holdings of 2.5 acres of less, the proportion of those not sending anything nor receiving anything was also high among these workers. Of the 35 workers who did not send or receive remittances, 20 of them had holdings of 2.5 acres of less.

Land Management

We have noted earlier that 191 of the 250 workers covered owned land. Each of these respondents was asked how their land was cultivated. Was this done through family labour, hired labour or did they lease out their land to sharecroppers? The findings on this aspect are shown in Table 9. We have made four categories. Firstly, those who used only family labour, secondly those who employed agricultural workers to supplement family labour, thirdly, those who employed only hired labour and lastly, those who leased out their land to sharecroppers. We can see from Table 9 that a majority of the workers owing land depended on family labour for cultivation. There were 107 workers, accounting for 56% of the landholders, who used only labour available within the family. This is quite natural because a majority of the landholders (100 out of 191) held less than 2.5 acres each. If we take a total of the next column, i.e. showing instances where both family labour and hired labour were used, we find that 177 of the families (92.7% of the landholders) were engaged in cultivation. This perhaps indicates that though the workers showed little interest in cultivation, their families were more enthusiastic.

TABLE 9.9
Cultivation of Land

Size of Holdings (acres)	*Family Labour*	*Family+ Hired*	*Only Hired*	*Leased Out*	*Total*
Below 1 ac.	28	-	-	2	30
1 to 2.5	59	6	-	5	70
2.6 to 5	19	24	-	-	43
5.1 to 10	1	25	2	3	31
Above 10	-	15	2	-	17
Total	107	70	4	10	191

TABLE 9.10
Purchase or Sale of Land

Size of Holdings (Acres)	*Bought Land*	*Sold Land*	*Neither*	*Total*
No Land	-	6	45	51
Below 1 ac.	5	4	21	30
1 to 2.5	11	3	56	70
2.6 to 5	7	1	35	43
5.1 to 10	6	2	23	31
Above 10	3	2	12	17
Total	32	18	192	242

Table 9.9 also gives the cultivation of family and hired labour according to size of holdings. As expected, we find that the incidence of employing hired labour increases with the increases in the size of landholdings. However, it is also worth noting that though the larger landholders employed agricultural labour, their families too participated in cultivation. We have only four cases where cultivation was done only through hired labour. Two of these cases were in holdings of 5.1 to 10 acres and the other two in holdings of more than 10 acres. Another interesting finding is that very few workers had leased out their lands. There were only 10 such cases (5.2%) seven of whom were among those owning 2.5 acres or less. This low incidence of leasing was because the workers' families were engaged in cultivation. They would not like to lease out land when they were capable of cultivating it themselves. We found that in all cases where land had been leased out, the workers' families were residing at Bokaro and not in their villages.

Dependence on family labour was higher among the smaller holdings. We can see that 87 of the 100 who held 2.5 acres or less cultivated their lands only with family labour. In addition, there were six cases in holdings between 1 to 2.5 acres where hired labour supplemented the efforts of the family. Employment of agricultural labour by the workers was quite significant, even if not widespread. There were 74 workers who used hired labour for cultivation. This accounted for 38.7% of the total workers holding land. In other words, more than one-third of the landholders engaged agricultural labour, which is not a small proportion.

Purchases or Sale of Land

Since land seems to be a major attraction for maintaining contact with their villages, we tried to find out how many workers had bought or sold land during the preceding five years. The findings are shown in Table 10. It is interesting to note here that a majority of the workers (192 out of 242) who were rural based did not buy or sell land during the preceding five years. It we take only those who had land (i.e. 191) we find that 147 of them (77%) did not buy or sell land during this period.

Apart from this, we find that the number of people who bought land was higher than those who had sold land. There were 32 who had bought land and 18 who had sold land, six of whom had no land at the time of the survey. The number of people who had bought land was evenly divided between the smaller holders with 2.5 acres or less and those with more than 2.5 acres; each category had 16 workers. At the same time there were 13 workers with holdings of 2.5 acres or less who had sold land and only 5 with holdings of more than 2.5 acres who had done so.

Though a majority of the workers did not buy or sell land in the preceding five years, we find that they had a marked preference for purchasing land if the opportunity arose. Table 11 gives the data on this aspect. Each worker had been asked whether he would like to purchase cultivable land in the future. The workers from urban areas have been excluded because all of them said no. We found that of the 242 workers, 163 wanted to purchase land and only 79 did not want to purchase land. We therefore find that 67.4% of workers from rural areas were in favour of purchasing land in the future.

We have given the breakup of the workers' responses to this question by cross tabulating the different landholding sizes with whether they had bought or sold land in the preceeding five years. We can see from Table 9.11 that most of the people who had bought land wanted to buy more. Only three of the 32 who had bought land did not wish to buy any more. Among those who had sold land there were 10 who wanted to buy land. Of these five had sold their land earlier and had become landless. However, what is striking here is 124 of the 192 workers (64.6%) who had neither bought nor sold land were in favour of buying more land. This indicates the high value placed on land by these workers. The reason perhaps lies in their rural backgrounds which places greater importance on land as a form of security and prestige. In contrast we find that the eight urban based workers showed no interest in possessing land, though of course their number is too small in this sample to indicate any definite trend.

Conclusion

We find two distinct features among the workers at Bokaro. Firstly, they are all (with one exception) first generation industrial workers who come mainly from rural backgrounds. Secondly, their level of education is fairly high. This would in fact suggest that these workers are not from the rural poor. After all how many agricultural workers, impoverished Harijans, or tribals can afford to educate their children beyond middle school even if education is free. The individual land holdings of the workers would again indicate that they were not from

TABLE 9.11
Preference for Buying Land

Size of Holding (acres)	*Preference for buying land*		*Bought Land*	*Sold Land*	*Neither*	*Total*
No land	Yes		-	5	23	28
	No		-	1	22	23
Below 1 ac.	Yes		4	-	20	24
	No		1	4	1	6
1 to 2.5	Yes		9	1	36	46
	No		2	2	20	24
2.6 to 5	Yes		7	0	25	32
	No		0	1	10	11
5.1 to 10	Yes		6	2	12	20
	No		0	0	11	11
Above 10	Yes		3	2	8	13
	No		-	-	4	4
Total	Yes	163	32	18	192	242
	No	79				

the poorer sections of society. We therefore find that only 17 workers came from families of agricultural workers. One can in this way contrast these modern rural based workers with the traditional rural based workers in the jute mills of Calcutta and the textile mills of Bombay.

Since a majority of workers are from rural backgrounds we find that the workers have strong rural links. Their frequent trips to their villages is further proof of where their preferences lay. At the same time their attraction for their villages was not caused by a fascination for agriculture. Few of them were actually interested in cultivation. They would rather own land and supervise agricultural activities back home.

The workers obviously prefered working on machines and not on land. They felt that as industrial labour engaged in well paid jobs their status was higher than those of cultivators. This becomes clear from the preferences of the workers towards the type of work they would like to do. We had asked them whether they preferred working on land, with machines or in an office. Only 16 workers gave their first preference for work on land. Ther others all preferred working on machines or doing office work. This indicates that agriculture as a source of livelihood has low priority for these workers.

We find that though family labour is an important component in the cultivation of land, a sizable section of the landholders employ agricultural labourers. One has to follow up further and investigate how far this affects the workers' political behaviour. A contradiction may arise here. These workers may be vocal in demanding higher wages for industrial labour but they may not show the same enthusiasm when the demand for higher wages for agricultural labourers arises.

It may appear from the data we have that there are some contradictions among the workers which may have a bearing on their class outlook. We also find that these workers are quite eager to possess land, they have strong rural links and they employ agricultural labourers to work for them. These factors may affect the proletarianization process among the working class here. One can argue that they still have a lot to lose besides their chains. On the other hand we find that there is a marked preference for industrial work and the workers are proud of their new status. It is therefore possible that these workers view ownership of land as a form of security and not only as a form of prestige. For these workers, who are mainly from rural areas, land is a form of investment, just as the urbanized people view shares, savings certificates, fixed deposits, etc., as forms of investment. These workers are more familiar with land than with the other forms of investment. Perhaps if we look at the problem from this angle, the workers' choice of holding an industrial job while increasing their landholdings may not appear contradictory. However, a more detailed study of this process is necessary.

ACKNOWLEDGEMENTS

I wish to thank Coms. N. Rajashekhar Reddy, the then Secretary of the National Council, and Mohit Sen, then member C.E.C., of the CPI, who were incharge of this project for their encouragement; Gaya Singh, Anuriddha, Ahmed and the workers of BSP for the help they gave me; and Prof Sunil Sen Gupta for helping in designing the lengthy questionnaire.

CHAPTER 10

Town-Country Nexus: A Case of the Food Processing Industry

—Manorama Savur

Urban-rural relation, history shows, is an exploitative one. Marx posits such a relation to division of labour, starting with the differentiation between the mental and the manual labour. He goes on to show the various forms of exploitative relations that develop as the town and the country grow at different pace. In *German Ideology,* he also took pains to point out the contradictions that emerge among the classes during the historic process of growth. In Gordon Childe's reconstruction of history, an urban civilization was possible only through appropriation of the rural surplus by the newly emerging ruling classes, the priests and the chieftains. The Dependency Theorists, whatever the variation of the main theme may be, have generally shown that modern Western societies, viz., the metropolitan countries have grown by sucking their colonies which have consequently been reduced to the level of hinterland or satellites.

There is a great deal of data on imperialist policies and the current mode of exploitation by the multinationals (MNCs). What is significant is that they have first turned to their own country side and then to the 'Third World' for the exploitation not only of raw material, but also to set up simulaneously cheap production centres to overcome the rising production costs in their own metropolitan centres. A host country's willingness to provide the infrastructure has exacerbated the process. The state's active intervention is understandable as it is the handmaid of the ruling classes.

Urban exploitative relations within the countryside takes a variety of forms. The food processing industry (FPI) is one such and is gathering strength. This is a world-wide phenomenon. Our focus is on the consequences of the growth of FPI on various classes in rural India. Since the West has reduced many countries to the status of hinterlands we shall also show, how this process operates with respect to FPI in India.

USA as a premier metropolitan country is believed to have set the trend. Its shift from urban-based industry to agro-industry in the sixties was historically necessary to overcome repeated recessions. It not only took to manufacturing farm machinery and farm chemicals, but simultaneously started biological research to increase farm produce whether it be cereals, fruit or vegetables, meat, dairy or poultry. The inevitable next step was to process the increased output to give them longer shelf life, convert them into a variety of ready-to-eat or at least ready-to-cook products to catch the urban market where the growing middle class was ready to absorb any time-saving device. Sales promotion did the final trick, of course. What is important is that bourgeoisie of the advanced industrial countries undertook R and D work in all the three related fields in their own corporations (Lester Brown, *Seeds of Change*). If their business must go on, food production of raw material for food processing has to expand, and that expansion inevitably was in the third world. It was also an outlet for sale of their agro and FPI machinery and chemicals. Such a shift to the hinterland meant a change in the cropping pattern—from cereals for subsistence, for the vast mass of poor peasantry, to temperate and tropical fruits, vegetables and only specific cereals such as recommended by influential bodies like FAO and the World Bank (WB, 1972 and 1985).

In India the trend was remarkable parallel and yet there was a distinct difference possibly due to resource constraints. The Indian bourgeoisie confidently entred into agro-business in the sixties, but most often in collaboration with MNCs to manufacture agro-chemicals and agro-machinery. Simultaneously, attempts were made to bring some changes in the cropping pattern —first through village spontaneously adopting and then through IRDP—but they too were not properly articulated as in the West due to the short sightedness of the Indian bourgeoisie, who like the merchant and the local money-lender sought immediate petty gains (Savur, *Corporate Sector in Rural Development*, 1985) and hence they lost. Although the apex bodies like the Maharashtra Economic Development Council, on the basis of its studies in 1970, predicted that "agro-industries hold out a great promise and that surplus agricultural and allied produce is indeed a spring board for rapid and sustained development" (MEDC, 1970, p. 12). Yet it is the Government and not the corporation that carries out research. For instance the Managing Director of the HPMC revealed that its R & D is provided by 22 agri-universities, 2 horticultural research centres at Bangalore and Lucknow, besides the numerous branches of Indian Agricultural Research Centres and are funded by ICAR and by Central and State governments (R.S. Raina, "India" in Asian Productivity Organization, *Fruit Production and Marketing in Asia and the pacific*, pp. 302-303, Tokyo, 1985). In order to assist in a shift in the cropping pattern the Government provides extension services which are put to use by industrial houses to induce poor peasantry to grow profitable market crops. Barring the rather old fashioned cash crops like sugar and oil, FPI was a low ebb till the end of the last decade and were confined to small scale and even cottage industries. This was done, inspite of the fact that agro-indusries corporations were set up, as early as in 1964-65, at the advice of the Central Government (N. Kothari, Agro-Industries Corporation in India in RBI *Bulletin*, Vol. XXXII, No. 2, February 1978).

The negative impact of FPI on the countryside can be seen at two levels, one at the point of raw material production and the other at the level of processing. We shall separate the two artificially, for the sake of convenience.

Since organized industry in India was essentially agro-based (cotton and jute) during the colonial period there is a certain amount of commonality and some new differences that have emerged due to changing historical reasons. If during the colonial period railway tracts were laid as an infrastructural measure only in raw cotton cultivation areas[1] (D. Thorner, *Investment in the Empire*, p. 7) the present government has gone much beyond and has, to state one instance, recklessly built roads through protected forest areas in sub-Himalayan region to open out the area for apple growing. This was done at the behest of USAID and the World Bank (WB) and has led to land slides resulting in silting of rivers and floods every year all along the Sutlej, Ganga and Yamuna river tracts. Annually crops and livestock of all peasant classes were destroyed along with the homestead of the poorest section. Even the British had shown some enlightened self interest and had banned felling of trees in catchment areas, and such areas were designated as protected forests. Within a decade the entrie sub-Himalayan region became a catchment area for growing apples and other temperate zone fruit sfor the WB aided Himachal Pradesh Fruit

Production and Marketing Council[2] (HPFMC). It had persuaded only the feudal elements of the region to take to profitable apple cultivation. Apple orchard owners need packing cases to transport the fruit which led to further indiscriminate felling of deodar chir and pine forests in the same protected forest area.[3]

As in the British period, so too now, if the rich peasants were enticed to grow cash crops (Barrington Moore, *Social Origins of Dictatorship and Democracy*, 1966, p. 345) even poor ones joined in. It continues to be so now, even if it is fruit trees (A.L. Nanda, *Economics of Apple*, 1987, p. 89) which begin to yield only 7 years after they are planted. It is inevitable as the poor peasants are caught in the web of a cash economy and an unknown unreachable metropolitan market both Indian and overseas. Their only contact are contractors and commission agents (Negi, *op. cit.*, P. 11.1) who serve urban merchants and large scale FPI respectively. This is true for both temperate and tropical fruits (M. Savur: *Political Economy of Mango Pickle*, 1978).[4]

The present Government of India provides a variety of other infrastructural facilities to ease and facilitate a possible change of cropping pattern. These include leasing of farm machinery by Agro-industrial corporations, credit through nationalized commercial banks and Land Development banks; a variety of subsidies for the necessary inputs for poor and tribal peasants. They were been induced by the large industrial houses which had diversified into agro-industries and had entered into backward and tribal regions to convert them into catchment areas for raw material and also for sale of their agro products. The modus operandi is now different from the colonizers who had set up plantation and lured tribals and scheduled caste members as indentured labour much against their will (Griffths, *Tea*). During the VI Plan period the big industrial houses under the guise of rural development (RD) and modernization of agriculture had quietly channelized their own products, whether it be Mafatlal's PVC or ACC's cement pipes, or Kirloskar's motors, or Escorts' tractors, or Tata's farm implements, or Hoechst's animal vaccine, or even BAIF's frozen Danish Bull's semen, etc. through the Government IRDP. The Indian Government buys and distributes them at subsidized rates to selected poor peasants under the IRDP scheme. Our study of Mafatlal's RD programme revealed that in reality it was a formidable combination of Mafatlal, Shell, Hoechst and BAIF which operate under a trust like all large houses in India. In this instance, it was the Sudguru Seva Sangh Trust (SSST) set up in numerous tribal and backward areas in the country. In its RD work SSST patronized only the relatively better off, most often the village sarpanch or a police patil and a couple of others who by chance have their landholdings close to perenneal water source. All this created class differentiations where none existed. This first families to be converted along rich peasant lines were well above the poverty line. They in turn now began to engage wage labour - a vast army sometimes. This pattern is in strong contrast to exchange of labour and is tending to break the strong tribal community ties, their last vestige of strength. This is particularly so since the newly emergent rich peasants also tend to indulge in share-cropping and money-lending. The "modernization" process has a negative impact on the women in the favoured households. They are no longer permitted to work in the fields but are now confined to their homes as sole household drudges and compelled to cook enormous meals for an army of hired labour during the agricultural season. The industrial bourgeoisie have brought in very uneven development in the countryside. This study indicated that because of Mafatlal's short-sighted policy of narrow immediate gains, unlike its counterparts in the West, failed to bring a total change in the cropping pattern and could not enter into the FPI. It did however succeed in bringing about a change from coarse grain to rice in which this controlling business house alone stood to gain. SSST, provided the seed and took control of the grain to be sold in the market. Only the 'market' in this case happened to be Mafatlals' textile industry's ration shops in Bombay, Ahmedabad and Navsari. By this the Mafatlal house stood to gain. The industrial house was able to buy the grain immediately after harvest when the price is at its lowest and also to simultaneously eliminate the cut that a middle man would take. On the contrary, it took 1/5 of the produce as charges for servicing the bank loan for fitting the lift irrigation scheme. This is a three-fold gain and a fairly typical behaviour of industrial houses that had participated in RD under IRDP. Utilization of small holders is also recommended by such international bodies like UNTAD.

There are important reasons for not setting up colonial style plantations today. The most important of these are land ceiling acts and the growing threat of organized labour, especially in countries where peasant movements are endemic. It is therefore not surprising that UNTAD recommends that increase in spice production in India should be undertaken as a small holders backyard crop, and "as a secondary or even a tertiary crop," but it should be made a part of the cropping system. It also calls on the Governments of spice growing countries to provide extension service to increase the crop output. Strangely, like the agro industries and like the Government of India, UNTAD also insists that such a recommendation is meant purely to supplement the income of the small farmers. Like important commercial crops spices in India too have statutory backing of two prominent agencies viz., the Cardamon Board and the Spices Export Promotion Council. And, not surprisingly, it is an Indian Giant—the Tatas- that have entred into the present lucrative spice export business.

Small and marginal farmers, the target group of the modernization programme, ostensibly patronized by big agri-business, does not benefit. This can be illustrated through Cadbury's activity in India which dates back to 1964, when the major cocoa growing countries, Nigeria and Ghana, were growing politically conscious. Cadbury's first experiment in cocoa cultivation in India had revealed that the Indian soil did not yield cocoa that was suitable for chocolate. It therefore commissioned various agricultural research institutes to carry out intensive research. Seedlings were raised at the horticultural research institute at Calicut, and from here Cadbury began a campaign of "grow more cocoa" in Kerala and started distributing cocoa seedlings free to urban[5] and especially to all the rural households to cultivate cocoa even in their backyard. Irrespective of class and status it was accepted, although Kerala had hardly recovered from its "grow more rubber" fiasco. The promise held out by Hindustan Cocoa to buy the entrire output of cocoa pods at Rs. 300/- a ton was attractive. But in 1978 cocoa prices slumped to Rs. 12/- a tone. The reasons for this are clear: Cadbury had found a cheap substitute in Sal for its cocoa butter and with its use Cadbury's sales also jumped from Rs. 1.85 crores in 1977 to Rs. 5.29 crores in 1978 (Stock Exchange Directory, 1982). India is now the major raw material producer for Cadbury - now Hindustan Cocoa. The installed capacity of its new Sal-based cocoa butter plant is 3,000 tones per annum (*Financial Express*, 24/8/1988). The wound that a MN-FPI inflict go very deep.

Traditionally, the Sal seed was crushed for oil and the oil cake dried and pounded into flour for bread by the tribals in and around the whole stretch in the central and northern forests. This area was, therefore, known to be free from famines even during the British period. It is no longer so today with Cadbury and many other powerful FPI contenders like Godrej and Hindustan Lever contending for Sal seeds. There are many other nuts in the forests like Mahuva, Kanag, Dupa, Kususm, Kokam, Nahar which are intensively tapped for their oil content, although oil seed is the most important cultivated crop, second only to cereal in India. What is tragic is that KVIC is instrumental in getting hold of these oil seeds (K. Laksmikanthan, *Sources of oil seeds*, Gram Udyog, 1979, Vol. 17, No. 11. p. 711) for big corporations and thereby depriving the tribals of their only source of fat, as price of oil is soaring. The Government of India is responsible for this state of affairs for it set up an eighteen-member committee with representatives from powerful Hindustan Lever, Tata Oil Mills, Vanaspati Manufacturers' Association, Indian Soap Toiletories, KVIC to name some, to explore this forest resource (Forest Archieves vide letter No. 11/9/70-EP dated 23rd September 1970) Hindustan lever has now gone beyond and started oil palm plantation by clear felling virgin forests, the most notable of which are in Andamans. This act has deprived the Andamanese, incidentally the world's most primitive tribe, of its habitat and therefore its right to survive. This is an instance to show that the Government's stated concern "to lift the poor above the poverty line" (Planning Commission, *Sixth Plan*) and its actual support to MNC in FPI do not match.

For that matter the whole sub-Himalayan region its now being persistently converted into mainly temperate zone fruit growing area. In fact the overall growth rate of fruit today exceeds grain and even wheat, which is only 1.5 per cent per annum, whereas apple is 5 per cent per annum. The annual rate of growth of pineapple is as high as 14 per cent (Asian Productivity Organization (APO): *Fruit Production and Marketing in Asia and the Pacific*, 1985, p. 291, Tokyo) and as a tropical-cum-sub-Himalayan fruit it is concentrated in the tribal North-East, with a factory in Silchar for processing. The rate of growth of Mango is only 2.1 per cent (APO, *ibid*). But then mango is spread out in the plains region and is therefore not amenable to super exploitation. But as it is a native of India and grows untended even in little patches of the poor, it is not surprising that 60-70 per cent of mango is exported - thanks to the help from Export Promotion Council (Shard Mistry, *Indian Express*, 2-6-1988). Incidentally export of Alfanso alone fetched Rs. 15 crores this year (*ibid*). The 1985 level of fruit and vegetable production was 54 million tons, the target for the Seventh Plan being 68 million tons (*Indian Post*, 6-8-87). It is not a shift in the cropping pattern from coarse grain for consumption to potentially profitable fruit production for market *per se* that is being questioned. Instead attention is being drawn to the damaging effect such changes in cropping pattern have in a highly class structured rural society. Here the traditional elite has had a head start in life. In alliance with the ruling class the traditional elite uses its clout to corner all the state aid for its own growth and closes the opportunity for the rest of the peasantry to get to the market. That the urban merchant operates through the rural merchant and through the richer peasant to get the rural produce of all the classes is a known phenomenon (*vide* Ila Shah). The actual producer, particularly if he is a poor peasant gets the worst in the deal as also one unpublished study for Punjab shows. Punjab has taken to horticulture in a big way. Iyer shows the returns for apple varies from 17 to 70 per cent for the cultivator and chief beneficiary is the middle man who is no other than Voltas (Gopal Iyer). There is very little doubt that the powerful orchard owners are the ones who get 70 per cent profit whereas the poor peasant who has ventured into this "profitable" apple cultivation ends up by yielding his profits to Voltas and makes no more than 17 per cent on his small investment.

Despite intensive research for both high and quick yielding fruit trees the maturation period of a fruit tree varies from 5-7 years. Yet the poor peasants in a bid to survive, and lured by potential profitability of fruit is compelled in a cash economy to cultivate the prevalent cash crop. This is true for apples too, even when its profitability is on the decline (A. L. Nanda, *Economics of Apple*, 1987, p. 89). In Himachal Pradesh (H.P.). the apple country, the gross cropped area under fruit jumped from 792 ha. in 1950-51 to 1,00,084 ha., thanks to WB, USAID[6] road building in the sub-Himalayan protected forest area and in the process broke the eco-system and the back of the poor and middle peasantry whose kharif crop is washed away every year in floods.

Having successfully converted the western section of the sub-Himalayan region into apple and other fruit cultivation area, and the local peasants into fruit cultivators, (which itself creates surplus labour force) the WB and USAID embarked on fruit processing with the local Himachal Pradesh agro industrial corporation as its front. It created Horticultural Produce Marketing and Processing Corporation (HPMC) with several sub-collection centres and the most sophisticated processing plant costing Rs. 17 crores, inevitably with expensive imported machinery at Parvanu and "run with the assistance of personnel of international repute" (P.S. Negi, *Horticultural Produce Marketing Technology and Marketing Management*, 1982, pp. v.4 and II 28-29). The Indian Food technologist have no place in it. Although this plant has monopoly over the region's produce it has belied GOI's expectation and has not generated any employment. The plant is automated at all levels even at the levels of washing, grading and packing. The fresh fruit is packed in imported telescopic cell pack corrugated cartons. Economics of scale necessarily operates and it has throttled the numerous small FPIs in the region. Surplus fruit used to be converted to brandy, but now the licences of these small manufactures have been withdrawn, says HPMC's Managing Director (P.S. Negi, *op. cit.*, p. iv 1). This brings to mind Susan George's prediction that "agri-business is capable of destroying everything it touches, local employment patterns, local food crop production, consumer tastes, even village and traditional family structures" (Susan George, *How the Other Half Dies*, 1975, p. 133).

Government of India's IRDP programme meant for income generation of the small/marginal farmers and landless labour through production and sale of milk or poultry have only strengthened the very large FPIs and not the lower peasantry. Distribution of hybrid high milk yielding heifers to 'poor peasants' or whoever it may be, and the establishment of extension services to maintain such cattle in rural areas where the local people by and large have no purchasing power, results in such milk being sold to numerous Government collection centres. This milk either reaches some urban dairies or the milk processing plants like those of Hindustan Lever's, Glaxo's or Cadbury's. MNC's private dairies are well-supplemented with milk produced cheaply and with Government subsidies. Many of the industries, like Glaxo and Lever, which diversified into milk processing often did it as a package deal, as baby foods and veterinary products; or as Hoechst has struck through BAIF a big package deal including livestock breeding, animal vaccines medicines, and fodder production. (Savur, *Corporate Sector in Rural Development Under IRDP*). They have all indulged in the RD game to create the necessary catchment areas for both their input and their output.

This is also true for TRYCEM programme of training unemployed rural youth. Although the Government's target group is the small and marginal farmer, it is often the middle peasant who gets selected for the progrmme. One such programme is training in poultry keeping and breeding of high yielding exotic varieties both for their eggs and their meat. Not only a chicken, but even an egg is a luxury for most villagers. The consequence of this is that their output reaches only the urban rich or urban middle class not directly but through powerful agents who give them their brand names and sell them. The most notable of them today is of course Venky. 66,000 middle peasants mainly from Andhra, Karnataka, Tamil Nadu and Maharashtra do not know that they supply and strengthen Venkateswara Hatcheries with their eggs and chicks which they have handed over at the Government collection centres. Venky now has over 70 per cent of the market share in India. Every fourth egg that comes in the market is Venky's. It's net work is spread through 10 associate companies and 42 franchises and its turnover by 1986 was Rs. 120 crores. The use of the hallowed name of the most sacred deity of the South is deceptive, so too the notion that this network is the brainchild of Sri B.V. Rao. On the contrary, Babcock, an MN, and the largest poultry organization and Cobb, an associate of American Pharmaceutical Company, Upjohn, operate through Venkateshwara. The group has a strong presence in poultry vaccines in India, which are necessary to maintain the vulnerable exotic breed alive and healthy. The rural poor and middle peasant, again, with Government support and training enrich the international bourgeoisie with little evidence of generating wealth for rural India. Not more than a couple of farmers in a cluster of villages get selected for poultry training.

True Venky has put India on the world poultry map and she now ranks fifth in the world. But Venky also holds rural India in thrall. The MN as a part of its strategy ensures that its franchises are dependent on it for supplies. In this case the MN retains the seed stock and sells patents to franchises on a regular basis. If U.S.A. employed an embargo it would mean closure of poultry industry and the TRYCEM poultry programme (*Business India*, May 5-18, 1986, No. 213, pp. 60-63). Despite this, Venky's RD work is recognized by CSIR who in collaboration with ICICI was planning to set up Venketeshwara Poultry Management Institute in 1986.

The problem created by the big FPIs are endless. A great deal has already been written on the hardship caused to the fishermen who have been driven out of their occupation by trawlers owned by MNs and by FPIs. It also simultaneously means that the local coastal people are deprived of the once inexpensive protein, in their otherwise poor diet. Despite the ban, the trawlers poach on the 6,535 km long coastline with the large continental shelf which again used to be rich in certain types of fish like the prawns which have a ready market abroad. The creeks are where many species of fish come in to spawn but these areas are also under attack and besides that intensive fishing in the coastline prevents the fish entering the creeks. Due to intensive fishing India by 1980, occupied the 7th place in fishery production. It is the second largest shrimp producer. The impressive figure of 88,000 ton annual catch of all varieties worth Rs. 2,400 million has tragically reduced the per capita Indian consumption of fish to 2.8 kg a year (GOI *Indian Industries* 17th Ed., Section 10, p.1, New Delhi). The victims again are the poor in the coastal areas - fishermen or otherwise.

A part of the raw material that is either collected from the forests or produced by the poor peasants in the backward districts under the newly introduced system of change in the cropping pattern initiated by industries is often meant for the export market. Exports have moved up from Rs. 487 crores in 1970-71 to Rs. 2,057 crores in 1980-81 and with the establishment of FPI, the rise is even more rapid at the rate of 10 per cent per annum in the next four years (Kamala Suri, *Economic Times*, May 19, 1988). The close link between the bourgeoisie and the state became clear only in 1978 with the Government buckling under the pressure to permit industries to enter rural area and even granting a 85 cc tax concession to boot (M. Savur, The Relations between Capitalist Class and the State in *Capitalist Development in India*—ed. Ghansham Shah, forthcoming). It was only a step forward for GOI to consider FPI as a thrust area in the Seventh Plan[7] and in 1988 June to set up a separate Ministry with Jagdish Tytler in charge of it. It is in keeping with this trend that the Government announced various fiscal concessions for 1988-89. These include: (1) Reduction of custom duty from 55 to 35 per cent ad valorem on 34 items of food producing and packing machinery. Excise duty on other parts of a plant has been halted (*Economic Times*, 14-3-1988). That is a boon for the MNCs. (2) Reduction of excise duty from 10 to 5 per cent for vegetables, fruit and nuts if manufactured in rural areas by a registered co-operative. (3) Certain types of meat, milk foods and preparations of certain types of cheese and butter made without the use of poor are also exempted from excise duty (*Financial Express*, 27/4/1988). It is well known that partial processing is done in villages for big FPI Corporations at the cooperative cottage level and through KVIC. And now government offers 5-22 per cent cash compensatory support on export of certain raw agricultural products as consumer packs as well as for 50 processed items (*Economic Times*, 19/5/1988). Government has delicensed fruit and vegetable processing industry from March 1988, unless it is set up by a MRTP/FERA Co. (*Economic and Commercial News*, Vol. 17, No. 52, 26 December 1987). Subsidiaries, franchises and ancillaries, are part of the game played by MNC's and the definition of small scale industry itself has changed from the original Rs. 5 lakhs to less than

Rs. 35 lakhs for very small, and less than Rs. 45 lakhs for ancillaries in the Seventh Plan.

Today there are 2,300 units licensed under the fruit production order. The total installed capacity of the fruit and vegetable processing industry alone, both in organized and unorganized sector, is 3.79 lakh tons per annum, and there are another 32 units listed under DGTD with the total capacity of 1.20 lakh tons per annum (*Financial Express*, 27/4/1988).

In the food production industry as a whole the current production is estimated as 140,000 tons valued at over Rs. 150 crores. Yet, it represents only 36.9 per cent of the installed capacity in 1988 (*Financial Express*, 27/4/1988). This confirms Malkhan's observation that most units are losing on all items in the international markets. But this is not true for a few internationally well established FPI who have set up associate companies in India like Food Specialities an associate of Nestle's, Britannia Industries; an associate of Huntley Palmers, Hindustan Cocoa of Cadbury, and HMM of Horlicks. These companies have emerged with a whopping success so much so that their shares are in demand at 9 to 10 times their face value. Their prospects have brightened further because of the Government's new thrust in FPI. But the new entrants even if they hail from well established Indian industrial houses like Kothari's, and are in collaboration with an MNC like General Food Corporation; or Godrej's Noble Soya which is in collaboration with Kibu of Japan, or Hindustan Foods in collaboration with Glaxo, have failed to take off. This is true too of an FPI like the TGL group which has used public sector CFTRIs and Defence Food Research's findings. CFTRI, one must remember, was thoughtfully set up in the early years of independence with high ideals to create nutritious but inexpensive ready-to-eat or easy-to-cook foods to cater to the needs of the vast starving masses that were created by the colonial rule. But it has always catered to the needs of FPI, be it idli and dosa mix or high protein Triptin. Devan Malkan puts down the reasons of the failure of big houses on the food processing front due to their low investment, (not exceeding Rs. 5 crores), and their inadequate sales promotion to catch the new rising middle class. This is a small but potential class with double incomes and like the Western urban middle class too busy for time consuming traditional cooking. He also noted that the sales began to dip with rising prices. In other words, the main limitation of the Indian market is the low purchasing power and the small size of the urban rich and the upper middle class which is unable to sustain the growth of FPI.

Several FPI including Swedish WIMCO which has been processing tropical fruit exclusively for export mart faced a catastrophic loss with the withdrawal of Russians from Indian Food Processing Market[8] (WIMCO Ltd., 65th Annual Report for the year ending December 1987). Soon enough a newspaper announcement read, "Indo-Soviet tie up in fruit processing on the anvil." The object was to set up an export-oriented vegetable and fruit processing unit in India (*Indian Post*, 26/12/1987) which would again spell disaster.

SUMMARY AND CONCLUSION

Our survey of the growth of FPI indicated that the actual producers and collectors of raw material viz. some middle, but mostly a mass of poor peasantry (mainly in the backward areas), fishermen and tribals get the worst of the deal. The whole process was spanwned by international bourgeoisie which was driven to it by a historical necessity and then supported by multilateral organizations like the WB and FAO and by international development agencies like USAID, SIDA ,etc.

The sophisticated urban based Indian industrial bourgeoisie, sensitive to changing economic situations had at about the same time entered the rural areas. But in the international game of agro business and industry based on food processing lost its independence in relation to the powerful MNs. This bourgeoisie has in collaboration with MNC's either destroyed the numerous small rural bourgeoisie which had entered FPI or put it in limbo. The Government's all-out support to the FPI by identifying it as a thrust area has also not generated any employment. On the contrary it has driven the very raw material producers and collectors out of their traditional occupations and has left them high and dry—all in the name of "development."

We have not touched on the question of the nutritive value of processed food not deny its convenience and have pointed out that one of the main reasons for the failure of FPI in a third world country is due to the disarticulation of the town and country the roots of which can be traced back to colonial rule. The persistence of the problem in India 40 years after the colonizers have left (we only hint for lack of space), is because the Indian bourgeoisie chose to take an ostensibly capitalist path of development when it was too late in history to do and in the process has kept the country in a "satellite" position.

NOTES

1. Also for quick troop transport to political trouble spots, Thorner, *op. cit.*)
2. A similar unit has been set up at Jammu and Kashmir and was mooted in UP (P.S. Negi, *Horticultural Produce Marketing Technology and Marketing Management*, 1982, p.11, 31, Simla).
3. In Himachal Pradesh alone it rose from 645 meters as late as in 1975 to 74,083 meters by 1982.
4. The Ratnagiri peasantry who have long lost their precious Alfanso mango crop to the Bombay fruit merchants and FPI are now getting wise. They chose to eat rather than cultivate the cashew nut that was distributed to them for cultivation by the President of the Bombay Chamber of Commerce in 1978, with its promise to bear the cost of maintenance for 5 years. This was the same period when Konkan Development Corporation and Ford Foundation were negotiating cashew production in Ratnagiri (Rajadekshay). If this is an exception to the rule, it is also important to remember that the poor peasants of Ratnagiri are part proletariat of Bombay.
5. Even Professor K.N. Raj was a victim. CDS has many sprawling unattractive cocoa bushes in its compound - thanks to Cadbury.
6. The process is replicated in JK and mooted in UP (P.S. Negi, *op. cit.*).
7. The target for fruit and vegetable production for the end of the Seventh Plan is 68 million tons and the actual achievement till 1987 is only 54 million tons in 45:55 ration, *Economic Times*, 29/6/1987.
8. Incidentally for the first time it was unable to declare dividends. With the falling sales of matches WIMCO shifted its interest in FP and set up a very sophisticated plant to process tropical fruits under the brand name Sun Sip.

CHAPTER 11

Rural-Urban Nexus and Labour Mobilization in the Raniganj-Jharia Coalfields

—*Anjan Ghosh*

Miners all over the world constitute a special breed of industrial workers. Their isolated workplaces, hazardous and trying conditions of work and usually repressive management regimes created a sense of community which often underlies their militancy. It also makes them strike prone as Kerr and Seigel have noted.[1] But working in a rural environment the characteristics of the peasant are retained and adapted for industrial purposes. In this, as in India, colliery owners were not averse as it reduced capital costs. On the other hand this meant that mine workers were not completely 'habituated' to industrial work.[2] Not only did they maintain links with the land but it served as a source of autonomy and bargaining vis-a-vis work in the collieries. In other words miners were not completely proletarianised by virtue of their work in the mines. This has led observers to characterise their militancy as 'agrarian radicalism'[3]

A considerable body of literature has pointed to the persistence of communitarian rituals and loyalty[4] among migrant miners. These have contributed to the solidarity of mine workers importing a resilience to their opposition to managerial aggrandisement. Even in industrially advanced economies the community of miners remain a distinctive part of the industrial labour force. Thus the lore of the Appalachian coal miners or of the South Wales pitman in U.S.A. and Britain respectively, transmits a sense of community rarely found in other kinds of industrial work. The sense of affinity was exemplified by the 'pit villages' in Britain where the lives of the people revolved around the 'pit' or coal mine. The nature and rhythm of work in the mine, the proximate living enhanced the intensity of social interaction among the families of mine-workers, the inevitable pub and miner's tales, the sense of comaraderie born out of a knowledge of the dangers of underground work, defined a way of life in which the individual was subject to the community.[5] In modern Britain these 'pit villages' have remained as a significant vestige of community life.[6] Perhaps an understanding of these communitarian ties enables us to comprehend how the British miners sustained their historic 1982 strike for as long as they did. For one of the causes for which the miners were struggling was to preserve a way of life in the mining communities threatened with dismemberment and extinction by large-scale mechanisation and redundancies.

Hence the mobilization of mine-workers implies the construction of a community, demarcating the interests of the miners from that of the owners and management. It presupposes a notion of difference emanating from the process of production but ensconed also in the perception of different ways of life. In this paper I seek to present this difference in terms of the rural-urban differential in the coalfield and its impact on labour mobilization. The paper will focus on the post-independence period schematically representing the situation up to the contemporary period. Information will be pulled from several sources including my fieldwork as a non-participant observer in two collieries of the Raniganj-Jharia belt in 1979-81, as well as documentary and published sources.

Aspects of Rural-Urban Difference

The Raniganj-Jharia coal belt is not only the oldest coalmining region but even till today continues to produce the bulk of the coal in the country. It is also the principal supplier of coking coal. In 1984 there were 6,59,003 men and women employed by the coal industry with approximately a little over half of them working underground.

Most of the collieries in the Raniganj field are located in Burdwan district, more specifically in the Asansol subdivision of that district. In the Jharia- field the bulk of the collieries are located in the southern part of the district of Dhanbad. The railway line (chord line) connecting Howrah to Gaya bisects the district. The collieries of the Jharia- field are situated south of the railway line and spread in a south-westernly direction towards Baghmara and Chas. Both Burdwan and Dhanbad districts are more industrially developed in their respective states of

West Bengal and Bihar having a larger proportion of people engaged in non-agricultural pursuits than the state's average. Some aspects of these two districts are given in Table 11.1.

TABLE 11.1

People Employed in Non-Agricultural pursuits in Burdwan and Dhanbad Districts

	Burdwan	*West Bengal*	*Dhanbad*	*Bihar*
Total Population	3,916,174	44,312,011	1,466,417	56,353,369
Rural Population	3,024,184	33,344,978	828,389	50,719,403
Urban Population	891,990	10,967,033	638,028	5,633,966
Scheduled Castes	24.51%	19.90%	15.18%	14.11%
Scheduled Tribes	5.84%	5.72%	10.61%	8.75%
No. of towns	22	223	26	202
% of workers to Total Population	27.93%	27.91%	33.73%	31.03%
Other workers (% to Total workers)	45.19%	41.57%	64.92%	17.74%

Source: District Census Handbook, West Bengal-Burdwan District, 1971.
District Census handbook, Bihar-Dhanbad District, 1971.

From the information given above the relative salience of rural-urban relationship is evident. Thus in Burdwan, notwithstanding the presence of industries, the rate of urbanization is 22.78% compared to the West Bengal state average of 24.75%. To understand the situation in Burdwan it is necessary to keep in mind the fact that industrial growth and urban development have primarily been confined to the Asansol sub-division. According to an independent estimate the percentage of non-agricultural employment to total employment in the Asansol-Durgapur region increased from 42.61% in 1951 to 54.95% in 1966. In this, employment in manufacturing as percentage of total employment went up from 16.48% in 1951 to 25.63% in 1966. A significant aspect of urbanization in this region was that migrational flows contributed considerably to the urban population growth. They accounted for over two-thirds of the additional urban population between 1951-66.[7] More recently in 1985 a survey of coal mine-workers by the Asansol-Durgapur Development Authority (ADDA) found that while only 32% of the workers in Raniganj field were from West Bengal, 40% were from Bihar and another 23% from U.P.[8] Together Bihar, U.P. and Orissa provided 65% of the workers in the Raniganj coalfield.

In Dhanbad on the other hand the rate of urbanization is very high, 43.51% compared to the Bihar state average of 10%. As Vidyarthi noted that out of 29 new towns added to the Chhotanagpur region during 1951-61, 16 were added to Dhanbad district.[9] In the next decade out of 39 new towns in Chhotanagpur, 7 were found in Dhanbad district. Table-2 below shows the growth of urban population in Dhanbad city.

TABLE 11.2

Growth of Urban Population in Dhanbad City

Year	*Population*	*Decadel increase*
1951	79,475	36.8 (1941-51)
1961	2,89,913	264.79 (1951-61)
1971	6,38,028	120.08 (1961-71)
1981	1,066,866	67.21 (1971-81)

Source: (Vidyarthi: 1982).

In Dhanbad too migration has considerably augmented the urban growth of the district. The sex ratio of the district which is 792 compared to Bihar's 954 (females per 1000 males) in 1971 indicates the nature of migration which is primarily single working class males. Out of a total of 2,18,381 inmigrants to the district in 1951, the main contributory regions were Patna division - 46,414, Bhagalpur division - 41,313, Chhotanagapur division (excluding Purulia and Dhanbad) - 51,052 and states adjacent to Bihar - 46,816.[10] Thus the bulk of the migrants have come from within the state and the neighbouring areas. Among the migrants the Bhojpuri speaking people constitute a significant section. In 1961, 1,13,000 Bhojpuri speaking people were enumerated by the Census in the Chhotanagpur - Santhal Parganas region. In Dhanbad district the 1961 Census reported that 25% of the population was born outside the Chotanagpur—Santhal Parganas area[11]. An approximate idea of the social composition of the people categorised along rural- quasi urban-urban lines is given in Table 11.3.

TABLE 11.3
Spatial Distribution of Castes in Dhanbad District

Rural		*Quasi-Urban*		*Urban*	
Mahatos, Santals, Backward & Scheduled Castes	75%	Overrepresentation of Backward & Scheduled Castes	c. 50%	Brahmins, Kayasthas	c. 33%
Muslims	10%	Mahatos under-represented.		Banias, Backward castes Similar to Rural	
		Santals negligible compared to rural		Mahatos, and Santals grossly underrepresented.	
		Muslims	10%		

Source: (Rothermund: 1972:96)

Having discussed the nature of urban growth and development a few words on the agrarian characteristics of the two districts are in order. As the data above indicates both the districts are essentially rural with the bulk of the population in both residing in rural areas. Yet the nature of agricultural development in these two districts is distinct. The difference lies in the extent of irrigation. Burdwan district, especially its eastern part, is agriculturally well-developed. Ever since the introduction of the IADP in the district from the early 1960s rapid agricultural development has taken place leading to the emergence of a stratum of capitalist-farmers.[12] But this could happen primarily because the district has an extensive network of canals for irrigation. Thus in 1970-73, it had 50.18% of its gross cropped area under irrigation .[13] However, the Asansol subdivision remained agriculturally backward compared to the eastern part of the district because of its dependence on monsoons for cultivation. Moreover, as the land of the western part is undulating and less fertile, where centuries of mining having also damaged the land both in terms of subsidence as well as eroding its capacity to retain the moisture on the surface, the rural areas around the collieries in Burdwan district are not agriculturally prosperous. In Dhanbad district only 2.1% of its gross cropped area was irrigated in 1971.[14] Even this meagre irrigation was mainly derived from ponds and tanks, and therefore agricultural improvements were tardy. Most of the cultivating households were engaged in subsistence production with 83% holding less than 5 acres of land.[15] This means that the agricultural sector in Dhanbad is far more homogenous than in Burdwan. Also the communitarian response is more characteristic of Dhanbad than Burdwan in terms of state policy and industrialisation.[16]

Mobilising Coal Labour Patterns and Perspectives

Coal mines were dispersed in the rural areas. The mining settlements which accompanied a mine comprised of a few quarters primarily for the colliery officers, some *dhowrahs* or one room tenements for the workers lacking any kitchen or bathroom. The *dhowrahs* would be located in lines and were meant for the migrant workers. For some kinds of migrant workers like the CRO labour from Gorakhpur there were exclusive barracks which were specially guarded and the CRO labour was not allowed to mix with the other workers. They were in fact even paid a separation allowance. The *dhowrahs* were often allocated along ethnic lines and workers from particular areas or of particular castes tended to congregate together. However, only a few ever got accommodation in these *dhowrahs*. About 15-20% of the total workforce obtained such tenements and lived in unhealthy, unhygienic and overcrowded circumstances. Along with these mining settlements had a few shops. The habitat of the mine settlement was thus entirely under the control of the colliery management who could easily restrict entry of 'undesirable' elements like trade-union organisers. Hence the site of the mine constituted the hegemonic space of the management and they often resorted to policing it through their own 'watch and ward' staff, a nomenclature for the company's musclemen. All this made it difficult for union organisers to mobilize the workers at the mine site. Consequently they had to start from the village end and work their way into the colliery. I will illustrate this proposition through two case studies culled from my fieldwork data. I shall describe the way in which the workers in these two collieries were mobilised to form Left Unions. Later I will briefly indicate the patterns of mobilisation at the level of the coalfield to construct a comparative view.

Chinakuri colliery is not one of the old working mines of the Eastern Coalfields Limited (ECL). It is one of the largest mines of the ECL employing over 5,000 people for its four units comprising of 3 pits and 1 incline. Pit Nos. 1 & 2 together employ over 3000 people. The colliery became operational in the early 1950s and experienced one of the worst accidents in 1958 when a series of gaseous explosions killed over 200 people working underground. Before nationalisation in 1973 the colliery was owned by the Bengal Coal Company (BCC) of the Andrew Yule Group.

BCC was one of the largest coal companies and as a result its collieries were better managed and more technologically advanced than many of the smaller companies. Yet the Comapany was hostile and wary of any kind of autonomous unions. Coal-workers unions had been a transitory phenomenon before independence in the Raniganj coalfield. Unions or organisations had sprung up in collieries during times of dispute but soon became defunct after its resolution. As a result there was little continuity in workers organisations.

Soon after the "raisings" started in Chinakuri in 1953, the astute Bengal Coal Company management invited the newly formed INTUC to set up their union in the colliery. Thus from the beginning the INTUC union was identified with the owners rather than the workers' interest. It was the company's *chaprasis* and *gomasthas* who manned this union. Such an authoritarian management system was sporadically resisted, but an attempt to form an alternative union was initiated by a school teacher from neighbouring Mithani, Madhu Banerjee (MB) in 1954. He had earlier been involved in nationalist politics during his college days and had veered leftwards. His estrangement with his family because of his politics brought him in search of a job to Mithani, a small colliery close to Chinakuri. His political inclination led him to investigate the condition of colliery workers in the neighbourhood and soon involved him in trade union organisation both at Mithani colliery and at Chinakuri. At Chinakuri he could initially gain an entry into the *dhowrahs* because of his standing as a teacher on the pretext of visiting his students. In the beginning organisational work was carried out clandestinely among particular section of workers. The organising was done by individuals contacted by MB who generally came from the ranks of skilled workers like electricians.

The coal cutting machine drivers were the first to be organised. Meetings were held in the *dhowrahs* and soon they demanded higher basic wages. After the machine drivers it was the turn of the wagon loaders. They were made to work as casual workers as no appointment letter was issued to them. They demanded that proper appointment letters be issued to them. After this the stone-cutters engaged in pit-sinking were mobilised over their demands of absorption in the labour-force. These stone-cutters were mostly tribals (Mundas from a neighbouring village) who were utilised for digging work during the sinking of the pit purely as casual workers. Scarcely were they retained in the colliery work-force permanently after the sinking of the pit.

Faced with the inroads of workers' organisation the BCC management resorted to charge sheets, suspensions, arrests and intimidation of worker- activists. The 'Watch and Ward' staff and the *chaprasis* of the Company including its *gomasthas* maintained a strict vigil so that MB could not enter the Chinakuri mine area. But this could not stem the popular support of the workers for the new organisation. In December 1954, during the elections to the canteen committee the candidate of the company union got one vote while the workers' representative Janardan Singh got 226 votes. In July 1956, the workers of BCC and Equitable Coal Company collieries struck work in the wake of the Mazumdar Award. The wage award which had been eagerly awaited by the workers turned out to be a disappointment since very meagre increase of wages was proposed. The resentment of the workers was vent through a month-long strike led by the erstwhile INTUC leader Deven Sen. During this long strike of colliery workers in the Raniganj field Sen mobilised the workers through *haat* meetings and meetings in the villages. The strike of the miners was sustained by the assistance of the villagers.

Soon after this strike MB led a procession into Chinakuri which turned the tide against the company's musclemen. The procession was 1000 strong, made up of Mundas, Bauris, Santals and Nuniyas armed with their rough and ready weapons like bows and arrows, *lathis*, *da* and *bati*. They confronted the Company's musclemen led by Rajbali *gomastha*. The workers got the better of the *pahalwans* and thus broke the back of the Company's terror tactics.

However, even thougn the BCC management carried out informal discussion and negotiations with the AITUC union at Chinakuri yet they were not recognised for bargaining purposes or invited to wage negotiations. It was only in 1958 that the Company invited 3 Trade Unions - Colliery Majdoor Congress (Sen faction affiliated to HMs), Colliery Majdoor Congress (INTUC), Colliery Majdoor Sabha (AITUC) to the wage negotiations thus acceding de-facto recognition. The Chinakuri union was affiliated initialy to AITUC but later was affiliated to UTUC.

The situation in Dharmabandh Colliery of the Bharat Coking Coal Limited (BCCL) is symptomatic of the Jharia Coalfield. Located away from the main Katras-Chas road and about 16 kms. from Dhanbad City, the story of Dharmabandh is one of violence and counter-violence. The colliery which was commissioned in 1925 has changed hands many times. Initially owned by Shaw Wallace and Co. it was later sold to the Sethias before being incorporated into BCCL in 1971. The colliery has difficult working conditions as the coal seam is only 3-4 ft. high.

As early as 1947, Sadhan Gupta had formed a workers union in Dharmabandh affiliated to the AITUC. In May 1947 there was a month long strike over payment of wages which caused damage to the colliery equipment. In July 1951 the manager of the colliery was assaulted as he had charge-sheeted some trammars. On April 28, 1952 the agent of the colliery B.N. Banerjee was lynched by some workers when he was returning home from work. The immediate cause of the provocation was that some workers had been dismissed previously. This led to the hanging of 3 workers in 1954 who were convicted for the murder—Gupteshwar Pathak, Dukhit Dusadh and Mahabir Teli. Sadhan Gupta as the trade union leader was implicated in the case and was given life imprisonment.

For a time the labour movement at the colliery suffered a setback. But around 1958 the INTUC union became powerful. Under the leadership of Shri. B.N. Jha the Congress union consolidated its position. But in 1967 facitionalism among the union leaders led to a clash and ultimately to the decline of the union.

In 1968 again some workers took the initiative and invited A.K. Roy to form a trade union in the colliery. Roy held a meeting at the colliery where he asked the workers to form their own union branch at the colliery and said that he wanted the workers to become their own leaders and not depend on outside leadership. However, he maintained that if they formed their union branch with majority support then he would cooperate with them. The arrival of Roy on the scene initiated a series of violent clashes as the management sought to neutralise the BCKU union. In April 1968 and again in February 1972 clashes ensued between the Company's musclemen and workers. The latter incident was especially important involving the CRO labour and the *pahalwans*. The CRO or Gorakhpur labour were the most oppressed sections of the colliery labour force. They were a form of bounded labour brought to the mines on 11 months contract and kept segregated from the other workers in guarded barracks. They were kept under constant surveillance and not allowed to be members of unions. It was these CRO workers who rebelled and became ardent supporters of the BCKU union. This incurred them the wrath of the management and the Personnel Officer instigated the attack of the musclemen against the CRO workers. Four workers were killed in the clash of February 1972, two by the *pahalwans* and two more in the subsequent police firing. Since that time February 4 has been observed as a Martyr's Day by the BCKU in the colliery.

The workers of Dharmabandh colliery were able to establish an autonomous union. But this they could achieve because the people of the neighbouring villages assisted and supported their struggle. The people in the rural areas not only sustained the struggle through providing shelter to the workers in times of distress but also mobilised in their favour and fought against the *chaprasis* of the Company. Moreover many of the workers came from these villages like Dharmabandh, Tetulia, Kharkharee. Consequently the worker-peasant alliance was forged 'spontaneously.' It was not for nothing that the BCKU dominated collieries were located in outlying reaches of the Jharia field contiguous to the rural areas rather than Jharia town.

CONCLUDING REMARKS

The above narratives are symptomatic of a pattern of interest articulations between the town and country. Even while recognising the 'quasi-urban' nature of the mining settlements yet the nature of its relations to the countryside is not entirely different from that of the town/city. Essentially it is a relation of power where the hegemonic space established in the urban settlements seeks to extend its control over the rural hinterland. In order to do so it must continuously fragment the sense of solidarity which persists among the peasants. As long as this solidarity remains and is directed towards addressing their demands against the city it remains a potential threat to the industrial production process which works unilaterally. The so-called rural links of the industrial work force is thus a source of its autonomy from the control of industrial but predatory capital.

NOTES AND REFERENCES

1. C. Kerr, & Seigel, 'The inter-industry propensity to strike', in Dubin & Kornhauser (eds): Industrial Conflict, New York, 1954.

2. H. Braverman, Labour and Monopoly Capital, New York, 1973.
3. J. Petras, & M. Zeitlin 'Miners and agrarian radicalism', American Sociological Review: 32: 578-86, 1967.
4. J. Clyde Mitchell, *Labour and Monopoly Capital,* New York, 1956. See also J. Clyde Mitchell, The *Kalela Dance*, Manchester, 1956; M. Taussig, Coming Home: migration and ritual in a Gautemalan village, CDAS, Montreal, 1981.
5. T. Hall, King Coal, Harmondsworth, 1981. See also N. Dennis, & Others, *Coal is Our Life*, London, 1969.
6. R. Frnyknberg, *Communities in Modern Britain,* Harmondsworth, 1971.
7. A. Bhattacharya, 'Urbanisation and employment trends: A Case-study of Asansol-Durgapur region', *Economic & Political Weekly:* 5 : 7 : 345 - 6, 1970.
8. Asansol-Durgapur Development Authority (ADDA), *Survey of Coal-mine workers* 1985, Asansol, 1986.
9. L.P. Vidyarthi, 'The Emergence of Industrial Anthropology in India', Eastern Anthropologist: 35 : 3 : July-Sept., 1982.
10. P. Pradeep, & A.N. Das, 'Organisation of the future? A case study of the Bihar Colliery Kamgar Union', *Human Futures:* Autumn, 1979.
11. N. Sengupta 'Background of the Jharkhand Question', in N. Sengupta (ed): *Fourth World Dynamics: Jharkhand,* New Delhi, 1982.
12. S. Haldar, 'Economic classes in a Burdwan village', *Socialist Perspective*, 1988.
13. N. Shah, *District-level data for key economic indicators,* CMIE, Bombay, 1982.
14. Ibid.
15. R.N. Maharaj, 'The impact of state policy on agriculture', in D. Rothermund & others (eds): *Urban Growth and Rural Stagnation,* New Delhi, 1982.
16. G. Heuze, *Dhanbad, exception or model,* CSSSC, Occasional Paper No. 92, 1987.

CHAPTER 12

The Country-Town Nexus : A Case Study of Entrepreneurs in Eastern Uttar Pradesh

Sheobahal Singh

Introduction

A net rural-urban dichotomy is hypothetical and not real. The two extremes are ideal-typical forms of society with heuristic significance for understanding the evolutionary process of social and cultural change.[1] Sociological literature is full of typologies like rural-urban, community-society[2], mechanical-organic solidarity,[3] and sacred–secular social organisations.[4] Generally, the first part of it is considered to represent the traditional rural society and the second part is equated with the modern urban society. In fact, the concept of rural-urban dichotomy is irrelevant and misleading.[5] Several studies reveal that many characteristics which are considered to be typical for a village are not absent even in the metropolis. As far as smaller towns are concerned it will be difficult and also futile to distinguish them from the village community in terms of their social and cultural forms. There are evidences that joint family structures considered to be a characteristic of the rural-agrarian society are found to be predominant in the urban centres.[6] Caste and kinship as the basis of neighbourhood relations are not uncommon in the Indian cities. Hoselitz writes : "that Indian cities...even some of the largest ones..show sizeable quarters which have preserved their rural character and in which life is carried on under general conditions only little different from those of the villages".[7]

Country-town nexus in India

Country-town relationship in India is a reality. Most of the urban people are immigrants from rural areas and the commuters form a sizeable group of people who play an important role in the cultural symbiosis that takes like place between the town and the country. Sellers of agricultural produce, vegetables and milk and labourers and servicemen who are the inhabitants of the villages not far off from the town go to the urban centres for appropriating their economic interest.[8] But the natural corollary of this is a direct culture-contact and social and ideological transformation of the rural way of life. The influence of culture and communication expands not only to the hinterland but to a whole region and in some cases to the country as a whole.[9] Geographical literature is replete with the contributions on rural-urban nexus. The concepts like urban-fringe and urbanization[10] have emerged out of the continuing relationship between the urban centres and their rural counterpart. Semi-urban pocket is yet another concept which refers to a partly-rural and partly-urban situation of the hinterland. There is a group of people in the village who mediates between the country and the town and helps in interpenetration of each other's social and cultural aspects of life. Early geographical studies concentrated only on physical delimitation and identification in defining the rural-urban fringe, but recently some scholars have started looking into social and cultural transformation taking place in the rural areas lying in close proximity with the urban centres.[11] A tendency towards social and spatial segregation, selective immigration, and collapse of geographical and social hierarchy have been observed on the fringe.[12]

A sociological analysis of country-town nexus is somewhat complex. Changing dimensions of rural-urban interaction have not been adequately researched. A macro-level analysis of rural-urban relationship would require an identification of the hierarchy of the towns on one hand and a similar gradation of the villages according to the extent of physical proximity with towns on the other. The nature of relationship and cultural influence offered by the urban ecology varies from town to town. Today the towns of the categories IV and below exhibit very little differentiation compared to most of the villages except of course some physical and demographic differences. A hierarchy of the villages too may be discerned as far as urban impact is concerned. The urban impact on the villages which are close to a town is found to be different from the ones lying in remote areas. While the impact on the fringe villages is more or less general and uniformally spread over whole of the village community, it is specific and sectoral in the distant villages. It is the middle and upper class people of these villages who are under the influence and therefore sufficiently urbanized. It is a fact that the people of these classes due to their educationally and economically advantageous position have easy and frequent access to the cities. The urbanization generated economic development varies from one set of villages to another. Land use and behavioural pattern in the villages near a city are rational, commercially motivated and enterprising, whereas the distant villages have not yet shifted much away from the traditional outlook and economic activity despite several programmes for rural transformation having been planned and executed.

Urbanization is equated with industrialization. It is only partly true. Cities existed in India even before industrial revolution.[13] The period of 1950's experienced a slow rate of urbanization despite rapid industrialization in the decade.[14] History of cities in India goes back to Indus-valley civilization. The cities, then, were primarily the centres of religious and educational activities and the place of commerce and trade. Growth of cities with industrial character in India began as a consequence of entrepreneurial upsurge in the country mainly from the beginning of the twentieth century. Migration to cities, induced by the industrial expansion did contribute to urban explosion, but the root cause of this process is not as much the pull of the cities - as a 'push' from the villages, no longer able to accommodate the surplus population and to satisfy the new kind of needs and modern social and economic outlook of the people. The flood to the towns in the Third World no longer bears any relationship to expanding urban economics and opportunities; underemployment in the villages is being exchanged for increase in unemployment in the towns.[15] Opportunities for advancement in the rural areas are poor, and subsistence agricultural economy prevails over much of the developing world including India. Agrarian over-population and exhaustion of soil, incidences of drought and famine make farming a hazardous way of life.

Urbanization in India has been slow as compared to that of the West. The main cause of this slow urbanisation is a lack of needed economic development.[17] The decadence of country-town connections is another factor leading to slow urbanization. The 1921 census reports:

"It will be observed here that while the towns with population above 50,000 have increased by over sixteen per cent in the last decade (1911-21), the increase has been considerably less in those between 5000 and

50,000, while the population of the towns between 10,000 and 20,000 has not even kept place with the progress of the general population of this country. The significance of these comparisons lies in the strong indication which they give of the gradual decadence of the mediumsized country-towns and the growth of the larger cities and towns under the influence of commercial and industrial development."[17]

This kind of process in India has led to over-urbanization of big cities which are turning to become a menace. Solution to this lies in the development of entrepreneurship in rural areas and availability of other avenues for greater country-town nuxus.

The case of carpet industry in Bhadohi

The carpet industry of Bhadohi—a town in Eastern Uttar Pradesh (U.P.) is an apt example to show how entrepreneurship leads to the establishment of a close rural-urban nexus. Bhadohi is internationally known for the woollen carpets manufactured there. No other industry or business exists in the town. Woollen carpets are a luxury commodity to be sold at an exhorbitant price. The carpet industry has played a big role in the economic development of the town. Although carpet weaving was a traditional occupation of Muslims,[18] today the Hindus of different castes have not only out-numbered the Muslims, but also have beaten them in business performance. Caste has not played much role in entrepreneurial involvement. However, the fact that *Banias* are more adaptive to occupational opportunities is fairly evident.

While many Indian handicrafts have succumbed to the challenges of technological modernization, the carpet industry-one of the urban handicrafts[19], which dates back to about 400 years, has not only successfully withstood the onslaught of technological revolution, but has flourished over the years due to its adaptive capability.

Carpet manufacturing involves a good deal of specialization. The whole organization opens up employment opportunities to a large number of workers and represents a tightly knit nexus of interrelationships among people engaged in the industry at different levels ranging from weavers scattered in the villages to the manufacturer-entrepreneurs in the town. The processes in the carpet manufacturing include picking and sorting of wool, carding, spinning, dyeing, weaving, trimming and washing.

Although the carpet industry is a cottage industry, it has many characteristics of the capitalist system of production. The industry runs in a putting-out manner. A major part of carpet manufacturing involves weaving, which is carried out on looms by weavers in the villages around the town. In most of the cases weavers have their own looms. Only a few weave on the looms owned by master-weavers. In certain cases manufacturers or commission agents give some amount of money in advance to the weaver enabling him to instal a loom. In this way he is contractually bound to the creditor-manufacturer for weaving the carpets. Weavers are mainly from among the lower castes and the Muslims. The high caste people in the villages do not weave carpets themselves. They work either as commission agents or suppliers of the, woven carpets to the manufactures in the town. Some high caste men have become carpet manufacturers and exporters.

The manufacturers have installed workshops in the town where trimming, washing and finishing are carried out. The number of workers in a workshop ranges from two to fifty dependeing upon the magnitude of the work. It is physically impossible for the manufacturer to employ a large number of weavers under one roof who can work for him at the same time. A weaver is happy with this system as he finds it economically more gainful to undertake the weaving work in his own house where he is able to take care of his household liabilities too. In addition to his earnings from weaving, he carries out his agricultural work on the small piece of land he possesses. The whole region in a radius of about fifty kilo metres is involved in the carpet manufacturing. The manufacturer provides raw material to the weaver who after having woven it hands it over back to the manufacturer. The industrial relationship forms the basis of a wider social interaction between the manufacturer in the town and the weavers and commission agents in the villages.[20]

Entrepreneurship and economic development

The entrepreneurship pattern in the carpet industry of Bhadohi has built a profound country-town nexus. The town which is known exclusively for carpet manufacturing depends chiefly on the surrounding villages and their primary economic activity. The labour-intensive industry of woollen carpets is able to meet the demands of rugs only on the basis of involvement of the village people on a large scale. The carpet industry of Bhadohi contributes about 90 per cent of the woollen carpets being exported from India. Around fifty per cent of the total cost incurred on the production goes to the weaver. There is probably no industry in the world where capital-labour ratio is entirely in favour of labour as in the carpet industry. Weaving is a semi-skilled labour, hence relatively scarce. The excessive demand of carpet from foreign countries has created a cut throat competition among manufacturers. Since the quantity of output in the industry depends on the number of efficient weavers, the manufacturer has to have healthy and cordial relations with the weavers in order to meet the demand in time. The form of exploitation generally attributed to by the capitalists is almost non-existent in the carpet industry of Bhadohi.[21]

A rapid growth of carpet industry in Bhadohi has given a big fillip to economic development as seen in the form of reduced unemployment, problem, increase in the proportion of secondary and tertiary industry and decrease in the primary industry,[22] and further in the form of changes taking place in the existing production pattern from within.[23] Unlike towns, in the villages, it is very difficult to discern any reduction in the primary sector, as even the introduction of secondary and tertiary industry does not necessarily lead to a complele withdrawal from agriculture under normal conditions. The villages in the Bhadohi area, due to urban contact and entrepreneurial expansion, have been blessed with considerable degree of economic development. There is no conspicuous loss in agriculture. Instead it has been added with an enormous growth in secondary industry in the form of one or the other kind of carpet work being carried out by the people in their homes.

Social Consequences of carpet industry

The development of carpet industry has led to a drastic economic change and has disrupted the traditional so-called organic structure of the caste system. Since almost all lower castes barring a few (which who form the basic components of traditional jajmani system which still (persists) in the villages ofcourse not in such a rigid form), have switched over to carpet weaving, the social and economic relationship among the village people has undergone a drastic change. It is less sacrosanct, less authoritarian and less inequalitarian. The village community has become modern. The most affected by the industry is the agrarian set up. New kind of class formations are coming up. The Brahmins and Kshatriyas who enjoyed the highest social and economic position are gradually loosing their economic supremacy over other castes. The main confrontation is observed between the Kshatriyas (ex-zamindars) and Ahirs (an agriculturist caste). The Kshatriyas who abstained from tilling the land themselves and are still not psychologically prepared to do so, have suffered a decline due to non-availability of agricultural labourers, who have now shifted to weaving. The Ahirs on the other hand earn handsome amount of money from weaving and simultaneously cultivate their own land. They are much better– off and expanding their landholdings by purchasing land from the Kshatriyas. This has resulted into the enhancement of status of the middle castes engaged in agriculture to the higher class due to the relegation of the economic status of the higher castes.

The caste-based economic inequality ingrained in the rural social structure has been thwarted by the proliferation of carpet industry in the Bhadohi-Mirzapur belt. a considerable degree of urbanization, style of life, interpersonal relations and social and economic orientation have been affected by the economic development brought about by the carpet industry. The industry has served to build a deep nexus between the town and the villages around it and opened a gate for faster rural-urban interpenetration of material and non-material aspects of social life. However, the interaction between these cultures may not be uniform and equal. It is most likely that in the material sense the interpenetration of rural-urban elements may be substantial, but in terms of non-material aspects of change the interpenetration may fall short.

It is needless to emphasise that the present trend of urbanization in India is lamentable in so far as a large number of rural people are forced to migrate to the large cities in search of a job, resulting into an economous growth of metropolitan cities leading consequently to problems of housing, transportation, slum-dwelling, civic facilities and hygiene. One of the solutions to the menace of such a trend would be to put a positive check on migration to urban centres and this can best be done by bringing about rural transformation, promoting entrepreneurship and encouranging self-employment in rural areas. Several attempts for rural uplift have been made by the government since 1950 but none has been effective enough to meet the objective. The Community Development Programmes and Land Reforms could not bring about desired results. The growth of small and cottage industries would probably be the only solution to the problems of poverty, unemployment and hazards of urban growth. India's industrial policies have always been favourable to the large sector and big business houses leading to the concentration of economic power, ignoring the merit of small and medium sized industries in reference to a developing country in which people have small capital to invest and large number of persons to wait for employment. From the beginning of 1970's the government has been paying some attention to rural industrialization but due to administrative lapses and structural constraints, industries have not grown in rural areas. Large funds supplied by the financial institutions financed projects in large urban centres rather than in the rural areas. Further the funds instead of benefitting small entrepreneurs and artisans for whose benefit again the programme was launched actually benefitted large industrial units.[24]

Currently the government has shown a keen interest in integrated rural development and entrepreneurial growth but simply announcement of various schemes and extension of financial assistance will not bring concrete and substantial results unless the government is directly involved in the programme, and a conducive industrial climate is created and the people are infused with entrepreneurial aptitude and acumen. What is required on the part of the government is to counter the forces which are successfully active in the misutilization of governmental resources. The concessions and assistance meant for the rural poor and the small sector are quite often manipulated by the rural elites and the owners of medium and large scale industrial units in their favour. The administrative staff is observed to be just unmindful of the proper utilization of funds. The recipient of the assistance is either wrongly chosen or he wrongly spends the offered money abandoning the project for which it was meant. There is an administration-rural elite nexus to dispel and frustrate the intended objectives of the programmes.

Concluding Remarks

The country-town nexus can be strengthened and be made gainful by planning a systematic industrial growth, and direct economic interdependence between the village and the city. This will be possible by confining small and medium scale industries to rural areas and allowing large scale heavy industries to grow in the main urban centres. The decentralized manufacturing would not only promote interaction between the country and the town but also reduce the rate of migration by eliminating the 'push' factor, cut the concentration of economic power and alleviate poverty. To achieve this end, a long range economic policy has to be adopted to create social, political and industrial climate, conducive to entrepreneurial supply and dissolution of administration-elite nexus.

REFERENCE

1. R. Redfield, The *Folk Culture of Yucatan,* Chicago: Chicago University Press, 1941. See also P.A. Sorokin, C.C. Zimmerman, *Principles of Rural-Urban Sociology,* New York: Henry Holt, 1929.
2. Ferdinand. Tonnies, *Gemeinschaft and Gesellschaft* tr. and ed. by C.P. Loomis as *Fundamental Concepts in Sociology,* New York: American Book Co., 1887.
3. E. Durkheim, The *Division of Labour in Society,* Illinois: Free Press, 1947.
4. P. Becker, Howard *Through Values to Social Interpretation, Greenwood.,* 1968.
5. R.D. Lambert, 'Some Impact of Urban Society upon Village Life' in Roy Turner (ed.), *Indian's Urban Future, Berkeley,* California Uni. Press, 1962.
6. K.M. Kapadia, 'Rural Family Pattern: A Study in Urban-Rural Relationship', Sociological Bulletin 1956: Vol. V, No. 2.; See also Singh, Sheobahal, Entrepreneurship and Social Change, Jaipur: Rawat Publications, 1985.
7. B.F. Hoselitz, 'The Role of Urbanization in Economic Development: Some International Comparisons' in Roy Turner (ed.) Indian's Urban Future, Berkeley; California Uni. Press, 1962.
8. R.L. Singh, Banaras: *A Study in Urban Geography,* Banaras: Nand Kishore and Brothers, 1955.
9. R.B. Andrews, , 'Elements in the Urban-Fringe Pattern', J*ournal of Land and Public Utility Economics,* Vol. 18, 1942. and Kishore and Brothers, 1955.
10. H.W. Balk, 'Rurbanization of Worcester's Environs', *Economic Geography* Vol. 21, 1945.
11. R.O. Harvey, & W.A.B. Clark, 'The Nature and Economics of Urban Sprawl', Land Eco., Vol. 41, 1965.
12. R.E. Pahl, The *Metropolitan Fringe in Hertfordshire,* London : London School of Economics, 1965.
13. R.K. Mukerjee, *Man and His Habitation*—A Study in Social Ecology, London: Longmans Green & Co., 1940.
14. A. Bose, 'Six Decades of Urbanization in India, 1901-1961, *The Indian Economic and Social History Review,* Vol. 11, No. 1, 1965.
15. Alan B. Mountjoy, *The Third World: Problems and Perspectives, London* : Macmillan Press, 1980.
16. K. Davis, *'Urbanization in India : Past and Future in India's Urban Future'*, ed. by Roy Turner, Berkeley, California Uni. Press, 1962.
17. *Census of India* 1921, Vol. 1, p. 66 See also *Census Report* 1974, On Carpet Looms and Weavers of Varanasi, Mirzapur, Allahabad and

Jaunpur Districts of Uttar Pradesh (U.P. Bhadohi All India Carpet Manufacturers Association).

18. A. Mukhtar, *Report on Labour Conditions of Carpet Weavers of India,* New Delhi : Government of India Pub., 1942.
19. D.R. Gadgil, *Indian Revolution in India in Recent Times,* 1860—1939. Delhi : Oxford University Press, 1942.
20. Sheobahal Singh, *'Organization of the Carpet Industry of Bhadohi',* Economic & Political Weekly, Review of Management, May 1979.
21. Sheobahal Singh, 'Marxian Theory of Surplus Value and The Carpet Industry', *The Eastern Anthropologist,* Vol. 32, No. 4, 1979.
22. C. Clark, *The Conditions of Economic Progress,* London : Macmillan & Co., 1957.
23. J.A. Schumpeter, The *Theory of Economic Development,* New York : Oxform University Press, 1967.
24. V.S. Mahajan, *Growth of Agriculture and Industry in India,* New Delhi: Deep & Deep Publications, 1983.

CHAPTER 13

Role of Merchants in Town-Country Nexus

—*Ila Shah*

SECTION 1

Any society undergoing social transformation must take into consideration the town and country nexus. This is largely because town predominantly specializes in the production of industrial goods and the country in agricultural production. Such a specialization results in exchange between them and our contention in this paper is that this exchange is largely in favour of the town and goes against the countryside resulting in uneven development. It is important to note that in the process of exchange, large transfer of surplus[1] takes place from country to town and this transfer, not only leads to capital accumulation and development of the towns but also adversely affects the development of the countryside. This hypothesis is evident from a case study of cotton trade[2] between Surendranagar town and its rural hinterland. Thus the present paper is an attempt to study the nature of exchange relations between cotton merchants of Surendranagar town and their counter parts in the countryside viz., the village traders and landlords who are also village traders-cum ginner and presser. The latter get hold of this surplus and even the product from within the countryside, from small and marginal farmers, landlords and landlords-cum-village traders.

The contribution of this paper lies in applying the historical method within the centre-periphery framework, to the study of town-country-nexus at the level of circulation. It is suggested that the present unequal exchange relations have roots in history. These are influenced and conditioned by many factors, in our area, for instance the most crucial being the social institutions of *Vyavhar* and *Sambandh* (to be discussed in Section 4). We also hold that the agro-climatic conditions are contributory factors to unequal exchange relations between town and country, leading to transfer of surplus from the countryside to the town. It is suggested that this transfer prevents development of the countryside and simultaneously leads to the development of the urban areas.

In order to get an integrated understanding of the processes and the nature of unequal exchange relations, the present paper is divided into 5 Sections. The following section briefly introduces the area of our study: Surendranagar town and Surendranagar District. In section 3 we briefly discuss the history of cotton cultivtaion in Surendranagar District and unequal exchange between town and country. Section 4 discusses the importance of the social institutions of *Vyavhar* and *Sambandh* and its integration and strengthening of the processes of unequal exchange. The last section briefly concludes the paper.

SECTION 2

Introduction to the area of our study:

Surendranagar District (SD) is one of the 19 Districts of Gujarat State. It holds a very strategic position as it links the Kathiawad peninsula to the rest of Gujarat. Hence, it is termed as the "Gateway to Saurashtra."[3]

The District headquarters, Surendranagar town (ST) is centrally located in Wadhwan taluka of the District. It is well connected by an efficient network of road and railways. The town is an important railway junction, which joins the peninsula in all four directions.

Rural Surendranagar District has specialised in the cultivation of cotton and has more than half (56.37) of its total cultivated area under cotton. Traditional Wagad and the modern 0-2 and V-797 varieties of cotton are cultivated. Cotton continues to be cultivated in SD due to favourable agro-climatic conditions of coastal, deltaic, alluvium, sandy, black, *goradu* soils, hot summers and cold winters. A hot climate is good for the cotton plant to grow and cool conditions are good at harvest time. Its arid climate inhibits the spread of pests.

Its average rainfall is 517mm (1961-80). This rainfall is very erratic and unevenly spaced during the rainy season. Failure of monsoon is one of the major causes of droughts, famines and sudden rains give rise to floods. Cotton generally requires 510 to 1150mm of rainfall in rainfed areas, but its spacing is very important. For instance, the September rains benefit the crop most when it is "flowering time". If water is not available, cotton fibre remains immature, weak and of low quality.[4] The quality of cotton in SD can decline by 6 - 10 counts. While irrigation just before harvest time can increase its output by 25-33 per cent, the lack of it can reverse the situation. To ease the situation, the district has 4 medium and 31 minor irrigation schemes [5] but inspite of this only 11.64% of the total area under cultivation is irrigated. This 11.64% of the irrigated area is shared in the ratio of 85:15 between cotton and non-cotton crops but this is capable of irrigating only 16% of the total area under cotton cultivation.

Geographically viewed, the arid and the extreme climate of Surendranagar District and the type of soils available in the Surendranagar District, seem to be two of the important reasons why cotton continues to be cultivated in the countryside despite its major limitations in the form of erratic and unevenly spaced rainfall and meagre irrigation facilities.

According to Dikshit[6] wheat generally grows where cotton grows. He shows how the economy of Gujarat gradually switched over to the cultivation of cash crops from food crops, almost totally in the post-independence period, specially to cotton cultivation "at the expenses of wheat". One of the reasons he mentions is that "the farmer is assured of an advance against cotton or tobacco which he finds helpful in keeping his general farmer economy in shape"[7] Our field work observation confirms that the above reason is the most important reason for the cultivation of cotton in the district. But it is important to note that rural Surendranagar District switched over to cotton cultivation "at the expense of food grains" not recently but around 1870s, under different socio-economic-political conditions. This is discussed in the next section. Today, the merchants of Surendranagar Town (STT) and the rural village traders (VTs) and land lord-cum-village trader-cum-ginner and presser (LLVTGP) enter into social and economic relationships of Sambandh and Vyavhar. The VT and LLVTGP, who take the loans from the STT, are forced to grow what is required by the STT, i.e. Cotton. This is largely because the STT is a trader in cotton. The VT and LLVTGP who refinance it at the rural level, compel the rural farmers to grow cotton, because at the rural level, the loans are prepaid "in kind". This credit nexus acts as a major constraint to the rural peasant's choice of crop and also his access to the free market. In other words, the pattern of specialisation of crop in the countryside is indirectly dictated and maintained by non-farmers: the STTs (Details in Section 4).

SECTION 3

History of Cotton Cultivation and Surendranagar Town (ST)

Surendranagar Town was established as a Cantonment Town by the British in 1864. It was known as Wadhwan Camp till independence. With the merger of Native States with the Indian Union, its name was changed to Surendranagar, after the last Native Prince of the state. By 1872, it was connected by railways to Ahmedabad in the East and to Bhavnagar in the South (1879-80). A criss-cross network of railways and roads linked up the rest of Kathiawad Peninsula to Bombay either *via* Surendranagar Town and Ahmedabad or by railways from Surendranagar Town to Bhavnagar and then by ship to Bombay.

The development of this infra-structure must be viewed in the context of events taking place all over the world, especially the American Civil War (1861-64). Till the war, America was an important source for the supply of raw cotton to the British textile industries. American supply of raw cotton was curtailed with the advent of war. Hence, when England was looking out for alternative sources of supply of raw cotton India was an ideal choice as it was already an exporter of cotton.[8] With this spurt in the demand for raw cotton, there was a massive switch over to cotton cultivation in many parts of rural India especially Gujarat and Surendranagar District.

In 1872, Wadhwan was already an exporter of cotton (1152 tons) and importer of food grains (1119 tons). Within a short span of 7 years viz. by 1879, the whole trend was intensiftied with cotton exports reaching the hall-mark of 5520 tons and the imports of food grains to 1937 tons.[9] This shift in the cropping pattern indicates the integration of the rural interiors of Surendranagar District and the Kathiawad Peninsula in the world economic system. The opening of the Suez Canal in 1869, which shortened the distance between the two countries by over 3000 miles had acted as an impetus.[10]

But it is important to note that the cost of construction of this infra-structure was predominantly borne by the Native States[11] and these were paid from the revenues collected from the peasants. So indirectly the impoverished peasants were compelled to cater to the British requirements and this further encouraged the process of peripherilisation of the rural economy of Kathiawad Peninsula, over and above establishing the processes of unequal exchange relations.

By nineteenth century the East India Company, a monopoly British trading company, had already entered into exchange relations which tended to be biased against the peasants, at two levels : buying the peasants produce at cheaper rates and by supplying what they required at higher rates.[12]

We have no direct evidence of unequal exchange of cotton during the British period, but the methods employed with the producers of indigo[13] or manufacturers of Salt[14] or the weavers[15] elsewhere in India should presumably also apply to the cotton growers of the same period. However in Gujarat, Rao Bahadur Ranchodlal does speak of unequal exchange of cotton in these terms:

> The Britishers are taking raw cotton through the middlemen (*dalal*) to their country for the use of their mill and the finished products are imported to our country. So, though we are producers of raw cotton, we have to depend upon other countries and above all have to pay double charges and the profits to the other country. [16]

Historical sequence leads us to believe that inspite of commercialisation of agriculture and development of infra-structure, especially transport, Indian industrial development which could have fostered the growth of Indian agriculture had received a death blow from the colonizers who established cotton industry in their own country.[17] So Indian agriculture and specially agriculture in Gujarat did not show much sign of development. So too was the case with the textile industry in Kathiawad[18] and industrial development in Surendranagar District. In fact, Surendranagar District was declared as an Industrially Backward District in 1971. Such a tendency, has further been aggravated by the exchange relations between town and country in modern times. This we propose to study in the subsequent section.

SECTION 4

Processes of Unequal Exchange

We had already noted in the previous section that unequal exchange between town and country and with the metropolis was exacerbated by colonial policies. In this section we propose to highlight the rôle of two Indian social institutions viz. *Vyavhar* and *Sambandh* in the perpetuation of cultivation of cotton in the countryside and the processes of unequal exchange between merchants of Surendranagar Town (SST) and the rural village traders (VT) and landlord-cum-village trader-ginner and presser (LLVTGP).

The dictionary meaning of the term *Vyavhar* is "intercourse"– mutual give and take relations. In the course of time there was a subtle change, which, we found in our field work, such that *Vyahar* actually now refers to pure *loans* given by the SSTs to VTs and LLVTGPs, which in turn, was given as *advance* by the latter to cultivators (small and marginal farmers, landlords and landlords - cum - village traders) and agricultural labourers[19]. It is of great significance that both the parties (SST and VT & LLVTGP) involved in this exchange insisted on the use of the term loans, as loans are always repaid "in cash" whereas advances in this area are generally repaid "in kind" - cotton. The former transaction is between town and country whereas the latter, was within the country side. In order words, *Vyavhar* is an economic relationship or a financial transaction.

The dictionary meaning of the term *Sambandh* is relationship or connection. The Gujarati meaning is given as "Sagai" which it explains as "betrothal or blood relations". In other words, a kinship bond. In Surendranagar District, however it refers to social interaction between SST and VT and LLVTGP. This interaction is generally restricted to social occasions such as weddings, *kathas, poojas* etc. It is not extended to marriage relations between them. It is not clear, at what point of time, the social relations got compounded with economic relations. But in some cases, they have continued for generations.

The whole process of exchange relations of cotton trade is hierarchical. Cotton passes through a chain relationship from country to town (Surendranagar Town) and then to metropolis. When expressed in terms of categories involved, we see that cotton trade passes through four inter related stage. It can be observed that at each stage of exchange, some classes are eliminated from the exchange relations and this generally happens with the economically less powerful classes. For instance in the second stage of exchange relations between country and town, the actual producers of cotton, the small and marginal farmers and the landlords are eliminated and in the third step of exchange relations, *i.e.* between urban area and metropolis, the VT and LLVTGP (from rural areas) and small STTs are eliminated. In the fourth stage of exchange relations between metropolis and metropolis, even big STTs are eliminated. Therefore, when we study the town-country-nexus, we study the exchange relations between merchants of Surendranagar (SST) and rural VT & LLVTGP. An understanding of this "chain" relationship is important because any changes such as failure of rain at the starting point (rural) will affect the end point (metropolis) and vice versa *i.e.* any glut or fall in prices at metropolis, will affect the countryside. To illustrate further, suppose the price of the cotton candy (2 bales) in the metropolis has gone down by Rs. 200-300 per candy, then the price at the rural level falls by Rs. 20 per maund, which is equivalent to Rs. 1,000/- per candy, (as 50 maunds of *kapas* make a candy). The effect is hardest at the lowest hierarchical level.

Of the two classes involved in exchange relations, the STTs are economically more powerful than the VTs and LLVTGPs, as the former gives loans to the latter. The urban SSTs are in a dominant position to dictate the terms of trade to VT and LLVTGP, who are in a dependent position, as they take loans. Thus the economic unequals of urban and rural areas (because of *Vyavhar* relations)become social equals due to Sambandh relations, especially when they participate freely in weddings, poojas, etc. but not in marriage relations. The interweaving of *Vyavhar* and *Sambandh* relations in the processes of unequal exchange relations, is the focus of this section. But before we go into the details of the processes of exchange we will briefly introduce STTs, VTs and LLVTGP.

Reasons Why STTS, VTs and LLVTGPs Enter Unequal Exchange Relations

STTs function in various capacities such as cotton merchants, traders in various forms of unprocessed raw cotton such as *Kapas*, *Kapasia*, and *roo*. As ginners and pressers of cotton, they deal in bales, as licenced financers/shroffs they finance VTs and LLVTGPs and as commission agents they sell to textile mills or cotton merchants in metropolitan areas. There are big and small STTs but the latter do not have direct access to the metropolitan markets, hence, they sell their products to big STTs in ST market intself.

The big STTs operate from a "pedhi". A "pedhi" is an establishment or an office. It is often over a century old and serves as the pillar of exchange relations over generations, bound through *Vyavhar* and *Sambandh*. The economic context of the two terms is possibly the result of the growing cash nexus in all relations including the network of kinship relations within the trading country. The big STTs employ 5-9 persons at the *pedhi*, the senior accountant being the most respected. He is the final authority in sanctioning the loans. Since *pedhis* continue from generation to generation, the young STTs find their senior accountant to be a valuable aide in initiating them into the intricacies of business.

The VTs are usually village grocers, money-lenders and traders in cotton. About 75-85 percent of the cotton produced in countryside is sold through them. VTs generally do not own land. But some money-lenders have become LLVT over a period of time and some of them have even taken to ginning and pressing of cotton in the district giving rise to the category of LLVTGP. They sell the remaining 15-25 percent of the cotton to STTs. Their number is very small in rural areas, less than 5% of the rural population. Of these 2-3% hold a valid licence for cotton trade. They require larger quantity of cotton because they gin and press their own bales, in near-by towns. Generally this category is present in villages which are well-connected by major roadways.

Of the two, LLVTGP have a better credit standing than the VTs because the former owns land and has over the years also become farmers by profession whereas VTs do not own land and are traders by profession. Hence, after 2-3 successive failure of monsoons, VTs are known to have run away as they could not repay the loans to the STTs. This does not happen in LLVTGPs case as he is tied to land. Hence, the nature of relationship with STT varies according to the risk taken by the STT.

It is important to note that both VTs and LLVTGPs are economically powerful classes of the rural society. They enter into unequal exchange relations at lower hierarchical level, *i.e.* within the rural area. They give cash advances to small and marginal farmers and landlords. The recovery is made "in kind" through cotton. Thus VTs & LLVTGPs are in a dominant position in the rural areas and dictate unequal terms of trade and benefit from it. But this is beyond the scope of the present study.

Although VT and LLVTGP take loans from STTs and because of Sambandh relations, they are forced to sell their cotton to STTs. This dependence is further aggravated because they do not have a direct access to the consumers - the mills in the metropolis. The dependence on STT increases in times of natural calamities when STTs continue to *ply* them with loans. Thus VTs and LLVTGPs continue to depend on STTs, for loans and for marketing their cotton, and considering the "benefits" they derive from the STTs, they are williing to accept a "price-cut".

There are many other reasons why the exchange relations are maintained by both the parties. By giving loans to VTs and LLVTGPs, the STTs secure for themselves a regular supply of a particular variety of kapas from different regions within the District. Again, the villages are widespread and collecting cotton from distant and remote villages would be a difficult and time-consuming process for a STT. This would reduce the quantum of his business. Hence, by financing a *few* VTs and LLVTGPs he is able to expand his business as the VTs and LLVTGPs "refinance" *many* cultivators at the rural level.

The reasons why the VTs and LLVTGPs borrow from the merchants is not the non-availability of institutional credit at the "right time" or the "lengthy" procedures involved in obtaining these loans but because they have to maintain "healthy working relations with them". This is largely because they are totally dependent on the merchants for marketing their cotton, as they have no direct access to the textile mills. Thus the VTs and LLVTGPs are in a dominant position with rural areas but in a dependent position with an urban area. This neutralises or softens the unequal exchange relations between the town and the country.

Methods of Trade and Unequal Exchange Relations: Here we discuss in detail the various methods by which the merchants benefit in the processes of exchange with the rural VTs and LLVTGPs. There are two methods by which cotton trade takes place: (1) by forward trading and (2) by trading in ready.

Forward Trading and Unequal Exchange : It takes place in *Kapas* after 2-3 months of sowing, much before the crop matures. Surendranagar town traders get hold of 50-75% of the VTs cotton through forward trading (1978-79), although officially forward trading was banned (1977). The remaining cotton is sold in the "open" market or "in ready". This method (forward trading) of transaction is confined to only those VTs who were indebted to the STTs. Therefore, indirectly it also restricts trade to local varieties of cotton produced in the SD viz. C-2 and Wagad. STT is particularly interested in the Co-2 variety as it is a superior long-staple variety, which is used for mixing with the even more superior *Shankar-4* variety, and the mixture can be sold as pure *Shankar-4* at higher rates.[20]

Forward trading begins on an auspicious day - the New Year Day[21], which falls sometime in October-November. On this day all the VTs ceremoniously sell about 10-50 percent of the cotton to the STTs which they themselves have bought through forward trade from the farmers. Forward trade in the remaining cotton takes place any time after the New Year and continues almost till the harvest, which is referred to as late forward trade. The time of such forward trade depends on the VTs requirements for funds to be given as "advances" to the farmers. Here, a VT forward sells small quantities of cotton to a STT. He could do this as often as he wishes until the crop is ready.

Unequal exchange takes place in both these methods but the degree of unequal exchange depends on the degree of risk that the STT takes. The higher the risk, the lower the price offered by STT to the VT. New Year Day represents a relatively high risk day as the crop is still immature and has yet to go through an unpredictable winter, which if severe, could be fatal. In other words, forward trade really amounts to borrowing by VT from STT. So in an early or New Year Deal, a VT is offered Rs. 10-20 less per maund than the ruling market rates. For instance if the rates are Rs. 60 per maund then the VT gets Rs. 40 per maund. At the aggregate level this difference becomes very large as each VT sells huge quantities of cotton to STT. For 1,000 maunds of cotton a VT loses out as much as Rs. 20,000. An STT is involved with as many as 20-25 VTs.

Besides the above mentioned disadvantage in terms of prices, the VT also faces another problem. The STT pressures the VT to forward sell maximum quantity and further reduces the rates. The rates that STT offers, he claims, is meant to cover interest and the risks he takes for the four to six months period that the cotton crop takes to mature. In the late forward trade deal the VT is offered Rs.5 less per maund than the ruling market price because the cotton crop has matured and is almost ready for harvest; and the waiting period and risk involved is reduced, the price difference is less.

Whether through a New Year deal or otherwise, the VT generally loses through forward trade on the grounds of price. Again, he has first to deliver the cotton that he has forward traded to the STT. Therefore, he surrenders the first pick of the cotton which is the best quality and when it would have fetched the best price, if sold in the open market. Even if it is not the first picking or the best quality, still the VT loses through price difference between forward trade and ready rates. In case of a failure of crops and non-delivery of kapas to the STT, the account between STT and VT is settled around April and the latter continues to pay interest on the money borrowed. And if the rates in the ready are higher than the Diwali rates then the VTs have to pay the price difference to the STT, in case of non-delivery. If the rate in ready are lower than the Diwali rates then the STT does not come to collect the cotton, for the VT, who has no storage facility, has to store it in the open yard. If there are pre-monsoon showers, this cotton may be spoilt and the VTs have to bear the losses, as the deal is not yet completed.

VTs also lose on interest, as part of the loan is repaid through the delivery of cotton by February-March. But the VT is expected to pay interest upto April. This is particularly so in the CO-2 variety of cotton which gets ready by February-March and *Wagad* gets ready in April-May.

Trading in Ready Cotton and Unequal Exchange : Only 25-50% of the cotton is sold in "ready" or in the open market, but even here VTs and LLVTGPs lose out to STT. In contrast to forward trade, trading in ready is based completely on the sample of cotton. By and large, it is the second picking of cotton that is sold in ready, the quality therefore is not as good as in the first picking, which the STT has already got hold by its forward trade deals. The sample method of sale is absolutely necessary for fixing prices because the quality is not the best. We first point out how both VTs and LLVTGPs slose through trading in ready.

Unequal Exchange for both VT and LLVTGP through Trading in Ready Cotton : As already seen both VTs and LLVTGPs are indebted to STTs which determines their methods of selling cotton to STTs. When VTs and LLVTGPs bring the trucks "in ready" to Surendranagar Town market, in principle they need not sell their *kapas* immediately, if the rates are unsuitable. Because of *Sambandh*, they have the option of emptying these trucks in STTs ginning factory, without actually selling it on that day. STTs also know that VTs and LLVTGPs do not have any other storage place in the villages and the STT is also aware that the VT and the LLVTGP will require money immediately for redistributing it at the rural level as consumption loans to the peasants. So the STT strikes a bargain. This uneqaual exchange is rationalized in the following terms: "The VTs and LLVTGPs are free to sell this cotton as and when convenient rates are available to them".

True, the STT permits the VTs and LLVTGP to use his gining yard as a temporary storing place for the latter's cotton. But the latter usually do not have any choice but to sell to the same STT as they are already tied down by the loans it has given. In other words, it indicates a monopoly of a STT over a VT and a LLVTGP. Even if market rates are rising STTs will not offer the ruling market rates and VTs and LLVTGPs will not be able to sell the cotton they have procured to any other STT because of the high costs involved in reloading and unloading the trucks.

The price are dictated by the STT. He cuts down on the firstly the market rates because of the "advantage" he offers to the VT and LLVTGP, viz. of emptying their trucks in his ginning factories. STT pays 25p to 50p less per maund than the ruling market price. Economic obligations compel the VT and the LLVTGP to accept this price. Besides, the relationship of *Sambandh* intervenes. The VT and the LLVTGP acquiesce in this arrangement because they have to go to him again next year. Secondly the STT often cuts down the ruling market price by another 50p per maund because the system of payment is "cash against delivery". This cut in prices is accepted. What is strange is that VTs and LLVTGPs do not collect the cash payments from STTs immediately. Their own explanation is that they belong to the well-to-do classes of the rural areas and do not need the money for immediate consumption. Their second argument is that "they can wait for payment" and "prefer to keep it 'safe' with the STT for the fear of being robbed in the rural areas". They do not deposit the money in the banks because they say "it involves a lot of official procedures". This strange pattern of behaviour makes sense if we view it from the *Sambandh* perspective. The STT also takes loans without interest from the VT and LLVTGP during the business season. The VT and the LLVTGP proudly declare : "when we need money they give; and when they need, we give". The VT and LLVTGP lose their interest charges. But then they are not economically equal and therefore they cannot get even with the STT neither can they survive without the STTs loans. In other words, they prefer a symbiotic relationship which saves the STT the trouble of taking loans from the banks and paying interest. The STT nevertheless will make a claim for a loan from the bank for the cotton that he has not yet acquired but hopes to acquire at a later date from the VTs or LLVTGPs, who have emptied their trucks in his ginning yard, thereby adding further to his gains.

Unequal Exchange for VT: After delivering the best cotton as loan repayment, the VT is obliged to sell the remaining cotton of the first picking to the STT because he has to take into consideration his long term interest *i.e.* need for new credit in the next season. That is why the VT 'prefers' to sell to the STT with whom he has *Sambandh* relations.

It would also be uneconomical for the VT to bring second quality of cotton or cotton in small quantities to the Surendranagar market, as the major part of the superior variety of cotton is repaid against forward traded cotton. The remaining stock is not enough for one truck-load. As transport is expensive, the VT is forced to sell his cottonto the STT on the latter's terms. The STT collects this stock along with the forward traded 'maal'.

Again there is a limited market for the second and third picking of cotton as the quality of cotton deteriorates with each picking and, therefore, fetches a lower price. The STT will not buy unless he sees the sample. He may further reduce the price and claim that he has done "favour" to the VTs by buying their cotton as otherwise, the VTs would have faced the problem of selling it. The VT is again caught in the trap of *Vyavhar* and *Sambandh*.

The other way in which the VT loses is when he is forced to provide free labour when the STT's truck is being loaded. The VTs have to check on weight, quality, etc. and as the STTs say, "the villagers have become smart and can cheat us". Our field trip to village Khodu showed that this kind of work was not voluntarily accepted by an average VT. He felt he was made a slave (gulame) by the STT, just because he had borrowed money from him. Very rarely does the STT send his own men to the village for this type of work.

Unequal Exchange Relations for the LLVTGP : The LLVTGPs are well-to-do landlord-farmers, who can wait till the *kapas* is ready and then sell it to the STTs in "ready". Hence, they do not fall prey to forward trading. They generally trade in the local variety of cotton : CO-2 and Wagad. But due to regular contacts with the same STTs over a number of years, the LLVTGPs have also started borrowing from them, for "doing business", as well as for moneylending at the rural level, but the amount borrowed is much smaller than the amount borrowed by the VTs. The LLVTGPs may buy cotton from neighbouring villages also and for that they hold a valid licence for trading in cotton. They borrow from the STTs to gin and press around 100-200 bales per annum. They even hire a tractor which carries 50-60 maunds or a truck with a 200-210 maunds capacity and bring it to ST market. Generally they bring it in *kapas* form but sometimes, as *roo* in sack loads. This is possible if they have their own ginning factory or they get the cotton ginned in a neighbouring village or town where ginning facilities are available. This is mainly done because the ginned cotton fetches better price due to its quality[22]. The LLVTGP revealed that this cotton may fetch as much as Rs. 5 more per maund if it is brought in substantial amount that is around 1500-2000 maunds.

The LLVTGP contacts *Phatak dalals* and the transaction with the STT are done through them so that they are not cheated. As stated earlier not every LLVTGP has his own ginning and pressing factories. If an LLVTGP brings '*roo*' or *kapas* to STT's processing factory for pressing into bales, he is permitted to do so only when all the members of the Co-operative Ginning and Pressing factory have finished pressing their own bales (these members are all big STTs) . Till then, the LLVTGP's *roo or kapas* is allowed to lie in the open yard of the factory. It is important to note that SD's harvest of cotton, specially Wagad, continues to arrive till late April early May. Therefore,the real threat comes when the *kapas* and the roo lying in the open would be ruined with pre-monsoon or early June showers and the LLVTGP will have to bear this loss. The same fate awaits his bales of cotton stored in the open yard. It also results in a loss in weight by about 3 kg. per bale and the quality of the cotton deteriorates, which in turn means that the LLVTGP will fetch lower prices .

The LLVTGP might still delegate the STT to wait and sell his bales at specific rates when he goes back to his village. Even in this arrangement the STT may get the better of the LLVTGP by selling the stocks at even a higher price than the limit set by the LLVTGP, and by keeping the difference for himself. At other times the LLVTGPs bales will not be sold at good prices because the STT will push his own bales first, for after all the STT lives in the town itself, whereas the LLVTGP lives in the countryside and has to rely on the STT for selling the bales at whatever rates the latter chooses to. This is because the LLVTGP does not have direct contact with the mills, the eventual buyers of raw cotton, whereas the STT is often a commission agent for mills or for large metropolitan cotton brokers or merchants. Again the LLVTGP cannot afford to wait for long periods of time, as the farming operation begins sometime in June or July, when he will require cash for agricultural purposes. [23] In which case he will sell his bales to STT, who as we have already seen, is in a better bargaining position .

When the STT functions as a Commission Agent, he gets his commission from the LLVTGP, but if relations between them are very good then the former states that he "does not charge commission". In reality however, he makes up for this generosity in the price differences which we have alluded to earlier. He may also make a claim on the VT and on the LLVTGP in the form of "majoori kharch" *i.e.* "money spent on labour," for transporting bales, stacking them in the shade, loading them on to trucks, etc. In other cases, the STT gets a commission from both the LLVTGP and from mills, when the STT is a direct commission agent of the mills. In which case, the STT is expected to give to the LLVTGP the same rates that he has secured from the mills, and the payment to the LLVTGP is done when the mills pay to STT. But LLVTGPs have complained that in the last 5-7 years the STTs keep the price differences, as explained in the previous paragraph. Again, the LLVTGP incurs an addtional loss because he has to pay a commission to the *Phatak dalals* through whom he sell to the STT.

It is important to note that there may be some cases of defaults, *i.e.* non-repayment of loans, more so by VT and less by LLVTGP to STT. These cases occur in times of depression or consecutive failure of monsoons, which incapacitates the farmers to repay the advances they have taken from the VT and the LLVTGP. The same is often the plight of the latter vis-a-vis the STTs. But such cases are few because of *Sambandh and Vyavhar*, The debt is carried forward to the next year in case of failure of the monsoons and the STT provides them with a fresh loan, for the new season. This morally binds the VT and LLVTGP to repay the loans. "There is no need for the musclemen or thugs to recover the loans" says an STT. But the STT's explanation gives them away. "The VT and LLVTGP generally pay back because next year they need us, they need money".

An STT may threaten to break or breach the compact if the quality of cotton does not tally with the sample, which also means that there would be a differene in the stated prices and the actual price. But the STT then bargains and pulls down the price further, irrespective of the market rate, for a given variety of cotton. But the STT would have us believe that he "never fails a VT or LLVTGP. He always adjusts and the deals are through". The STTs proudly state that "very rarely are court suits filed; they usually arrive at settlements outside the court". And this is mainly because of *Vyavhar* and *Sambandh*.

So far we have been dealing with unequal exchange relations between town and village traders, but STTs can be divided into small and big traders. Much of the unequal relations that we have discussed in the earlier pages are realised by both categories of STTs. The small STT get hold of only 5-10 percent of the total cotton produced in the countryside. As, we notice the village surplus product often passes through successive hierarchical levels, it would not be out of place to show how a part of the surplus of small STT passes on to the more powerful big STT. This happens for two reasons : (1) Like the VT and the LLVTGP the small STTs suffer from lack of storage space and danger of exposure of their cotton to the sun, and so they are compelled to sell at a price dictated by the STTs. (2) Eventually it is only the STT who have direct exchange relations with metropolitan traders and with cotton textile mills and benefit from them.

SECTON 5

Conclusion

The present study is an attempt to evolve a framework for the study of town-country-nexus in societies which are undergoing transformation. It highlights the role of credit-nexus and its impact on the rural areas. It further shows that this credit-nexus has definitely resulted in unequal exchange (over and above market mechanisms) between town and country *i.e.* between Surendranagar town cotton traders and village traders and landlord-cum-village trader-cum-ginner and presser. It further shows how the social institutions of *Vyavhar* and *Sambandh* reinforce this unequal exchange. Such an unequal exchange relation, leads to forced transfer of surplus from country to town and this we believe, is an important cause of backwardness of the district and the people affected by it *i.e.*, the village trader and landlord-cum-ginner and presser. They also feel that they are loosing out on this exchange and if facilites such as Cotton Corporation of India, institutional credit, marketing yards, or Gujarat Marketing Federation were accessible to them diretly, then they would have got a better deal. But it has already been shown that the institutional credit has failed in breaking this vicious circle of indebtedness. Even the Government's policy of purchasing cotton from peasants via the Cotton Corporation of

India or Gujarat Marketing Federation, has failed to make a dent on the nature of exchange relations between town and country.[24] It is further indicated how the agro-climatic conditions, especially the erratic and unevenly spaced rainfall, reinforce this credit-nexus, the pattern of specialization of rural Surendranagar district in cotton, and the subsequent unequal exchange relations between town and country. Above all, the study shows that these processes are rooted in history and have been going on for a long time.

NOTES AND REFERENCES

* The present paper is based on the author's Ph.D dissertation titled "Rural-Urban Relationship : With Special Reference to Surendranagar Town and its Hinterland". Department of Sociology, University of Bombay. I sincerely acknowledge Prof. Manorama Savur's contribution .

1. No attempt is made in this paper to calculate or quantify the surplus, which is crucial for capital accumulation and development of the rural areas.
2. Town and country nexus is predominantly established by economic exchange. We are analysing such a relation pertaining to cotton trade.
3. Government of Gujarat (1982), *Statistical Atlas of Gujarat, Vol.I* (Resource Profile), Bureau of Economics and Statistics, Gandhinagar.
4. D.S. Hamby (1977), "Cotton", Encyclopedia Americana, Vol.8, Americana Corporation, New York.
5. Government of India (1981), *District Census Handbook,* Surendranagar District, Ahmedabad, Gujarat.
6. K.R. Dikshit (1970), *Geography of Gujarat : India - The Land and People,* National Book Trust, New Delhi.
7. The other reasons he suggests are that cash crops ensure comparatively higher returns and show greater stability in their prices. Better marketing facilities may be another factor encouraging the cultivation of cash crops.
8. H.L. Dholakia (1942), *Futures Trading and Futures Markets in Cotton,* New Book Co., Bombay.
9. V.V. Janaki (1967), *Some Aspects of the Population in the Different Functional Groups of Towns in Gujarat,* M.S. University, Baroda.
10. V.M. Bhatia (1965), "Agriculture and Cooperation" - *Economic History of India : 1857 - 1956* by V.B. Singh (ed.), Allied Publishers Pvt. Ltd., Bombay.
11. *Imperial Gazetteer of India* (1908), Karachi to Kotayam, Vol. XV, Clarenden Press, Oxford.

12. The distress cry of Nawab of Bengal elsewhere establishes this point: "In every paragraph, every village and every factory, the Company's Gomastah, buy bamboo, fish, gunnies, ginner, sugar, tobacco, opium....They forcibly take away the goods and commodities of the raiets, merchants, and C, for a fourth part of their value; and by ways of violence and oppressions they oblige the raiet and C., to give five rupees, for goods which are but one rupee....(Dutt R.C., 1960)."
13. Pillai P.P. (1925), *Economic Conditions in India,* George Routledge and Sons Ltd. London.
14. Dutt R.C. (1960), *The Economic History of Indial Vol.*I *(1757-1837), Vol.II (1837-1900),* Publication Division, Delhi. Palme - Dutt R. (1955), "India Today and Tomorrow", People's Publishing House, Bombay.
15. Hamilton C.J. (1919), *The Trade Relation Between England and India,* Thacker, Spink & Co., Calcutta.
16. Parikh Nandkishor (1962), "Cotton Industry in Ahmedabad", Unpublished Ph.D. Thesis , M.S. University, Baroda.
17. Gadgil D.R. (1942), *Industrial Evolution of India in Recent Times,* Oxford University Press, Bombay.
18. Trivedi A.B. (1943), Kathiawar Economics, Bombay See also, *The Universal Practical Combined Dictonary : English into Gujarati and English, and Gujarati into English and Gujarati,* (1940), R.R. Sheth and Co., Bombay.
19. VT does not give advances to landless agricultural labourers, who can generally repay in labour. Since, a VT does not have any land, he has no use of labour of the agricultural labour.
20. In recent years in SD Shankar-4 is cultivated. Pure Shankar-4 bales are sold till about February when good quality of CO-2 or Gujarat-12 begins to come in the market, it is mixed with Shankar-4 and passed off as Shankar-4 bales.
21. It sometimes begins even on a Dushera Day.
22. There is no mixing of inferior varieties of cotton.
23. VTs have no land and therefore tend to abscond sometimes permanently whereas LLVTGP has land and is therefore tied down to his land.
24. For details refer the author's Ph.D Thesis 'Rural-Urban Relationship...., op. cit.

CHAPTER 14

Rural-Urban Nexus: Theoretical Formulations and a Research Design for Historical Analysis

—Atiya Habeeb Kidwai

Social scientists have studied urban and rural area either as discrete objects of social analysis, acting autonomously as causal forces, or, as interacting systems, coterminous with some more fundamental set of social relations. The distinction as well as the relationship between 'town' and 'country' were recognised and explicitly formulated even in the earliest social theories and have become of central concern in many debates on the societal transformations taking place in the Third World countries today.

The 'town' and 'country' as explanatory variables, or, as analyatical categories, were initially adopted in the historical analysis of many societal processes such as the origin of the division of labour and the market; the separation between production and consumption brought about by rural-urban exchanges and the operation of the processes of urbanization.[1] The town-country distinction and the differentiation of the 'urbane' and progressive from the 'rustic' and 'backward' provided the conceptual basis for the 'Whig theory of history' in which as ascendent, civilized urban particiate, operating from dynamic capitalist cities is at the centre of cumulative social progress.[2] The separation of town and country in the 'commercial stage' of civilization became the bench mark for the proponents of the new and revolutionary 'conjectural' history of 'civil society.'[3]

Within sociology the dominant framework for analysing the distinction between rural and urban was the concept of a rural-urban continuum. It appeared to be a more defensible response to the critque of urban-rural dichotomy.[4] The difference in social and cultural patterns were explained by reference to the place of communities along a continuum, which ran from the most urban to the most rural type of settlement.[5] A great deal of rural sociological research became organised around this specific conceptual scheme. Geographers and regional planners, primarily interested in analysing spatial interrelationships also contributed to the debate that raged around the rural-urban continuum or folk-urban continuum, their ideas being greatly influenced by the American Sociologists of the 1920s and 1930s and by the Chicago School of Urbanologists.[6]

The success of the idea prompted its exportation to certain European and Third World countries.[7] This varied application, however proved the inadequacy of these concepts and by the end of the 1960s the notion of a rural-urban continuum was considered theoretically bankrupt *(loc. cit.)*. The *received studied* had demonstrated that differences in social and cultural patterns did not coincide with, and hence, could not be explained by spatial and economic milieux.[8] This dissatisfaction had stemmed from the primarily dualistic nature of formulations and from the fact that they failed to include an adequate classification of urban and rural types, so essential for societal analysis.[9] The Fallacy of using urban and rural as generic terms also became apparent when one was confronted with discordant empirical material collected in trans-historical cross-cultural contexts.

However, the recent literature on rural-urban diffusion and transformation suggests that supra-local linkages need to be deciphered and adequately understood in any serious analysis of societal processes, specifically the developing countries where the rural-urban linkages, both functional and spatial, are in a flux. An alternative, and a more relevant framework of analysis is needed to capture the nuances of the changed situations. The country town nexus or more appropriately the rural-urban nexus appears to be a useful category for such an analysis. In this paper, which is no more than exploratory, we will attempt to assess the analytical potential of this concept and identify a possible 'entry point' for the analysis of concrete situations in order to evolve a researchable methodology.

The Country-Town Nexus-Theoretical Formulations:

The historically changing rural-urban relationships have been conceptualized and interpreted in terms of such diverse processes as separation, polarization, opposition, domination/subordination/ appropriation and more recently as nexus formation. Marx for instance, defined the town and country relations either in term of an 'undifferentiated unity' as observed in Asiatic history or as an opposition/separation which became the foundation of social division of labour in the Western societies. The same line of argument recurred in the Dobb-Sweezy debate on the origins of capitalism wherein the town-country opposition was seen as an opposition of economic-corporate spheres of sovereignty.[10] For Pirenne and Weber, on the other hand, town and country were opposed as spatial and structural forms and as cultural patterns only in feudal societies, the opposition being obliterated in industrial societies.[11] The town and country relation has also been seen as one of dominance of the town. This dominance, it is variously argued, emanates from the capitalist control of production which subordinates the country to urban capital.[12] It may also result from political hegemony, or arise from a concentration of decision-making/bureaucratic clout in urban centres.[13] The classic objective of revolutionary socialism hence becomes the abolition of the antithesis between town and country.[14]

Implicit in perhaps all the points of view mentioned above is the concept of a 'nexus' rather than simple rural-urban interaction. 'Nexus' signifies the end product, the 'bonds' that evolve over time through continued interation. The concept of a nexus and the process of nexus formation, if explicitly qualified by a set of fundamental social relations, hence, may prove analytically more relevant in the context of the developing world where the sharp edges of the rural-urban 'dichotomy' are in some respects softening. It may be mentioned here that in this paper the terms 'town' and 'country', used by many researchers, have been replaced by the generic terms 'rural' and 'urban' because the term 'country' in the contemporary context is nebulus and is not indicative of the components (peasants, farmers, tribals) of which the rural societies are made of. On the other hand, the terms 'town' conceptually precludes the other urban hierarchical categories, by now, well differentiated in social science literature in terms of the metropolis, the city, the intermediate or small town etc. It is important to appreciate this hierarchical structuring of urban areas because the internal dynamics and the interaction patterns governing each level in the hierarchy are different. For instance, in terms of the nexus the migration pattern to an intermediate town is different from that of the metropolis; the trade links are also structured differently and so are the socio-cultural bonds.

As the starting point of analysis the following theoretical formulations addressing the rural-urban nexus as a sociological category, are being put forward. These are knitted together in terms of a heuristic model given in Figure 1.

— The nexus is a product of the SYSTEMIC relationship existing between the rural and the urban components of a social formation and is historically determined.

— The nexus is not a separate structure with its own laws of construction and transformation but is reflective of a larger social reality.

— The nexus comes into existence when rural and urban areas mutually act and react, adapt and adjust in terms of a systemic relationship. These processes of reaction, adaptation and adjustment also qualify the nexus and lend it its potency.

— The nexus can be conflict -ridden, antagonistic or symbiotic.

— The nexus, once formed, may continue, change or come to an end. This depends on factors both internal and external to it. The internal factors include both macro and micro structural factors such as economic imperatives, local power structure, class/ethnic/caste alliances, linked familial and household decisions etc. The external factors consist of macro-societal processes important from the historical point of vew.

— The political, economic and socio-cultural imperatives in the nexus formation acquire varying relative significance vis-a-vis different interest groups.

— The nexus may evolve at various levels. It may evolve at a higher, more complex aggregative and permanent level through the interaction of interest groups, mass movements etc., or, it may form at a lower, simpler, less permanent level through individuals or households which are elemental units in a social formation.

— The nexus may be formed at the conscious level through idelogical propagation (generally mass-based) to fulfil specific economic, socio-cultural or political purposes. It may also be formed at the unconscious level through tradition, culture etc.

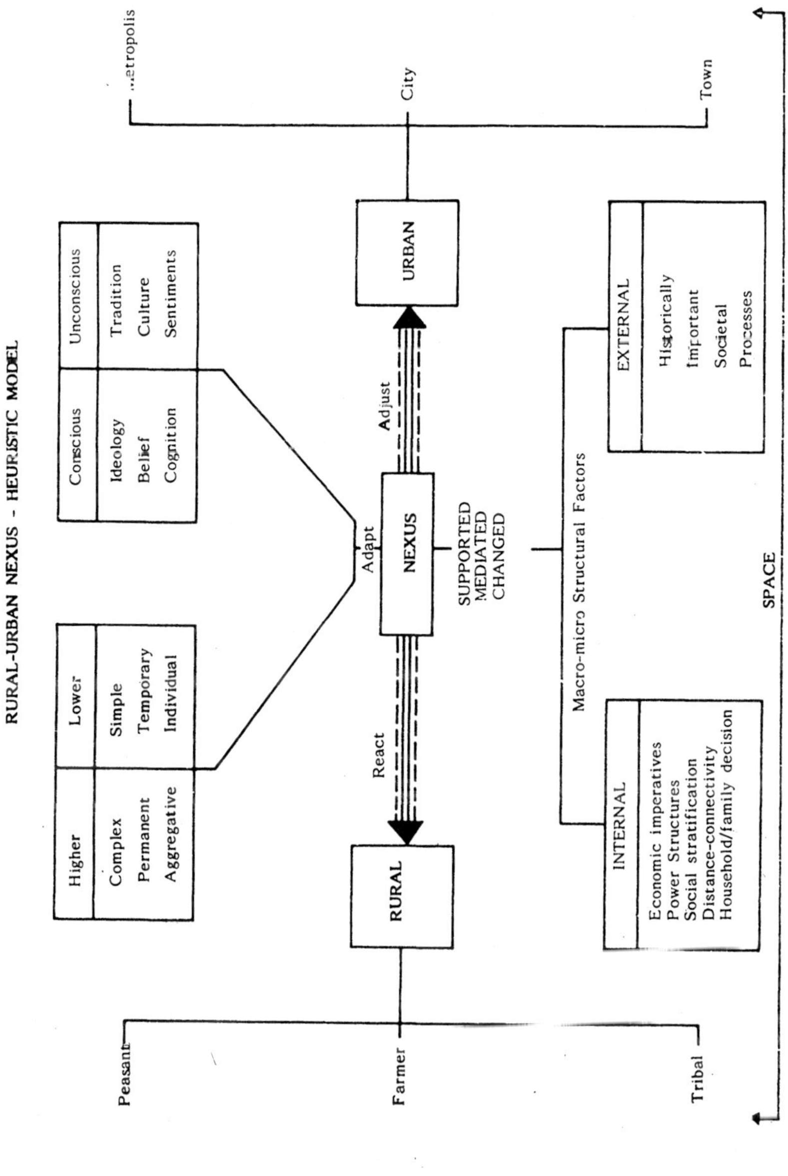
RURAL-URBAN NEXUS - HEURISTIC MODEL
Higher
Complex
Permanent
Aggregative
Lower
Simple
Temporary
Individual
Conscious
Ideology
Belief
Cognition
Unconscious
Tradition
Culture
Sentiments
Peasant
Farmer
Tribal
RURAL
React
Adapt
NEXUS
Adjust
URBAN
City
Town
SUPPORTED
MEDIATED
CHANGED
Macro-micro Structural Factors
INTERNAL
Economic imperatives
Power Structures
Social stratification
Distance-connectivity
Household/family decision
EXTERNAL
Historically
Important
Societal
Processes
SPACE

Fig. 1

— Since the rural and urban areas exist in space and since the systemic relationship which evolves between them over the time has spatial ramifications the nexus becomes an important factor in the organisation of space.

— The societal role of the nexus is partly determined and partly determining.

— The rationale of the nexus may shift either towards its urban or its rural components.

For analytical and methodological convenience, the nexus can be studied separately as an economic, social, political or a spatial system. These systems, however, are not mutually exclusive.

Explorations in Search of a Research Design

The discussion so far has suggested that the rural-urban nexus is multifaceted and each of its facets requires detailed enquiry. The analysis in this paper, hence, can only be a limited one. The endeavour would be to convert some of the stated theoretical propositions into the analysis of actual empirical situations which is the only way to test, and,if necessary, to reformulate them. In order to do this a choice can be made from a large array of research designs appropriate for rendering the various facets and levels of nexus formation researchable. The analysis can either be longitudinal or cross-sectional; a study of either structures or actors; a micro or a macro view.[15]

This study has been designed as a LONGITUDINAL MICRO STUDY OF ACTORS, a method considered useful for the expressed purpose of this paper. The contention here is that it is difficult to fully comprehend macro-processes unless they are linked with micro-level empirical work, however "complicated, variegated and intransigent human behaviour at this level may seem to be."[16] Large scale social movements need to be related with the behaviour of individuals within society.

The prerequisites of such a study are that it refers to a distinctly identifiable socio-economic and geographical milieu, a specific historical period and a group of actors which can be treated as representative of a segment of the society of their time. This enquiry has hence been focussed on a small area, the 'Qidwara', in the region traditionally known as Avadh in Uttar Pradesh, India. The period covers the last phase of colonial rule in the country and the four decades after independence. The baseline from which the extent of change is assessed is 1857, the year of the 'Mutiny' and crucial in the history of Avadh. The 'actors' belong to a family of the Kidwais which has not only been influential in its homeland, but, has developed significant supra-local linkages over time and in four geneological generations has been able to shift its base from a rural to an urban one. An inter-generational analysis of this family, it is hoped, would provide the appropriate data to address some of the theoretical formulations in this paper.

The nature of the approach adopted in this analysis is now explained and the terminology used clarified.

LONGITUDINAL in this context means 'following some-thing over time. Longitudinal studies can be distinguished into two main types, TRAJECTORY and STATION studies. In the former individuals are traced over time and spacc and in the latter a 'station' or a delineated area is selected and what flows in and out of this area is traced and studied, not further than the delineated boundary. It resembles 'historie/geographie totale.'[17] The drawback of the trajectory method is that it overemphasizes the invididual and not the society in which he lives, whereas the station method overemphasizes space. In this study the trajectory approach (inter-generational) has been adopted because our concern is with individuals in the nexus formation.

Individuals are not conceived here in the narrow sense of being 'subjects', but as 'actors', *i.e.*, supports of positions defined by macro-structural elements. Hence they may also be called SUPPORT AGENTS.[18] An 'Actor' can either be studied as a sequence of events or as a sequence of years. The former method, known as the 'life course' method, is centred on transitions and provides a summary record of successive eventful changes in a life course, while the latter gives an yearly account of a life history.[19] The life course approach involves two levels of behaviour; one is the relationship between individual life history and the collective history of one's family unit, and the other the relationship between individual and family change and changes in the larger society.[20]

Four events in the life of an 'actor' are considered important in highlighting aspects of the nexus. These are:

(i) Birth terms of calender time and demographic generations (periods of 30 years). This helps in the analysis of the effects of 'shifting environment' and 'shifting history' on the actors and generational cohorts.

(ii) Education in terms of the place where it is obtained and the level attained. The place informs us about facilities and opportunities available at a station and the level about the social attitudes and aspirations espoused by individual actors and succssive generations.

(iii) Marriage fields. Marriage knits actors and families together and indicate the extent of the area incorporated in the nexus.

(iv) Livelihood positions. These indicate the 'niche' an individual must occupy in society in order to survive. It is a spatial position at which the resources and facilities needed for a person's survivial are available. If no such niche is available he/she must migrate to an area where it is available. Livelihood positions are reflective of the economic and social 'openings' available in the society and the extent of diversification taking place in it. Economic growth means creation of new and varied livelihood positions. Spatial and social mobility, as well as the mobility of investible surpluses also depends on their creation.[21]

The Region, the Period and the Actors

Avadh has been a region of some historic individuality. Emerging as a successor-state, set up by a governor nominally under the Muguls in their eighteenth century decline, it was later converted into a British client-state and was finally annexed in 1856. Traditionally, it has consisted of about twelve districts in central Uttar Pradesh, ten of which lie south of the river Ghaghra[1]. Lucknow has been the socio-cultural and political pivot of this region.

Geographically, Avadh cosists of vast, featureless alluvial expanses and is one of the most intensely cultivated areas in India. It has been the domain of big land-lords (called *zamindars* or *taluqdars*), often absentees. Soon after the independence of the country the *zamindari* system was abolished and many a big landlords left their villages for Lucknow and other neighbouring towns. The partition of the country had also weakened them because the properties of those relatives who had left for Pakistan were confiscated by the government. Today, by and large the land holdings in Avadh are small, much too small for efficient cultivation; fragmentation is rampant. Population presses hard

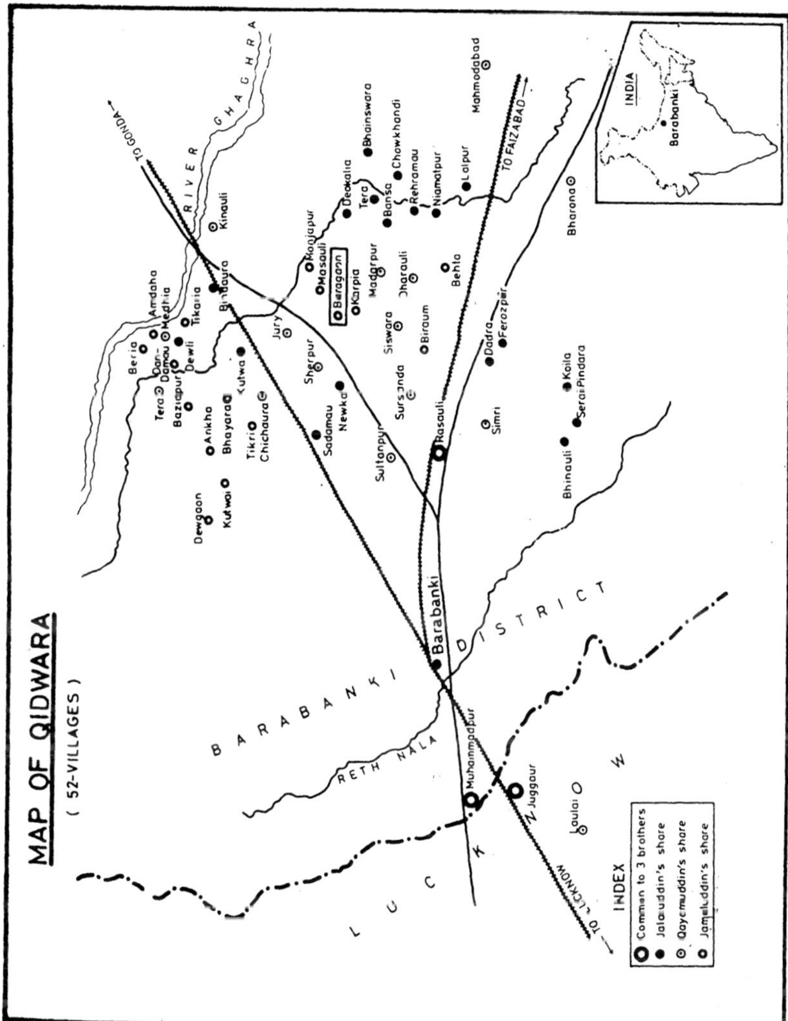
MAP OF QIDWARA
(52-VILLAGES)
RIVER GHAGHRA
TO GONDA
TO FAIZABAD
TO LUCKNOW
BARABANKI DISTRICT
LUCKNOW
RETH NALA
Barabanki
INDIA
INDEX
Common to 3 brothers
Jalaluddin's share
Qayemuddin's share
Jamaluddin's share
mza / cssd / jnu / new delhi

Map

on resources. Settlements are generally nucleated in large and remarkably evenly spaced villages. True urbanism is modest. Cities there are few. Most towns have something of the aspect of village life. Lucknow, the largest city in the region, built on the sordid exploitation of the peasant masses, was of little importance until the eighteenth century and was characterized by 'clumsy and garish' provincialism.[22] Today it is no more than a well equipped administrative centre.

It may be mentioned here that in terms of their rural interlinkages cities of north Indian differed greatly during the last quarter of the nineteenth and early twentieth century. If rural-urban migration is taken as a differentiating factor we had Kanpur on the one hand, which was a city of migrants and had grown very fast, and, on the other, we had Lucknow, Allahabad and Patna which were continuously declining. Most of the smaller towns in Avadh were also loosing their population. The economic base of these cities was weakening and in some of them the growth rate of the workers was much less than the growth rate of population .[23] This increased the dependency ratios in them. Most of the towns in Avdah had been reduced to *hats* (small market places) or at best were administrative and judicial centres providing employment in low-paid jobs. Rural populations could not look upon their neighbouring urban areas for sustenance or opportunities.

The Kidwais had settled in the districts of Barabanki, Lucknow and Faizabad in the middle of the thirteenth century .[24] Geneologically they can be traced as the descendents of Qazi Moiz-ud-din, who had left his homeland in Turkey and had travelled to India in the beginning of the thirteenth century to meet Khwaja Moin-ud-din-Chishti of Ajmer. The Khwaja asked him to proceed to Ayodhya. Shahab-ud-din-Ghori, the king of Delhi at that time was greatly impressed by the Qazi, and, not only gave him permission to go to Ayodhya, but also troops and money for his safe journey and a *farman* granting him property rights to all the territory he might conquer on his way. The Qazi eventually settled in Ayodhya and was greatly respected by all as a sufi saint. He was knwon as Qazi Qidwa in the area. The Kidwais (a surname derived from Qidwa and adopted in the 1920s) of Uttar Pradesh, Hyderabad and Pakistan are said to be descendents of his great grandson Salar Ahmad Turk Taj who was married to Balban's grand-daughter.

The clan initially owned 52 villages in Avadh (See map 1) which were either conquered or bestowed by the Delhi Sultans. The main families were known by the name of the villages where they resided and were generally addressed as Qazis. Some of their important villages were Bhayara, Baragaon, Rasauli, Masauli, Juggaur, and Gadia. Our actors belong to the family which had settled down in Baragaon in Barabanki. Baragaon is an old *zamindari* settlement situated forty kilometres east of Lucknow and thirteen kilometres east of Barabanki. Its population has always been split, almost equally, between Hindus and Muslims though historically Muslims have wielded economic and political power as well as a higher social status.[25]

Early Genealogical History

The Kidwais of Baragaon are the descendents of Jalal-ud-din, the eldest of the three sons of salar Ahmad Turk Taj. These brothers, because of their maternal connections with Balban, had spent a large part of their lives in Delhi. Jalal-ud-din was one of the fifteen most famous and revered *ulemas* (scholars) at Balbans court. After Balban's death these brothers migrated to their native land, Avadh and settled in Rasulpur, a village five kilometres from Barabanki. Sometime in the early eighteenth century, Mohammad Aman (fifteenth generation from Qazi Kidwa) migrated from Rasulpur to Baragaon. We shall here trace back the lineage of the family to Newazish-ur-Rehman (born 1823, fifth generation from Mohammad Aman and twentieth generation from Qazi Qidwa).

Newazish-ur-Rahman had inherited all the property of his father as well as four villages from the Raja of Mahmudabad through his maternal grandfather who was brother-in-law of the Raja. His younger and only brother, a loyalist, had been killed during the Mutiny in 1857, fighting against the British forces near Gorakhpur. He had left behind no children. Newazish was a generous man and his generosity proved such a strain on his resources that he died in debt in 1886 leaving behind only 10 annas (62 paise) in cash and four sons. The responsibility of the rehabilitation of the family fell on the eldest son, Nisar-ur-Rahman (1857-1929). He discharged his duties with exemplary courage, efficiency and perhaps ample manoeuvring. He not only paid back his debts but on his death left an estate worth Rs. 70,000, one of the largest in Barabanki. In 1909 he constructed the *haveli* in which some of the members of the family still reside.

In the following pages is traced the process of widening and the thickening of the webs of interaction between a landed rural-based gentry and the nearby *Shahars* and *qasbas* (big and small town) through the life course analysis of the next five generations of Baragaon Kidwais. The discussion has been grouped into two parts. Initially the individuals in each generation have been studied in terms of the four events in their life courses mentioned earlier. Subsequently conclusions have been drawn, generation-wise, from these eventful life courses with reference to some of the theoretical propositions stated earlier. It may be noted that demographic generations have been used, each comprising of a thirty year period, to group the actors and related data. This division of the sample population has been preferred to geneological generations because it makes it easier to correlate life course events with historical societal events taking place in calender time.

Generation I (1850-1880)

This demographic generation consisted of six men and two women. All the four men belonging to the first genelogical generation in this cohort received traditional, nonformal education at home in Urdu, Arabic and Persian and were married in to the Kidwai *biradari* (clan) in the neighbouring villages. The two men belonging to the next geneological generation (but born before 1880) were sent to Deoband and Firangi Mahal in Lucknow after being initiated into traditional education at home. Both these institutions provided scholarly religious education and allowed its students to dabble a little in 'modern' disciplines. Four out of these six male members (66%) derived their livelihood totally from the *zamindari* and two supplemented it with managerial jobs in neighbouring estates. Nisar-ur-Rahman, the eldest male member of this generation, having acquired respectability and social status after reconsolidating his property, realized that in order to further his interests he had to develop and maintain cordial relations with the British adminstration which was now in full command of the region. This he did and was amply rewarded. The title of *Khan Bhadaur* was bestowed on him and he was made an Honorary Magistrate for life which used to be the exclusive right of the *Taluqdars*. He held his court, once a week, in Barabanaki, the district headquarter. This strengthened and formalised his links with the nearest town and its events. For the family, the town now became much more than a place where household provisions were obtained or judicial matters settled. It now became an arena where family interests could be furthered.

Generation II (1881-1910)

The second generation multiplied into thirteen men and twelve women (the demographic and geneological generations during this period were more or less coterminus). The family had by now realized the importance of modern education and ten out of the thirteen male members were sent out of the village to obtain it. Most of them were first initiated into traditional and religious education at Firangi Mahal and were later shifted to colleges either in Lucknow or were sent to the Mohammedan Anglo-oriental (M.A.O.) College at Aligarh. One of them was even sent to Cambridge University for graduation. He subsequently completed his Bar-at-Law at London and started legal practice in Lucknow. Two other men also studied law at the Lucknow University and later practiced it in the neighbouring towns of Barabanki and Gonda. This generation produced the family's first engineer (who later returned to farming), an agricultural scientist, a religious scholar and four graduates. Five out of the thirteen male members in this generation (about 1/3) remained totallly dependent on the *zamindari* for their livelihood. The income coming from the land was, however, distributed amongst all family members, male and female, according to *Sharia* norms.

The marriage pattern did not change much but since women were now available in the immediate family they were preferred to women from the *biradari*. Only one marriage took place outside the *Qidwara*. The women of the family observed *purda*, were tutored at home and remained as housewives after their marriage.

The supra-local involvement of the family, however, increased significantly. Unlike in the earlier generation, there was an awareness of national level politics. This generation was responsive to social changes and to the growing Freedom Movement. Their stance, as opposed to the earlier generation was avowedly anti-British. This manifested itself in members either joining the Congress party (Jamil-ur-Rahman became the District Congress President in 1935) or the Muslim League (Ehsan-ur-Rahman, the barrister, became the General Secretary of the Muslim League in the United Provinces in 1938). Sayeed-ur-Rahman, an ardent nationalist, joined the Khilafat movement, became private secretary to Shaukat Ali for a while and later migrated to Hyderabad to spread the movement there. Shafiq ur Rahman joined the freedom struggle and the Jamia Movement in Delhi and later started the Maktaba-i-Jamia, a publishing house. In 1950, he became the Education Minister for the Delhi State. The family also pioneered the co-operative movement in Barabanki and produced two successive chairmen of its board.

Thus the area of interaction of the family gradually expanded beyond Barabanki and included Lucknow, Aligarh and Delhi within its ambit. Two of its members took up permanent residence in Lucknow. Two others migrated to Hyderabad (one because of his political involvement and the other for a government job) and one to Mainpuri (for a government job).

Generation III (1911-1940)

This demographic generation consisted of twenty men and twenty eight women (Geneologically, the third generation spanned fifty years between 1901 and 1951 and consisted of twenty-three men and thirty-nine women). Most of the children in this generation were initially given traditional and religious education at home and were not sent to a 'Madarsa' or to Firangi Mahal. Most of the boys and some girls subsequently attended schools in Barabanki or Lucknow and later either continued in the colleges there or were sent to the Aligarh Muslim University (A.M.U.). The educational attainment of the men in this generation were:

1 Doctorate	— Cornell University, U.S.A.
4 Engineers	— A.M.U., Aligarh
7 Post-graduates	— 4 (A.M.U., Aligarh)
5 (Science), 1 (Arts)	— 3 (Lucknow University)
1 (Commerce)	
3 Graduates	— 2 (A.M.U., Aligarh)
	1 (Lucknow University)
5 Intermediates	— All from Barabanki

The non-traditional education of the women in the family started with this generation and sixteen (55%) of the women were given some formal training. Their attainments were:

3 Post-graduates	— 2 (A.M.U., Aligarh)
(all in Arts)	1 (Lucknow University)
11 Graduates	— 5 (Lucknow University)
	2 (Jamia, Delhi)
	2 (A.M.U., Aligarh)
	1 (Allahabad University)
	1 (Barabanki)
2 High School	— A.M.U., Aligarh

Out of these women only seven (25%) took up jobs after the completion of their studies. Three remained unmarried and became school teachers, one became a programme officer with the All India Radio and three involved themselves with part-time social work and local level politics. The last three have been active members of the Congress Party; one of them was even nominated to the Rajya Sabha and one has been a Councillor in the Delhi Municipal Board.

The marriage pattern in this generation changed significantly. Though, like in the previous generation, about half of the men were married within the family, non-*biradari* urban women were preferred when marriages were solemnized outside the family. More or less the same pattern was observed in the marriages of the women. The marriage fields thus expanded considerably.

In terms of livelihood positions, it is interesting to note that dependence on land continued and six out of the twenty male members (about 1/3) remained dependent on it. Three of them, however, also tried to establish household factories or a family business but failed. Ten took up government or semi-government jobs, three became professional research scientists and one joined the Air-force.

It should be pointed out here that this was a generation which had to cope with the aftermath of the *zamindari* abolition in 1950. The economic imperative forced occupational diversification and migration to places outside the state. Along with expanding marriage fields this became another agent of nexus formation. More than half of the men of this generation migrated to places where the family had no earlier connections. It is interesting to note that the partition of the country did not affect this family and only one of its members left for Pakistan.

Involvement of the men in social and political movements at the supra-local level also reduced in this generation the extent of ideological commitment, as well as the sheer numbers of those involved. Three members joined such diverse parties after Independence as the Congress(I), the Janata Party and the B.J.P.

Generation IV (1941-1970)

This generation consists of twenty-two men and twenty-six women, out of whom only thirteen men and twenty-two women have acquired livelihood positions. The rest are still students.

It is interesting to note that fourteen (65%) of the men in this generation have been educated at the Aligarh Muslim University, the highest number and proportion in any generation, and more men have gone to the Delhi University than to the Lucknow University. Two men have also been educated overseas (Oxford and McGill). The level of education attained has been at par with the previous generation, but by and large, lower than that of the female counterparts in this generation.

The women in this generation have all received formal education. Amongst the twenty-two women who have acquired livelihood position, there are three physicians, two doctorates in science, five post-graduates and twelve graduates.

The marriage pattern has also changed. Out of the ten married men, only three have been married within the family and the rest outside the *biradari*. Amongst the nineteen married women, six have been married within the family, two within the *biradari* and eleven outside of it. All marriage fields have, however, been confined within the state. For the first time in all these generations some marriage ceremonies were held outside Baragaon.

In terms of livelihood positions, only one out of the thirteen settled men is dependent on his ancestral property in Baragaon (the other three men looking after this property today belong to the previous generation). Eight men are in government jobs and three are University teachers. Amongst the twenty two settled women there are four in government or private sector jobs, three are doctors, one is a university lecturer, four are school teachers and ten full time housewives.

The involvement of this generation in supra-local political activities is minimal, though commitment to certain social causes or movements is present at individual levels.

Genertion V (1970 to date)

This generation consists of seventeen males and seven females. All are students and all go to public schools.

Issues Pertaining to the Nexus

In this inter-generational micro-level analysis, the changing bonds of a rural gentry with supra-local spaces (both urban and rural) can be traced over the last hundred years. It is observed that in the first two generations, despite some urban involvement, the family is still wedded to the land and the logic in any supra-local involvement emanates from the rural component in the nexus. This is followed by a period of transition experienced both by some members of the second and almost all members of the third generation when both the rural and the urban components in the nexus formation become almost equally potent. A period of the weakening of the nexus begins in the fourth generaion which is predominantly urban-based. For the fifth generation, the nexus exists only at the ideational level, deliberately nurtured through family traditions.

The continuation of the nexus can be attributed to factors, both internal and external to the family. The first generation in the analysis is a generation which has seen better times and is aware of the possibility of the family again becoming influential in the local society. They know that the *Sheikhzadas* had always been a force to reckon with in the local power structure. They had valiantly, though unsuccessfully fought the British during the siege of Lucknow. Nisar-ur-Rahman, the man at the helm of affairs of this generation, however, realizes that the anti-British stance of the earlier generations would not help him achieve his purpose. He has to retrieve a lost *zamindari* and has to consolidate his social status. In order to do this he has to become influential in the local society. The apparent prerequisite for this is to maintain cordial relations with the British administrators of the region. His strategy is closely related to his economic interests as a *zamindar*. In order to climb up in the social hierarchy of the times he consciously aligns himself with the processes of modernization just beginning to manifest themselves in the region. He shifts his children from Firangi Mahal to M.A.O. College at Aligarh, to the University at Lucknow and to the Harcourt Butler Technological Institute at Kanpur. These institutions are symbolic of professionalism, now considered desirable in the elite groups.

These developments in the first generation have ramifications for the second. Some members of this generation have acquired professional qualifications and hence occupational diversification is possible for them. Dependency on land has become less of a necessity. On the political scene, winds of change are blowing and things once again appear uncertain. A national movement against the British is picking up and is offering many alternatives to the Muslims in the form of the Indian National Congress, the Muslim League or the Khilafat movement. Some in the family join these political parties according to their inclination, circumstances and calculations. However,the motive behind their choice is perhaps the same struggle for ascendancy in the local milieu.

TABLE 14.1
INTER-GENERATION ANALYSIS OF BARAGAON KIDWAIS

Actor's		*Education Urban*				*Marriage*			*Livelihood Position*				
Actor's	*N.F.*	*Local*	*UG*	*Grad.*	*P.G.*	*Family*	*Rural*	*Urban*	*Land*	*Govt.*	*Prof.*	*House Wife*	*Poli-tical Social*
Generation I (1850-1880)													
Total	8	2	6	0	0	1	7	0	4	2	0	2	—
Male	6	2	4	0	0	1	5	0	4	2	0	0	—
Female	2	2	0	0	0	0	2	0	0	0	0	2	—
Generation II (1881-1910)													
Total	25	10	10	3	2	11	12	2	5	4	3	12	1
Male	13	3	5	3	2	5	7	1	5	4	3	0	1
Female	12	12	0	0	0	6	5	1	0	0	0	12	0
Generation III (1911-1940)													
Total	48	13	9	12	14	19	6	20	6	14	3	21	4
Male	20	0	6	3	11	9	2	9	6	10	3	0	1
Female	28	13	3	9	3	10	4	11	0	4	0	21	3
Generation IV (1941-1970)													
Total	48	0	8	48	18	9	2	17	1	14	9	6	4
Male	22	0	4	10	8	3	0	7	1	8	3	0	0
Female	26	0	4	12	10	6	2	11	0	4	4	10	4
		(Only 34 members have settled in livelihood positions rest are students).											
Generation V (1971-to date)													
Total	24												
Male	17	(All Members are school students).											
Female	7												

Note: N.F. = Non-formal; UG=Undergraduate; Grad.-Grduate; PG=Post-Graduate; Prof. Professional.

When the third generation is at the helm of family affairs the options are quite clear. The *zamindari* has been abolished. It, however, does not come as a major economic calamity because most of the family members have a firm economic base in the urban areas. Moreover, they have been able to retain a considerable part of their land either in the form of mango groves (which are owned jointly by the family) or as agricultural land which is owned and cultivated by some members of the family who have not moved into towns and are now professional farmers. The family has also acquired considerable political patronage. It is important to note here that since the family could see an alternative to the *zamindari* system because of their urban based occupational diversification, its politically active members could continue to identify themselves with the socialistic programmes of the Congress party which were apparently against the rural gentry. Abolition of the *zamindari* was one such programme. They also responded to the changed political ethos after Independence and many members of the family joined different political parties. This further eased their adjustment in the changed circumstances.

All the urban-based families in this generation maintain their bonds with their village. No more because of economic compulsions, but because of the social pressure to continue the family traditions and the *bhaichara* (brother-hood) which has paid dividends in the past and which has been deliberately buttressed through family marriages. One positive result of this *bhaichara* has been that the land has at no stage been fragmented. The urban-based families also consider it prudent not to press for it because the small holding would not be viable and the management of the mango-groves impossible for them. All the marriages in this generation are solemnized at the family *haveli* and the family congregates every year during the summer vacations of the children who are invited here by the rural-based family elders expressly for the mango season. On these occasions the traditional bonds of give and take with the local population are also renewed.

In the fourth generation one observes a weakening of these bonds. Since the family is now mostly concentrated in Lucknow, Aligarh and Delhi, interpersonal contact is frequent and need to congregate in the village is not felt anymore. Moreover, the facilities needed for such congregations, specially in terms of domestic help are not available anymore because the obligatory relationships prevailing earlier between the *haveli* and the village folk no more exist. There is also no dependence on the landed property as most members have consolidated themselves economically. The village, however, is still occasionally visited by all because of reasons emotional and sentimental. It is perhaps at this level that the traditional bonds will continue to exist in future.

Thus through this analysis we have been able to illustrate, though very sketchily, how the country-town nexus transforms itself from one in which its rationale lies in the rural economy and society to one in which it shifts to its urban counterpart and then to an ideational level. It has also been possible to show that at the level of households and families the economic imperative is most important in the initial formation of the nexus and the process of modernization and political mobilization is linked to this imperative. Once formed the nexus can be sustained through tradition, culture and a framework of values.

Conclusions

Through these events and vicissitudes, the life courses of the actors in this study coalesce with the history of the region and provide a perspective on nexus formation. Through these 'actors' it has been possible to trace the genesis of a locally rooted rural gentry who like many others of their class build upon their base areas and gain a closer control over agrarian resources, perpetuate their identity and their economic and social dominance.[26] Like many of their class they respond positively to the solid British presence after the 1860s and to the fluid politics' of the later period and consolidate their economic and political base.[27] Like many of their class again, they give sustenance to the movements linked to the educational revival of their community[28] negate the myth that Muslims of the area are backward[29] and gain access to the new professions. They also emerge as the new Muslim elite of the nationalist period.[30] In the modern period, unlike many of their class, they build several bridges to the diversifying urban economy and society and join the band wagon of the upward mobile professional middle class. Their life courses thus act and react, adapt and adjust to the politics and social life of the region and the period.

The study finally raises certain questions:

—Can an explanatory social theory be based on the concept of the nexus?

—Can studies designed around the concept address the crucial issue facing current social enquiry, that of individualism versus holism?

— Are the qualifying characteristics of the nexus, its role and its potency predictable and replicable?

These and many other conceptual and methodological questions need to be answered if the concept of the nexus is to be invested with analytical strength and conceptual clarity.

REFERENCES

1. J. Merrington , "Town and Country in the Transition to Capitalism" in R. Hilton (ed.), The Transition from Feudalism to Capitalism, NLB, London, 1976.
2. T. Hareven, "Cycles, Courses and Cohorts: Reflections on theoretical and methodological approaches to the historical study of family development", Journal of Social History, Vol. 12(1), Autumn, 1978. See also: Holton, R.J. Cities, Capitalism and Civilization, Allen and Unwin, London, 1986.
3. Ibid. See also Merington, J. op.cit.
4. Ibid.
5. A. Kuper, and Kuper, J. The Social Science Encyclopaedia, Routledge and Kegan Paul, London, 1985.
6. F. Benet, "Sociology Uncertain: The Ideology of Rural-Urban Continuum", Comparative Studies in Society and History, Vol. VI, October, pp. 1-23, 1963. See also Lupri, E., "The Rural Urban Variable Reconsidered: The Cross-Cultural Perspective" Sociologica Ruralis, vol. VIII, No. I, pp. 1-20, 1967; H. Miner, "The Folk-Urban Continuum" in P.k. Hatt and A.J. Reiss Jr. (eds.), Cities and Society, pp. 22-34, 1959; R. Redfield, and Singer, M.B. 'The Cultural Role of Cities", Economic Development and Cultural Change, vol. III, No. I pp. 53-73, 1954; and Sorokin, P. and C.C. Zimmerman, Principles of Rural Urban Sociology, 1929.
7. Ibid.
8. R.E. Pahl, Urbs in Rure, L.S.E. Geographical Paper No. 2. London, London School of Economics, 1965.
9. T.G. McGee, The Urbanization Proces in the Third World, G. Bell and Sons, London, 1971.
10. Merrington, J. op.cit.
11. Pickvance, C.g., Urban Sociology: Critical Essays, Tavistock Publication, London, 1976.
12. Merrington, J. op.cit.
13. M. Lipton, Why Poor People Stay Poor: A study of Urban Bias in World Development, Maurice Temple Smith, London 1977.

14. J. Merrington, op.cit.
15. G. Hoppe, and J. Langton, Countryside and Town in Industralization, Kulturgeografiski Seminarium, Stockholm University, 1979. See also J. Merrington, Op.cit.
16. See E.P. Thompson, The Poverty of Theory, London, 1978.
17. Ibid. See also G. Hoppe, and J. Langton op.cit.
18. Pickvance, C.G. op.cit.
19. R.A. Carr Hill, and Macdonald, K.I. "Problems in the Analysis of Life Histories", Sociological Review Monograph No. 19, pp. 57-95. See also Hareven, T. opcit.
20. Hareven T. op.cit.
21. G. Hoppe, and J. Langton, op.cit.
22. O.H.K. Spate, (ed.), India and Pakistan, Methuen & Co. Ltd., 1967.
23. Kidwai, Atiya H., "Characteristics of Colonial Urbanization", Unpublished Ph.D. Thesis, Jawaharlal Nehru University, New Delhi, 1979.
24. R.R. Kidwai, Biographical Sketch of Kidwais of Avadh, Kitab Ghar, Aligarh, 1987.
25. Z. Bhatty, "Status and Power in a Muslim Dominated Village of Uttar Pradesh" in I. Ahmad (ed.), Caste and Social Stratification among Muslims in India, Manohar, Delhi, 1978.
26. C.A. Bayly, Rulers, Townsmen and Bazaars, Cambridge University Press, Cambridge, 1983.
27. Ibid.
28. D. Lelyveld, Aligarh's First Generation: Muslim Solidarity in British India, Princeton University Press, 1978. See also B, Metcalf, "The Reformist Ulema: Muslim religious leadership in India, 1860-1900", Ph.D. Dissertation, University of California, Berkeley 1974, Cited from C.A. Bayly, op.cit.
29. P. Brass, Religion, Languages and Politics in British India, Cambridge University Press, Cambridge, 1974.
30. C.A. Bayly, "The Small Town and Islamic Gentry in North India: The Case of Kara" in K. Ballhatchet and J. Harrison (eds.), The City in South Asia, Curzon Press, London, 1980.

Index